best wishes

Roy Hamilton

THE VOICE OF THE HILLS

Sunset from A'Cioch, Skye, June 1936. Photo: Ben Humble.

THE VOICE
OF THE HILLS

The Story of Ben Humble, MBE

ROY M. HUMBLE

FOREWORD BY JOHN HINDE

The Pentland Press
Edinburgh—Cambridge—Durham—USA

© Roy M. Humble, 1995

First published in 1995 by
The Pentland Press Ltd
1 Hutton Close
South Church
Bishop Auckland
Durham

ISBN 1–85821–249–9

Front: A view from the Cobbler across a cloud sea to Ben Lomond.
Ben Humble in the foreground. Photo: Geoffrey David.

Back: The Glenmore Lodge garden seventeen years after Ben's death.
Photo: Aviemore Photographic.

Typeset by Carnegie Publishing, 18 Maynard St., Preston
Printed and bound in Great Britain by Bookcraft (Bath) Ltd.

There is a voice the deaf can hear as clearly
as any other person – the voice of the hills.

B..H.H. (1934)

      . . . an unheard voice
That calls to higher lives, to nobler aims:
An unseen presence, beckoning us to leave
All artificiality behind
And be ourselves. For peace dwells in the hills
If we can hear her voice, and in the hills
We may escape the tired complexity
Of life, and in the silence vast, absorb
Into our weary spirits rest.

from "I to the Hills"

For Noreen, Morag, Áine and David, who were privileged to know the special handshake Ben reserved for all young people

and

to the memory of Ian M. M. MacPhail, teacher, historian and friend.

CONTENTS

LIST OF ILLUSTRATIONS

MAPS

ACKNOWLEDGEMENTS

My thanks are due to those who made their photographs available, and to the following for permission to reproduce previously published material: the executors of the estate of the late Frank Smythe for "Mountain Training in the Cairngorms", John Hinde for "Escape from a Stone Trap", W. H. Murray for extracts from the foreword to the facsimile edition of *The Cuillin of Skye*, and Tom Weir for extracts from the *Glasgow Herald* and *The Scots Magazine*. "Cairngorm Amazon!" and "A Cairngorm Rock Garden" first appeared in *The Scots Magazine* and "The Glenmore Story" in *Climber and Hill Walker*. The photographs from Ben's scrap book of accidents on the Scottish hills were kindly made for me by the National Library of Scotland, and the maps by the Cartographic Section, Department of Geography, University of Alberta. Being constrained by space, these maps are not all-inclusive, but rather show selected features from the text for the benefit of those less familiar with the places Ben enjoyed so much.

This is his story, not mine. It owes much to the recollections of all his friends. Sadly a number of them did not live to see the completion of the project, including his brothers John and Archie, Campbell Brown, Donald Campbell, Hugh Davidson, Ian MacPhail, John Mote and Angus Smith. Although it is now seventeen years since Ben's death, I know that they would understand that some aspects of his life have only gained in interest through the passage of time. Writing at a distance far removed from the scene of Ben's widely varied activities has also posed a number of problems, and the final appearance of the book can be my only public acknowledgement of the help of so many other people. I am especially grateful, however, to John Hinde, Diane Standring, and my wife Betty and our children.

Above all I am indebted to three individuals. Without the encouragement of the late Ian MacPhail, *The Voice of the Hills* might never have been started; without the sound advice of Bill Murray it is unlikely to have developed beyond the early draft stages; and without the unfailing support of Eric Langmuir it would certainly never have been completed.

Edmonton, Alberta, October 1994.

FOREWORD

It should be easy to write about Ben Humble, so well remembered by all, especially children including my own, but I find it difficult to write a foreword good enough for such a momentous biography as this will prove.

I knew him as a friend and a fellow hill lover and also because I was leader of the RAF Kinloss Mountain Rescue Team through most of the 1960s, sharing hill days, rescue exercises and a lot of committee work with him. He made a number of visits to Kinloss and our base camps and got to know us all. I must have quoted his forward-thinking ideas often to the team members, and they would sometimes sing, "Our Chief knows Ben Humble. Ben Humble knows our Chief," to the tune of "Onward Christian Soldiers". It gave them pleasure, not me, but I was indeed proud to have known him, one of the finest persons I have ever known. He was so intuitive that some of them could not believe he was stone deaf. To test him out one of the more brainless exploded a thunderflash a few inches behind him. He never moved a muscle.

In November 1968 Ben met me at 2,700 feet on my last Munro. Whooper swans were flying past in formation. He had tried to get to the top of Ben Lomond to photograph four of us who had walked for nineteen days from Ben Hope, re-traversing another forty-seven separate mountains. He could not reach the summit in time but sent Di Standring ahead with a camera. When we got down to Ben we were compelled to remove our boots so that he could take pictures of our feet, but they were too boringly normal for his Puckish humour.

He was a confident and excellent photographer and he got a better photograph on Beinn Narnain summit crags, near Arrochar. He was vigorous well into his sixties and spent some time with my son and me improving sites for howffing meets in the area. One January we had organised a night in snowcaves or rock howffs and met him on the summit of Beinn Narnain next morning for a complex rescue exercise. It was a glorious winter day with all the crags hoared like a wedding cake. I had everything set up for Ben to take his photographs. Volunteer patients were being lowered in stretchers, others were being winched up the cliff, or lowered in a Tragsitz (rescue seat). Somebody else was climbing a rope using the Prusik method, while rescue dogs and abseilers were operating at the same time amongst the snowbanks and crags – enough action in fact to provide illustrations for a whole treatise on rescue techniques. Ben produced a battered still camera with a bellows extension, and snapped one exposure before returning the Kodak to his daybag.

"Are you not going to take any more pictures – after all that setting up?" I wrote in his notebook.

"No, that's fine. I've got what I want."

And so he had, of course. His one picture was a masterpiece, and appeared as the front cover of *The Scots Magazine* some months later.

Ben was an avid collector of information and an enthusiastic recorder. He got material from all over the world, particularly Japan and the USA, for the 1968 Mountain Safety Exhibition, which may have been the first ever. He looked ahead so effectively that most of us were years behind him. He knew that mountain tragedies did not just happen, and that effective prevention should be taken when "the first domino fell" (not his quote) – a broken anorak zip, a lost map or deteriorating weather – before the chain of dominoes led to a catastrophe. His slide collection is less effective lacking his unique presentation style, but his scrapbooks of news-clippings and comments are now properly mounted and housed in the National Library of Scotland. His relentless collection of data was only matched by his readiness and need to impart it, so that he was a remarkable instructor.

He was only really annoyed with me once, and that was because of a communication failure on my part in the Cairngorm mountains. In July 1961 I had found the body of a man at the foot of Number 3 Buttress on Sgoran Dubh Mor in Glen Einich. I managed to recall some searchers with signal flares from a pistol, but I was unable to contact all the parties because of poor radios, so that Ben's group searched for several unnecessary hours.

I knew Ben for only fifteen years, so I have gained a lot from this book, increasing my admiration for him by learning the many other facets of his life, which deserve to be better known as he was such an inspiration to me and to countless others.

John Hinde BEM
Accident Recorder, Mountain Rescue Committee of Scotland
Mountain Instructor, Outward Bound, Scotland.

A RELUCTANT DENTIST

THE FIRST OF JULY

Benjamin Humble. How I hated that name. They used to tell me when I asked that as I was the seventh son, there was no room for me in the house, so Father said, "Ben Jam In!" Jammed in we were, with us four youngest boys sharing one bedroom, with constant fighting. Then when I went to school I wrote B. Humble on my books, and someone added "my motto".

Benjamin Hutchison Humble, Bennie as he was known to the family, was born at Dumbarton on 4 June 1903. His father came from the Parkhead district of Glasgow, where he had left school at the age of fifteen to work as an apprentice at Parkhead Forge. Rising rapidly over the next fifteen years, he was appointed Manager of Dennystown Forge, Dumbarton in 1886, and three years later married Jessie Marshall at Old Tollcross Parish Church, Glasgow. They set up house not far from the Forge at Comely Bank, but after the births of four successive sons were forced to move to a larger home on the high ground of Oxhill Road, overlooking the town and the River Leven. Hopes for a daughter faded over the years as the family size grew, finally to include eight boys. William, the fifth oldest, died from meningitis in 1901, at the age of two.

Life for the seven brothers was always well ordered in the early 1900s, with church attendance and membership in The Boys' Brigade dominating their out of school hours. Only one month of the year fell outside this disciplined pattern, the month of July. The enduring memories of Ben's childhood were all of this month, going back to the days following his sixth birthday:

School was irksome these last weeks of June; even the Sunday School picnic failed to thrill. For to us the first of July was the greatest day of all the year. Preparations had started long in advance, for our family of ten had to be transported to the wilds of Argyllshire. Together with our cousins, Father had discovered the village of Tayvallich, with houses for rent big enough for us all for the month of

July. We slept little that last night, but no matter how early we were up Grandpa had always disappeared. He had gone off early with the luggage. No porter would ever dare to check his management, for our treasured memory of him was the time our enemy the game-keeper tried to catch us when we were gathering brambles, and of Grandpa telling him to "rin awa and bile yer can!"

Five of us travelled with Mother on the first of July, with our elder brothers and Father waiting for the Glasgow Fair fortnight. A cab took us to the station, then a short railway journey to Craigendoran where we boarded the *Marmion* or *Waverley* to sail to Dunoon. We did not think much of these ships, but disembarked at Dunoon to await what to us was the greatest ship in all the world, the *Columba*, with its black and red funnels and gold paint on its paddle boxes. How we envied our cousins who had sailed on her all the way from the Broomielaw! Their family was almost as big as ours, and they always kept seats for us on the aft deck. Oh, the glory of that sail! There was the ship to explore, the engines to watch, stopping and starting at every pier, and of course we had to be up at the bow when going through the narrowest part of the Kyles. "Would we get a toss going around the point?" we asked, for to us Ardlamont was in the region of the Great Seas. The grown ups would go below for lunch, we being strictly enjoined to keep the seats, and content our-selves with sandwiches. At last we were round to Loch Fyne, up to Tarbert, and then on to Ardrishaig.

It was one of the delights of this journey that each succeeding stage provided still greater adventure, for now came the best part of all, to which we had been looking forward for weeks, the high brake with its three prancing horses! Whips cracked, and off we went with a flourish, north by Lochgilphead and then along the line of the Crinan Canal. There were always small yachts sailing through the canal, as it was busy in those days, and small boys would run alongside us, turning cartwheels, hoping to have pennies thrown to them.

At Bellanoch we left the canal and started up a steep hill. At least the brake did, with all the passengers dismounted. The road wound up and down, at one point almost round in a circle. We were constantly mounting and dismounting, for we also had to walk down the steep hills. For us boys the ploy was to wait till the brake had started, then run after it and jump on to the steps. A last climb, a long descent, and we glimpsed the upper waters of Loch Sween. Level ground now and we bowled along merrily, then round a bend, and the almost land-locked Tayvallich Bay lay before us. Our cousins had a

Humble and Hutchison families with friends, Old Carsaig Manse near Tayvallich, July 1909. Ben in foreground wearing hat.

house at Tayvallich, while our family crossed the peninsula to Carsaig Bay on the Sound of Jura. At that time there were only two houses at Carsaig, and one of them was our July home for all these years.

Soon we settled down, the day's programme varying little from year to year. Every forenoon our cousins and two other families whom we knew came over to Carsaig for bathing. Mixed bathing was unthought of in those days. The ladies undressed in a discreetly hidden hollow in the rocks, the men at a jetty a quarter of a mile away, while the wee boys used a boulder by the shoreside, being compelled to bathe with the ladies until they had learned to swim. Afterwards there was usually a game of cricket on the green in front of our house, and then the others would go back to the village for lunch. After lunch it was our turn to cross the peninsula, just a mile it was to the village shop. Much could be bought for our pennies then! Each of the four families had a rowing boat for the month on Loch Sween, and each had its own jetty. The bay was always interesting, for these were the days of the large private yachts, and Tayvallich Bay was a favourite anchorage; sometimes we were even invited on board. By five o'clock almost everyone in the village was to be found around the Post Office, waiting for the arrival of the brake with the mail and papers. We went with the brake to the stables, helped with the unharnessing, and took the horses to the water trough.

Evenings varied. Few memories remain, for we were sent to bed early. Sometimes the villagers would come over and have a dance on the green at Carsaig. If allowed to stay up, our job as children was to help make fires of dried bracken among the rocks to keep the midges off. Then at the start of the Fair fortnight the fathers and elder brothers arrived, and the tempo quickened. We were never old enough to fish at nights for mackerel and saith in Carsaig Bay, but there were glorious joint picnics to the Fairy Isles at the upper end of Loch Sween, or to the castle at the south end of the loch. With our four families we could muster almost forty.

The golden years flew by. How proud we were when we could at last join the men, and bathe from the jetty. But then came July 1914, and there was much anxious talk towards the end of the month, for our brothers and many of the villagers were in the Territorials. Soon they started to leave, off to the coming war. It was the end of an era. The families never returned.

When my brother Graham and I were growing up we often used to hear the name Tayvallich. It was spoken of almost with reverence by our father,[1] by all of his brothers including Ben, and by our grandmother.

Yet none of them ever went back, nor ever seemed to want to. I used to wonder why, as we often travelled the length of the West Coast but never made the short detour that would have taken us to Tayvallich. Reading Ben's words now, the reason seems obvious. They were supremely happy during those yearly holidays, happier as a family than they were ever to be again. The First World War broke the spell, and Tayvallich became a memory to be set apart, not one that could ever be recreated.

HOW I LOVED THAT HOUSE

The year 1914 started well for Ben and his family. Preparations had already begun towards the celebration of his parents' silver wedding anniversary when he heard of an impending change, one that was to bring him, after Tayvallich, to the second of his many loves:

> Then someone said something about moving. I didn't believe it at first, but the move took place in the early summer of 1914, to one of the biggest houses in Dumbarton, to Bellfield. How I loved that house! It was built around a courtyard, with sixteen rooms in all. The grounds covered three to four acres, with a tennis court at the top of the garden. There was a greenhouse with vines, and a larger conservatory with an entrance from the dining room, a lovely place. Upstairs the drawing room ran the whole width of the house; it was said to have the best dance floor in Dumbarton. There were many outbuildings, including a huge coal house, which took load after load of coal trucked directly from the station to fill up. We had two maids, a housekeeper, and a gardener with a flat above a coach house. How my parents did it I never knew,[2] but the move was in time for their anniversary in June. Bellfield was crowded with countless relatives and friends, and the celebrations extended over two days, with a garden party in the afternoon and a dance in the evening, first for the elders and then on the second day for the younger folk.

A plan of Dumbarton from 1818 shows Bellfield as one of only four named buildings west of the River Leven. During the second half of the nineteenth century it was occupied by one or other of the partners in Denny,[3] the famous Dumbarton shipbuilding firm. Walter Brock restored the house after an extensive fire in 1883, and subsequently leased it to Peter Denny, Jr, who had joined the firm in 1879. He was the third Denny of that name to follow the shipbuilding tradition. Although on a lower site than the house on Oxhill Road, the family's new home still

Twenty-fifth wedding anniversary of Mr and Mrs Robert Humble, Bellfield, Dumbarton, June 1914.

had a commanding view across Dumbarton, with an almost perfect location. For twenty-five years their lives had been centred jointly on Dennystown Forge and Bridgend Parish Church. The church now occupied the adjacent property, while the Forge was only moments away by way of the footbridge across the railway at Dalreoch. When they moved house in 1914 it must have seemed as though Bellfield had been built especially for them.

> But it was a short time of glory for us all. Events in Europe cast a shadow over our last holiday at Tayvallich. After war was declared, Father prevailed upon Bobbie, my eldest brother, to finish his studies in Law before joining up. He graduated in April 1915, and was commissioned 2nd Lieutenant in the Second (Dumbartonshire) Battalion of the famous Argyll and Sutherland Highlanders, the first Battalion having already been almost wiped out, down from 1000 to under 300 men. After a brief training, he left to join the British Expeditionary Force in France at the end of July. Within a month he was at the front line, and he was killed on the 7th of September.

Bobbie wrote many letters to his parents during his training at Hawick and the short time he was in France. Although Ben may have known much of their content, it is unlikely that he realised the full extent of the dangers faced by his older brother, a brother who probably seemed invincible to a boy of twelve. Bobbie prepared his parents for the possibility of his death by being totally realistic in all his letters, the more so the nearer he came to the front line. The detailed letters give a fine picture of the last brief weeks of a young officer at the front in 1915. In places he gives graphic details of the dangers, yet his mind was not always on the war. Just as Ben was to do in his own last days, Bobbie often thought back to the west coast of Argyllshire, to the peace and tranquillity of Carsaig and Tayvallich where the family had been so happy:

29 August 1915:
". . . During the last week we have had some splendid weather, with glorious sunsets and lovely moonlit nights. I could not help thinking while walking down with the Company to our work on the canal of some of the sunsets we used to watch over Jura from Tayvallich. There would be a glorious sunset sky overhead, and everything else in the world of nature at peace, yet all around you could hear the boom of the big guns and the noise of rifle fire – in total discord at times with the stillness of the night. Today there was heavy shelling going on during our forenoon church parade, but this afternoon there has been absolute quiet, and it is hard to realise that less than three miles from where we are many

gallant men are engaged in a death struggle. One cannot help thinking of these things, and I think it best to note them down in letters home."

5 September 1915:
". . . We are at work about a mile behind the front line, and there has been little doing for the past fortnight except for the continual artillery duels. I myself was up in the front line last week though, along with another officer. We were sent up for instruction purposes for 48 hours, temporarily attached to the 5th King's Own Yorkshire Light Infantry. As we were there for instruction we did just what the other officers had to do. I was out in 'no man's land' both nights seeing to some wire entanglements and listening posts. One felt rather strange the first time one got over the parapet of the trenches and out into the open with bullets whizzing about, but you soon get used to it all. The German line was only about forty yards away from one point of our line. I made a small sketch of the position just for practice, and for this I had to use a periscope pretty often. I could see the Germans moving about – in fact the beggars tried to smash the periscope two or three times. They gave us a pretty hot time in the evenings with bombs, shells etc. – this sort of display of theirs is called by our men the evening hate. The men at the front line where I was are mostly miners from Yorkshire. Their officers were exceedingly nice, and treated me handsomely. Just imagine, one of the evenings we were served some fine grouse. Not bad for the trenches, eh?"

Less than forty-eight hours after writing those words from the Flanders section of the front, Bobbie was dead, crushed when a dugout he was sheltering in took a direct hit. In earlier letters he had advised his father to try to persuade his brothers David and Alec to complete their studies before joining up, as he had done himself in the first nine months of the War. As Ben continues with his story of the family's life at Bellfield, he briefly describes how his older brothers fared:

> Of my other brothers, Archie the second oldest, who was a graduate engineer, became the first officer commissioned in the Third Argylls, but later transferred to the Machine Gun Corps, and came through the war unscathed. David, third, joined as a private in 1914, but was later sent home to finish his studies in medicine. Alec, fourth, was also sent back to complete his dental studies, but then rejoined his old Battalion as an officer. He was reported missing in action in 1917, with no word for six months, when we heard he was a prisoner of war.
>
> There were other tragedies for us in those war years. Deans Hutchison, one of our cousins who had enjoyed the Tayvallich days

with us, was also killed in France, and then my younger brother George died suddenly from appendicitis, a bungled operation done too late. George had been the only one in the family to show any musical talent, singing as a boy soprano at concerts at the Burgh Hall to raise money for the troops. Going to his funeral in 1917 was the first time that any of us had ever been in a car.

War brought double work for the Forge, and it sometimes seemed that my father worked all day and all night. Many and many a time when I was a schoolboy my mother would tell me around 11 p.m., or even midnight, "Go down to the Forge and bring Father back." I would usually find him watching the giant press, which was his pride and joy, one of the first of its kind on Clydeside. It was almost as big as a room of a house, pressing down on the red hot glowing ingots. The Forge was his whole life, his only other interests "his boys", as he called us, and his church. If anything needed fixing at Bellfield he just had one of the workers come up to the house. One of them, Old Moses they called him, built a hen house for me during the war. He used to say, "Does yer faither no ken I dae twa jobs, but just get paid for wan!"

After the war, when I was already suffering from deafness, I was taken away from 4th year at Glasgow High School and sent to a small school for the partially deaf in Norfolk. From there I was sent to specialists all over Britain, and given endless different types of treatment. I was already using a hearing aid when I started dentistry in 1921. Looking back now at those next five years I can't quite visualise it, but it seems I must have been busy and happy, with a normal life. Outside of classes at University, there was tennis in the summer, and cross country running with the Dumbarton Harriers. I often ran five to nine miles on a Saturday. I was a member of the Academical Debating Club in Dumbarton, and there were always grand dances at our house on winter weekends. All their lives my parents kept up with their old friends, and Bellfield welcomed them all. The best dances were always there, and we Humble brothers were famous for our own eightsome reels. Photographs were traditional at these dances, and were always taken on the stairs. That was where I got my first interest in photography.

The Bellfield dances were always formal occasions. Ben kept one of the printed cards as a memento, together with the large poster he made for the final gathering in 1930. Titled *Bellfield Again*, this poster includes life-like drawings of activities on and off the dance floor, accompanied by amusing *Punch* style quips. It must have taken many hours of work,

The last Bellfield dance, December 1930.

and remains as lasting evidence of the affection he felt for "his" house. A good friend from those days, John Mote, wrote to me from France in 1979 about the parties at Bellfield:

"They were the greatest fun, attended by up to fifty people, the young and the not so young. Full evening dress and dinner jackets were always worn, and there were lots of paper hats and streamers. We sat out between dances on the stairs, and photographs were always taken there. The dancing often went on till the small hours; even now almost sixty years later I still have the happiest memories; what fun it all was."

Another old friend also had memories from the 1920s. Archie MacAlpine was a fellow student in 1924, the third year of their dental studies. By then Ben was very deaf, and unable to hear any of the lectures. He remarked later that since he had passed the exams, this didn't say much for the lecture business! Archie commented on his reaction to the worsening disability:

"He spent the complete term carving B. H. HUMBLE on a desk. It was probably the best piece of knife carving in the College, and most certainly the largest, the letters being at least 3″ high. He was able to hear distinct conversation only, and my impression is that he greatly resented his oncoming deafness, and refused to accept it completely. The result was that quite often his natural humour was overlaid by a degree of 'touchiness'. If he failed to hear a sentence and had to ask for it to be repeated one could sense his irritation. If on the other hand someone leant towards him and spoke loudly he was likely to snap back, 'Well, do you think I'm deaf?' "

Despite the great difficulties which his deafness must have imposed on his studies, Ben had only to resit one exam during the whole of his training, and even then there was an unexpected bonus, as the delay gave him the opportunity to join his parents in America:

My father retired in 1925, and the following year he and my mother spent almost twelve months travelling in Canada and the States, visiting countless numbers of friends and relatives. By that time my brother Archie had settled in Toronto. When I was in my final year at University, waiting to resit one exam, my parents asked me to come out. I went on the first cruise of a new Cunard liner, which was a great time, then joined the family at Toronto. From there we went to Niagara, then on what was the dirtiest train I had ever seen to Philadelphia, and on to the old family home in Vineland, New Jersey. My mother's beloved Aunt Bella had married David Austin, and emigrated to the States in the 1880s; they were among the earliest settlers in Vineland. They had eight of a family, and I got all mixed up with the children and grandchildren. I went off with one who ran an ice wagon, and we went to Ocean City and Atlantic City, and right down the New Jersey coast. Then we had urgent word to get back to Vineland, where all the family had gathered for a farewell. The house was surrounded by peach trees, and every morning we plucked fresh peaches for breakfast, along with corn on the cob, hot and buttered. It was a wonderful time for me.

I graduated in 1926, soon after getting back from America, and joined my brother Alec in dental practice in Dumbarton. After two years I decided to take up dental radiology, and went to London for an extra year's training before setting up practice in rooms in Glasgow. Within the next few years first John, and then Alec, moved to the south of England, so despite Father's hopes of having all his sons settle in the area, out of the seven brothers only David and I were left in Dumbarton. I continued to live at home with my parents, sharing Bellfield with David and his growing family. Life was much slower there than in the years after the war, but we had a wonderful last dance in December 1930. I still have the poster I made for that dance. Father died only a few weeks later, early in the New Year, and all flags were at half mast across Dumbarton on the day of his funeral. It was a sad day for me when we left Bellfield in 1933.

Even more than Tayvallich, Bellfield has always been a name for me to conjure with. My brother and I were both born there, and almost every day we lived in Dumbarton we would pass by its front entrance. After it was sold, our family moved back to Oxhill Road, and when enough snow fell in the winter we made great sledge runs from the top of Oxhill down almost to the back wall of our old garden. For many years after the Second World War the house was used as a remand home for juveniles, but increasing age and upkeep costs forced its eventual closure. I managed to find my way inside after it had lain derelict for several years. As I wandered around trying to identify the different rooms, I had to pick my way through all kinds of debris; up past the landing at the turn of the stairs, where Ben had stood to pose and photograph the dancers, then up again into the long drawing room. The floor that had once been called the best dance floor in Dumbarton was covered now only by broken glass and masonry. Looking out across the town through the broken windows, the chimney stacks of the silent Forge still clearly visible, I wondered what Ben would have thought, to see his house come to this pass. Both Bellfield and Dennystown Forge have long since gone, but his memories remain, memories which hold the door open to life in a different Dumbarton.

A VICTORIAN AUTOCRAT

I never wanted to be a dentist, and never liked dental surgery. All I ever wanted was to take law, for I always enjoyed a good argument. But Father said no, I was not to oppose him in this matter. He insisted that I take dentistry, as my older brother Alec was a dentist.

What manner of man was Ben's father, and why did he force his son into a totally unwelcome profession? Although he lived in the same house as his parents for most of the first twenty-eight years of his life, Ben never felt as close as he would have wished . . . "I did not know him, for he died when I was just qualified in 1931."

In family photographs which have survived my grandfather appears somewhat stern and uncompromising, only on rare occasions showing a trace of a smile. My grandmother told me simply, "He was always a good man to me", while my mother remembered him as being dour and often uncommunicative at family gatherings. Ben kept all the letters his father wrote to him from America during his final year at University in 1926, and in the last few weeks of his life put down all his memories and reflections about the man who directed the whole course of his life, the man he called *"A Victorian Autocrat"*. The written picture which Ben left validates that title, while the American letters show the extent to which the autocrat was unable to release control over his youngest surviving son.

I did not know him, for he died when I was just qualified in 1931. My mother lived until 1959, and I was gradually able to get his story from her, and then see many of his papers after her death. He was born in poor circumstances in Glasgow, and only had schooling to 14 or 15 before being apprenticed at Beardmore's Forge at Parkhead, yet by the age of 30 he had been appointed Manager of Dennystown Forge, and later became a director of the firm and well known throughout Clydeside. I've always wondered how he managed all this, but looking back at his life and at the controlling influence he had on so many people, he must have been an autocrat almost from the start.

What did Sir William Beardmore think, I wonder, when Father took Parkhead Forge's six best workers with him to Dumbarton, including his brother David and brother-in-law Michael Young? Dennystown Forge was in a very poor state when he arrived, and the new owner left everything in his hands while he went out looking for orders. Later when the owner's son came into the business Father had to train him completely. All his life Father was junior to these two, but they had the sense to realise that his word was law as far as Forge work was concerned. Dennystown specialised in rudders and propeller shafts, and with Admiralty contracts made these for very many of the Clyde built ships, including all the Denny craft and the Clyde pleasure steamers. They had many foreign orders too, from such as the Irawaddy Flotilla Company, and when we were travelling back from America in 1926 on one of the big Anchor liners he mentioned to me that it had some of his work.

He was a non-smoker and teetotaler, and never knew any games, not even bowling. Until 1912 he was always up at six and off to work, home for lunch then back to the Forge again till six in the evening. After supper he would go off to sleep in a fireside chair, telling me, "Waken me at nine"; then he went back down again to the Forge to see that all the work was being properly done. He controlled everything and everybody, but was revered by all, for they knew none worked harder than he did. McEwen the head joiner and McLeod, who was in charge of the engine shop, both came from Parkhead with him, and they would often come up to Bellfield and sit for hours talking about the work in hand. Others too, but none thought it irregular or that they should get extra pay, for all thought it an honour to work with him. There was often labour unrest on Clydeside in those days, but there was never a hint of a strike at the Forge.

All his life he kept in contact with friends and people who had worked for him. Most were very ordinary folk who lived in tenements or semi-detached houses; I only remember one family who had a detached house. Many sought his help, and were set up in small shops or businesses. I doubt if he got all his money back, for my brother John mentioned one who could only leave an old violin as security. Others came looking for work, young men usually, and he got jobs for many of them overseas through his contacts in ship-building, for in those days Denny and Dumbarton ships really did sail the seven seas. Our house was full of souvenirs from places like Hong Kong and Rangoon, brought back by way of thanks to him. He put his six sons through University, and later enabled them to buy into medical and dental practices, but all had to be repaid, with interest, and everything was accounted for in a business-like way. It was his ambition to see all his sons working in prominent professions in the Dumbarton area, but Bobbie's death altered that plan, and in the end it was only David who spent his complete working life in the town. Our Uncle David's son Jimmy Humble, however, became a local lawyer, and his son in turn carries on that practice today.

At Bellfield we were next door to the gentry of the town, but Father had little to do with them. He was asked to stand for the local Council, and likely could have become Provost, but he was happier with plain folk, like the local grocer with a wee shop who used to come up to the house every Saturday night. They would sink into big armchairs in the parlour and talk away into the small hours. Sunday evenings were always different, for they were sacred to letter writing. The only thing I ever heard him boasting about was his handwriting, which was almost perfect copperplate. How did he manage that, I've always wondered, with limited schooling? He wrote to Archie in Canada each week without fail, and when he was in America in 1923, and again in 1926, he wrote long letters to each of his sons in rotation.

The only newspaper I ever saw him read was Blatchford's *Clarion*. Blatchford was one of the pioneer socialists, and that paper had great significance for me, for I am sure it was there that Father read about the special school for the deaf in Norfolk where I was sent for my last two years. The building and grounds there had originally belonged to Blatchford. I wanted to stay at Glasgow High School, where I was doing fine in spite of my increasing deafness, and resented being sent away, just as I later resented being forced into dentistry, but that was his way, he made the decisions and others followed.

When I was a young schoolboy I remember seeing the large letters KOSMOID all across the town. How I wish I had talked to Father about that name. He knew so much about Dumbarton and district I'm sure he could have told me everything about the great Kosmoid scandal that rocked the town in the early 1900s. A Glasgow doctor with a big practice was associated with a chemist who secretly claimed to have found a process for transmuting base metals into copper and gold. It was all very hush-hush. Several wealthy people subscribed towards the firm's initial capital, including one of the owners of the Forge, and all had great hopes for Kosmoid. It was almost like the famous South Sea Bubble! The initials which formed the name of the firm were said to have come from the first letters of the partners' names: K for Lord Kelvin, the two O's for Lord and Lady Overtoun, S for Dr Alexander Shiels the brains behind the scheme, M for a Glasgow business man George Millar, D for James Denny, and I for Lord Inverclyde. A huge factory was constructed in the Dumbuck region to the north of the town, ostensibly for the making of weldless steel tubes, and there was great talk of how many employees would be required. Shiels' grandiose scheme envisaged houses for six thousand workers, each with its own small garden. The Town Council were approached because of the firm's anticipated large requirement for water, while Kosmoid bored for water on its own ground at the same time. A plan to bring a water supply to Dumbarton from Loch Sloy was advocated, and a public enquiry was held to discuss this possibility, but in the end the whole scheme collapsed. Dr Shiels disappeared, and his death was reported only a few months later.

A number of years ago a well known Glasgow journalist had a fortnight's series on the affair. I became interested then and was able to go over all the company's records, and wrote to James Denny, the last surviving son of the Denny who was said to have been involved. He told me he was just a youngster at the time, but remembered Dr Shiels coming to visit their house. I also noticed the name of one of my father's partners among the subscribers, and as he was still alive I wrote to him. He replied with a short note saying, ". . . if you value our good name please do not publish anything about Kosmoid. As your father's son I trust you will take this matter no further." In other words he and others had been taken for a ride, and even now still wanted it all hushed up! Father was too careful ever to have been involved, but what a story he could have told.

I wonder, too, what he would have thought about another Dumbarton sensation that came about in the year he died. A. J. Cronin, who was born in Cardross, a few miles from Dumbarton, published his first novel, *Hatter's Castle*, in 1931. Its setting, the town of Levenford, was scarcely disguised from Dumbarton, the street names and localities easily recognisable by any local person even today. But Cronin went beyond that, for some of the sons and daughters of prominent people in the town were able to recognise clearly their forebears in many of the characters in the book. The doctor was of course based on Dr Graham, whom my brother David joined and later succeeded in practice, while the Latta Bursary and Sir James Latta of the story were quite unmistakable from the Denny Bursary and Denny name. Latta's house was even called Levenford House, the actual name of the house which stood next door to Bellfield, originally built by James Denny in 1853. The real Levenford House still stands today, in use as the Dumbarton District Library Store. My brother Archie was at University with Cronin, and years later he wrote and tackled him about all this, but of course Cronin replied that the characters of his book were fictitious. I doubt if he would have got away with it today. When the book first appeared they said that Cronin would have been lynched if he had returned to the Dumbarton area! *Hatter's Castle* is now in its thirty-seventh printing. Whatever would Father have said if he'd read it, for all the people Cronin based his characters on must have been his contemporaries in the years after he came to Dumbarton. Cronin's second book, *Three Loves*, again had a local background, for it was centred round the pub at Dalreoch, where I used to cross the railway bridge to fetch Father back from his work at the Forge.

In an interview given when he was in his eighties, Cronin confirmed what had always been accepted locally, that the main character in *Hatter's Castle*, James Brodie, was based on his own grandfather – a man he hated. As Ben said, there is no doubt that Cronin shaped many of his other characters from local people, and on re-reading the book recently I found Levenford instantly recognisable as Dumbarton. The house used for the filming of *Hatter's Castle*, located near Cairndow on Loch Fyne, later became a tourist attraction.

Following these digressions about Dumbarton's past, Ben's story returns briefly to his father's last years:

> In 1922 Father was desperately ill, and John had to sit up all night with him as his temperature climbed during the crisis of a pneumonia. Concern over his health made him cut back on his work load – with a consequent reduction in his earnings – and later precipitated his early retirement. As there were no pensions at that time, the Directors of the Forge simply asked him to state his terms. He replied that he had always trusted folk, and would leave the matter in their hands. They gave him one third of his salary for life, which was based on only £1000 a year, although at one time he had been making several times that amount. He was very grateful, but he deserved better after running the Dennystown Forge for almost forty years, and all of us regretted that our mother was left with only £150 a year to live on.
>
> Towards the end of his life he got great enjoyment out of motoring, and although I didn't have a car, David and John drove him all over Scotland. When John first started practice near Hampton Court in Surrey, he could only afford a motorcycle with sidecar. Father and Mother visited them there, and Father sat in the sidecar with John as he went on his rounds. He soon said that he didn't think this was quite the thing for a doctor, so he advanced John the money for his first car, a big Maxwell. Like everything else that loan had to be repaid, with interest, and I saw a letter he wrote to John complaining about the fact that he had given no security against the loan. There were stories about motoring in those days, for each trip could be an adventure that people today would wonder on. Going up the old Rest and be thankful road from Arrochar on one occasion John and Father couldn't get to the top of the hill because the radiator continually boiled over. Finally John had to turn the big car, difficult enough in itself on the narrow road, and then drive up the last third

of the road in reverse gear. Father would give one of his rare smiles when he talked about that trip! I think that old Rest road is still used for hill climbing rallies.

When I look back at my father's life, and the great influence he had on mine, I'm a little wiser these days, and can forgive more easily the control he wielded. If he hadn't been an autocrat from his earliest days, as a family we might never have risen above our poor beginnings, none of us might have got to University, and there might never have been Humbles as doctors, dentists and lawyers in the Dumbarton area. As I type these memories today, forty and more years since his death, that is quite a thought!

After Ben's death we found the fourteen letters he had received as his parents journeyed across Canada and the States in 1926. All were from his father. Since my grandfather wrote to his five sons in rotation, a fact that my uncle John also confirmed, that was quite an output. Surely a father who had done that must have had a close relationship with his sons, yet Ben said, "I never knew him."

The letters are very revealing. They are long, and affectionate, but full of concern and advice about every involvement, with an almost endless list of instructions and remonstrations. There was also one post-card. Not one showing a scenic view, or a panorama of the new American skyscrapers as might be expected, but instead carrying the following advice, attributed to C. W. Post:

Tackle the work just in front of you. Strive in an honest way to do the best you can, and if, having done your best, there seems to appear the hand of some over-ruling Power which hammers you, take it like a good piece of steel and come right off the anvil with a better temper and a keener edge.

Did Ben continue to think about that maxim, and equate it in any way with the loss of his hearing? One can only speculate, but he kept the card for fifty years. The letters often carried the same theme. At times they obviously upset him, for one begins with something of an apology:

"You must not think that I have wanted to push you in one direction. I may have been over anxious in planning for you, but Bennie if so, it was all done for the best, and you yourself as you say must be the final judge as to your Yea and Nay.

"I never thought on any one chaffing you because you weren't suc-cessful. Just one little thing wanting, and you were down, but by no means out; next time you will 'Mak Siccar'. Even if the exam is not held again until April, it would be better for you to do some regular study right through till then, so devote a definite time each week while the study habit is on; it is not so easy Bennie to sit down and begin study again after you have been off it for any length of time – the habit or ability to study is much easier lost than acquired again."

Even when Ben wrote of his social life, he might always expect something of a reproach in the reply:

"So you have come to the end of your galavanting. Mother and I are glad you have had such a good time with your running and other goings on, but now will you concentrate on your main business, dentistry. We note also that you have been playing a little golf. Good and well, but I don't know anything about that, or of drinking afterwards. Your father and his friends managed to carry through all of their activities, even their socials and dances, on a bottle of ginger or lemonade or a cup of tea, and I should not like to think that any of our boys or their companions had any desire for anything else.

"You must only work on your golf and other activities or recreations in such a way as not to interfere with your work and studies. You are now well into manhood Bennie, and man's <u>first</u> concern is his work well and faithfully done. Then he can enjoy his golf or other recreations with a clear conscience, but <u>work</u> <u>first</u> should be his motto always.

"Now last and not least Bennie, your last letters were almost indecipherable. Your composition and matter and way of putting things were quite good, but oh, my, the writing! As Grandpa Humble used to say about bad writing, it was like a hen scraping among snow. Take a little pains Bennie, and mend your writing."

Ben received a blank cheque from his father to cover his fare and other expenses in coming out to America, but at the same time he was also given some down to earth advice, and then suddenly a commendation that looked towards his true vocation:

"I see you have found out that money will disappear very rapidly unless carefully handled. Yes, laddie, you cannot be too careful in handling your money. It has a knack of getting away from those who are not careful, and in these particular days in which we live, it behoves each and all of us to keep as close a guard on our purse strings as it is possible to do without being really mean.

". . . We are glad to know that you are still following your bent for literature. As you say, there will not be many encouraged as you were by having your first ever contribution accepted and paid for. Keep on trying, Bennie."

How would he have reacted to this mixture of parental advice and exhortation, criticism and encouragement? Did it simply make him "come off the anvil with a keener edge", more than ever determined to go his own way? Referring to his University days, he himself wrote, "I suppose I must have been happy and busy during those years." The words "suppose" and "must" do not sound completely convincing. I think it is certain that what really kept him happy during those years were the very galavantings that his father was concerned about, his running, his debating, his outdoor activities in general, everything in fact except the profession that had been chosen for him. The evidence is also clear that my grandfather seriously underestimated his son's strength of character, never being able to release the autocratic role which was an essential part of his nature, always directing. He chose dentistry for Ben out of concern for his growing deafness, and in the mistaken belief that he would always be able (and want) to work under his older brother's wing, the mistaken belief that he required such protection. But Ben's spirit was not one that could be easily confined, and even in dentistry he found his own outlet through research and writing, and in original thought. His friend and climbing companion Bill Murray summed him up so well in his foreword to the facsimile edition of *The Cuillin of Skye*, beginning with this comment:

"The more important thing to know about Ben is that here was a youth of bright mind, force of personality, and vigour of body, who on leaving school had his hopes frustrated by a fast growing deafness. The experience induced later eccentricities and a stubborn will – both to be turned to the benefit of others."

It was the power of that stubborn will that my grandfather did not recognise, and with deafness hampering communication between them it seems likely that neither was able to give full expression to their mutual affection, leaving Ben with some lasting self reproach. But when he looked back at the end of his life, he recognised only too well the source of the opportunities that he and his brothers had been given.

THE DENTAL DETECTIVE

However reluctantly, Ben found himself qualified in dentistry at the beginning of 1927. He immediately started work as an assistant in his brother Alec's practice in Dumbarton, just as his father had planned. Although he found no great liking for the work, he was not too long content with a subservient role, and soon took over the running of two branch surgeries in Renton and Alexandria. In addition he helped with the dental care at Keil School, a local boys' boarding school, gaining

The young dentist on holiday in Iceland in 1930. Photo: Douglas Scott.

an early insight there into the need for preventive dentistry. He read the dental journals voraciously, and since virtually all of his learning at University had been by way of the written word, found no difficulty in keeping himself informed of the rapid advances that were taking place in dentistry.

"How many stories I can tell of those early days in practice," he wrote, but sadly, only a few brief glimpses of the more humorous aspects of his work were ever recorded:

> One of our patients in the Dumbarton practice was Lady Overtoun, widow of Lord Overtoun, the great Dumbarton benefactor. As well as seeing us on her own behalf, she once brought me her old mangy cat, and wondered if we could make dentures for it! Another of our best paying patients was an epileptic, who managed to break his dentures almost every time he had a seizure. He never complained, and always paid the full cost of the repairs. Not everyone did that. No doctors knew anything about teeth, but the patients always seemed to call them when they had severe toothache at nights or on the weekends, much to my brother David's annoyance. He was in general practice with our old family doctor, Dr Graham, and used to have fierce arguments with Alec every time he was called out at night for one of our patients. Years later they were still at it, when Alec insisted that the National Health Service was correct in paying more for removal of a wisdom tooth than the amount David was paid for the total care of a woman throughout her pregnancy!
>
> I took a cruise to the Canary Islands during that first year. There were six doctors on board including the ship's doctor, but none wanted to help when the Chief Engineer developed a raging toothache. They found out from one of the passengers that I was a dentist. I can still visualise that scene. The cabin crowded with onlookers, with the other engineers grinning round the door as I extracted the tooth – without an anaesthetic – with the one pair of ancient forceps that we found on the ship.

(Friends will have no difficulty in imagining the triumphant shout as the offending tooth was held high for the bystanders!)

When in Philadelphia the previous year, Ben had taken a chance opportunity to attend one day's sessions at the Seventh International Dental Congress, and heard there of the growing importance of dental radiology. Not every Dental School covered the subject adequately at that time, and he had been lucky that Glasgow was one that did. As he continued his professional reading he soon decided that here was a chance to join a new and growing sub-specialty, one that would perhaps take him away from the humdrum work of dental practice, which still held no great appeal.

Successive six-month training periods with the X-Ray Departments of King's College Hospital and University College Hospital in London provided the necessary training, using early equipment which often allowed dangerous amounts of scattered radiation. All the senior men under whom Ben worked eventually died from X-Ray burns or other side effects of radiation. At the end of that year he returned to Glasgow to open practice on his own account at Berkeley Street, becoming one of the first consultant dental radiologists in Glasgow and the west of Scotland. He worked closely with the Phillips Electrical Company, who were pioneers in the production of X-Ray machines in Britain, and installed in his surgery the first Phillips Metalix unit to be used in Scotland. Another pioneering role was in the early use of colour films of teeth.

Patient referrals were slow, initially only from the younger Glasgow dentists, so he turned to the research and writing that came easily to him, presenting papers at local dental meetings to gain a wider audience, while still continuing to help in the Dumbarton practice until Alec moved to the south of England. It is quite remarkable that within two years, at the age of 28, Ben had published two seminal papers in the dental literature, both of which have a permanent place in the developing story of dentistry.

My first paper, "Preventive Radiology", was published in the *British Dental Journal*,[4] then republished with an enthusiastic editorial in its American counterpart.[5] Apparently I was the first to stress the preventive value of dental radiology. This brought me more patients, but really the dentists sent patients only when they got into trouble, with broken roots and all sorts of obscure conditions. Then when I heard that the Eighth International Dental Congress was to be held in Paris, I decided to see if they would accept a paper from me, and got busy and wrote one on "Identification By Means Of Teeth", which became the first paper of its kind ever presented on this topic at an International Congress.[6] The transactions of the Congress were published in four different languages, and distributed throughout the world. The research was very involved, as I had to go over all the previous records on the subject, trying to get figures from all the major European centres on the number of unidentified bodies which they had each year. In 1926 a German had invented a very detailed procedure for identifying toothmarks on skin, using photographs and an etching printing process. I saw at once a way of simplifying his method, and made many experiments on skin and all sorts of other materials. After a general review of the subject of identification by teeth, identification of bite marks formed the second part of my paper, and my modification afterwards became the standard way of identifying human bite marks in criminal cases.

In the editorial column of *The American Dental Surgeon* introducing the first of Ben's two articles, the writer made the following comments, under the title "The Importance of Dental Radiology":

"On every hand one hears endless and varied discussion, pro and con, concerning the diagnostic value of radiography in dentistry. The attitudes range all the way from an extravagant enthusiasm to almost a bitter skepticism. One dental surgeon declares that he wouldn't know how to practice without it, another is just as positive in asserting that the X-Ray pictures are worse than useless, they are positively misleading, failing to show pathology when it is present, and deceiving one into believing there is pathology when there is none . . . In short, no one pretends that radiology is a final and sufficient key to the entire diagnosis, but the evidence is incontestable that properly evaluated and interpreted, the radiogram is an exceedingly valuable, if not indispensable, aid to diagnosis in appropriate cases. Now comes Dr B. H. Humble, in an article reproduced in this issue, showing us another field of usefulness for dental radiology – the field of preventive dentistry . . . We are inclined to agree with the author that 'soon radiology will be made a compulsory subject for every dental degree and license, and this will lead to its being given a much more important place in the curricula of dental schools.' No one, we think, can read this excellent paper without coming to the same conclusion."

An additional editorial comment by Dr Howard Raper, the author of the first North American textbook devoted entirely to dental radiology, stated:

"The paper is a particularly good one, and is also interesting because it comes out of Scotland, and the author, incidental to his subject, gives us little vivid flashes of what the practice of dentistry must be like in Scotland . . . One must not get the impression that dental Scotland is years behind us, however, for certainly the author of this paper is abreast of our best men in America, and far ahead of many."

Dr Raper was then considered the world's top authority on dental radiology, so that is no mean tribute to the ability of a young dentist. Never loath to stick his neck out in any debate, whatever the topic, Ben did not hesitate then. In this late twentieth century era of consumer knowledge, it is fascinating to look back at the last paragraph of his 63-year-old paper, remembering that it was written at a time when many denied the value of dental radiology:

> Prophecy is ever rash, but I would say this – the ordinary person is well informed these days. Soon all will come to know the value of the X-ray examination. Just as, at present, the dentist who does all his extractions without anaesthetics would soon lose all his practice, so, in the future, the dentist who does not at least offer his patients an X-ray examination, will be passed by.

As he researched the material for his second important paper, on identification by means of teeth, Ben showed the persistence which was later to characterise his work on behalf of the Mountain Rescue Committee. Enquiries over a two year period had failed to obtain for him any figures for the number of unidentified bodies found yearly in the city of London, although he had found no similar difficulty with other major centres. A reply from New Scotland Yard, dated 2 December 1930, reads:

"I am directed by the Commissioner of Police of the Metropolis to inform you that he regrets he is unable to furnish the information required, as no such records are kept in this office, and to obtain the figures would involve much research. I am, etc."

Such a reply might have deterred some, but not Ben. He wanted an answer, and immediately wrote to his Member of Parliament, Sommerville Hastings, a dodge he never hesitated to use subsequently when normal channels of enquiry proved fruitless. The following extract can be found in the pages of *Hansard* for June 1931:

"*Dr Hastings* – To ask the Secretary of State for the Home Department: can he give the number of unidentified bodies taken to the mortuaries in London in any one recent year?"

"*Mr Glynes* – The most recent year for which figures are available is 1927. 77 bodies of newly born infants, and 74 other bodies found dead in that year remained unidentified after the end of the year. It is understood that these numbers fairly represent the average."

His enquiries thus completed, Ben went to Paris to present his paper, "Identification by Means of Teeth". An international audience heard him conclude with this summary of the essential requirements for any forensic dental examination:

> Where it is necessary to examine the teeth of a corpse, the following conditions should be noted in addition to details regarding fillings etc. Note whether the teeth wanting in the corpse or skeleton were lost before or after death, and if before, how long before. Note also

whether any unusual condition of the jaws is the result of disease, or existed prior to death, or was caused after death. When the long bones are destroyed a radiograph of the mandible may show the state of calcification of an unerupted third molar tooth, and so assist in estimating the age of the deceased. By these means, even though only a small portion of the teeth and jaws remain, the dentist who has kept careful records can supply, beyond contradiction, evidence as to the identity of human remains.

Only five years had passed before a sensational British murder trial brought these words dramatically to light. The trial, Rex *vs* Ruxton, was held at Manchester Assizes in March 1936. Relatives of the children's nursemaid of Dr and Mrs Buck Ruxton had become concerned as to her whereabouts the previous September, as they had heard nothing from her for a number of days. Mrs Ruxton herself had not been seen during the same period, and among several different explanations which Dr Ruxton gave for their disappearance was his statement that the maid and her mistress had gone off touring in Scotland. A local rumour suggested that the girl's disappearance could be related to her concealment of an early pregnancy. It undoubtedly proved true that the missing pair had gone on a tour to Scotland, but not quite the tour indicated by Dr Ruxton!

Some weeks later a human arm was seen protruding through cloth wrapping in a ravine two miles north of Moffat, in Dumfriesshire, and eventually sixty-eight separate packages containing dismembered human remains were unearthed. A recent flood had apparently helped to disperse some of the smaller bundles in the area below the Gardenholme Bridge. Two separate heads and torsos were found, the torsos and most of the limbs having been disarticulated, and the hands and fingers badly mutilated, the latter presumably to prevent identification by fingerprints. There were indications that the dismemberment of the bodies had been carried out by someone possessing anatomical knowledge. A month later a roadman made an additional discovery ten miles further south, unexpectedly coming across a single left foot, covered by a rain-sodden newspaper, lying on a grassy bank at the side of the Glasgow–Carlisle road.

It proved possible to reassemble all the mutilated and partially burned remains, and determine that there were two adult female victims. The dental evidence was crucial to both the estimation of age and the identification of the bodies. Radiographs of the jaws showing unerupted wisdom teeth indicated that the age of the younger person was between 18 and 22 (actual age 20). The skull and facial remains of the older victim indicated that many of the teeth had been extracted after death, or shortly before it, while other teeth showed evidence of having been recently ground down by a revolving dental instrument. A partial upper dental plate made with the help of Mrs Ruxton's dental records fitted exactly into the reconstructed skull. Superimposition of photographs of the victims on the skulls, a technique being used for the first time, helped to conclude an extraordinary medico-legal investigation.[7]

"As God is my witness!" cried Dr Ruxton in the witness box, denying any violence to either his wife or his maid, but once the identification of the bodies was clear other damning evidence revealed the horrific nature of the murders. Blood stains were identified on pads underlying a stair carpet which the accused admitted having removed, and dustmen confirmed that he had asked them to clear away a quantity of burned carpets and clothing, while a witness reported seeing further blood stains on curtains and the walls of the bathroom. Dr Ruxton, in addition, had been observed repeatedly attending to two fires in his backyard, neighbours recollecting that unpleasant smells emanated from both in and outside the house at this time, three days after the last sighting of the victims. Portions of the *Sunday Graphic and Sunday News* found with the remains in the Moffat ravine were even traced back to the Lancaster store which regularly supplied the prisoner. There can have been little doubt left in the minds of the jury, who brought in a unanimous verdict of "guilty of murder". Although an appeal followed, Ruxton did not escape the gallows.

Ben was not called as an expert witness, perhaps on account of his deafness, but his opinion on the radiographs was obtained, and for many years he kept in his possession one of the actual radiographs that had established the age of the younger woman. His part in this dramatic murder trial is made the more remarkable by the fact that in his Paris presentation five years earlier he had foreshadowed every single aspect of the dental evidence that helped convict Dr Ruxton.

Writing in the *British Dental Journal* in 1951, the renowned Home Office forensic pathologist, Dr Keith Simpson, noted:[8]

"Dental data, it is now realised, have come to provide detail of a kind comparable with the infinitesimal detail that was previously thought likely to be provided only by fingerprints."

Ben had stressed that very fact in *1931*, emphasising then that identification by means of teeth was absolutely conclusive. His paper was later reprinted in the same dental journal.[9] Humble's modification of Sorop's method for identifying human bite marks became the accepted procedure in criminal cases in Britain, and remained so until well into the 1950s. In a standard textbook of forensic medicine published in 1973, Polson refers to both parts of Ben's paper,[10] and discusses the case of

Gorringe (Rex *vs* Gorringe 1948), where punctures in the skin of the breast of a murdered woman were found to correspond in position with the four lower and two upper teeth of the husband, stating:

"Identification was established by demonstrating a precise coincidence between the bite marks on the breast and casts of Gorringe's teeth, using Humble's modification of the Sorup technique, and a conviction obtained."

Ben's work came full circle in yet another notable murder trial, one which made legal history in Scotland in 1968. Bite marks were noted on the breast of a 15-year-old girl found murdered in a cemetery outside Biggar in Lanarkshire. Suspicion fell on an inmate of a nearby Approved School which rehabilitated boys in their late teens convicted of minor criminal offences. Although the youth was known to be an acquaintance of the murdered girl, the case rested on very shaky circumstantial evidence. However the expert dental witness, Dr Warren Harvey, and other medical experts including Dr Keith Simpson, were able to demonstrate exact coincidence between the bite marks and the very unusual spacing and notching in models made from the accused boy's teeth. Ben added a note to the press clippings he kept of this case, "seems like my method was used", but this was correct only in regard to the basic premises of identification of bite marks. Techniques had moved forward in the intervening years, and the prosecution presented much more extensive dental evidence, including experiments with working models made from casts of the teeth of the accused.

The Biggar murder marked the first occasion in Scotland in which the identification of an assailant's bite marks was successfully used to secure a conviction for murder. In an extensive treatise on Dental Identification and Forensic Odontology, which includes a ten page presentation of the dental evidence in this particular case, Harvey[11] refers to Ben's early work, and also gives him credit[12] for being the first person – forty years earlier – to suggest dental registration of persons working in dangerous occupations, for the purpose of possible later identification. Without question, Ben deserves recognition as one of the early pioneers of what later came to be known as forensic odontology, now fully established as a separate branch of forensic medicine. His role as a dental detective stands alongside that of his other early work in the field of dental radiology, a unique personal contribution in a profession that was not of his choice.

2

IN THE WORLD OF SILENCE

A FAMILY TRAIT

I am deaf, stone deaf. I hear nothing, absolutely nothing. Don't tell me of hearing aids, I have tried many types with no success. Don't tell me of the newer operations, stapes mobilisation or stapedectomy. I have had them both. Both failed. I have had other types of treatment from specialists in Britain and the USA; none of them have made any improvement. There are some of us to whom no operation, no treatment known today, will bring back our hearing.

Ben's deafness resulted from otosclerosis, the commonest cause of progressive hearing loss in adults. The hereditary nature of otosclerosis has been recognised for over a century, and this is clearly shown in our family by its occurrence through four generations, starting with Ben's father. Although he was not profoundly deaf, and his slight hearing loss explained by relatives as being an industrial deafness resulting from a lifetime of working in a forge, it is certain that he had otosclerosis. Only one of his five surviving sons had normal hearing, and my grandmother was never significantly deaf until the last years of her very long life. Hearing loss in this disease is not normally obvious in the first two decades of life, but the condition was so severe in Ben's case that his problems began around the age of eleven, and continued to progress very rapidly during his years at school and University.

In one of the letters he sent to his parents from Skye in 1929, he told them that he had been awakened by a severe thunderstorm, and added, "You can realise the intensity of the storm by the fact that it woke me up!" For all practical purposes his deafness had become complete by the time he was in his early thirties, although he wrote of a totally unexpected experience at the age of thirty-five, when he was almost jolted out of his wits whilst exploring Kilwinning Abbey:

> I wandered through the town till I was attracted by a notice informing me that the keys of the Abbey could be obtained at a shop in the High Street. That was all. I felt as though I had been presented with

the freedom of the town when I was handed a bunch of eight keys. One let me into the churchyard, where the ruins indicated that the Abbey must have been a very extensive building. Another key let me into an isolated square belfry tower. Ropes dangled down, and I had difficulty in restraining an impulse to lock the door and ring the bells.

Yet another key let me into the entrance to a spiral stairway, very dark and narrow. Above the first floor the weights of the clock – like huge curling stones – hung down. The next stairway was darker and narrower. Countless pigeons fluttered out from the narrow slits in the walls, for the tower is innocent of glass. Towards the top there were pigeons' nests on every step. I reached the belfry feeling something like the hunchback of Notre Dame. Suddenly there was a terrific booming. The whole building vibrated. I had the fright of my life, and thought of an air raid. The clock was striking twelve and I was within six inches of it!!

Ben made no mention of his deafness in telling this story, part of an article for the Glasgow *Evening Times*. In such a confined space, the unexpected sound of a large clock would come as a severe enough shock to anyone with unimpaired senses. Think what it must have been like for Ben. This incident took place in 1938, after roughly two years of being inured to the loss of his hearing. The sudden booming and vibration must have seemed like the Last Trump!

I recall clearly a much later occasion when he came to our house in Dumbarton to try out a new and very large type of hearing device which my father had obtained, and I also recall the intense look of frustration on his face when he realised he was hearing nothing, even at the maximum available setting. I think I must have been in my early teenage years then, so that was likely just after the end of the war, yet it was another twenty years before he would finally write, "There are some of us to whom no operation, no treatment known today, will bring back our hearing." By that time he really had tried everything.

There was nearly a disaster for him in the early 1960s. I was working in a hospital just outside London where one of the surgeons had extensive experience with stapedectomy,[13] the new operation for otosclerosis which had been introduced in 1958. After much discussion, despite one previous unsuccessful operation (stapes mobilisation) a few years earlier, Ben decided that he had nothing to lose by undergoing this latest procedure on one ear. Unfortunately that hope proved too optimistic. There was no change of any kind in his hearing, but he suffered from attacks of momentary vertigo post-operatively which continued for so long that it seemed that he might never be able to be out safely on the hills again. It was over two years before these dizzy spells more or less disappeared, two years during which I reproached myself on many occasions for having suggested that he consider the stapedectomy. I think that concern over the chance of sudden unsteadiness may have precipitated his decision to stop leading groups of students on overnight excursions from Glenmore Lodge.

Ben's inability to master or even try to master lip reading has surprised many people. His parents always put the blame on him, that he would simply not persist, but it was recognised in the family that a major share of responsibility also lay with his father and mother. They were told time and time again that there was no hope for any return of his hearing, yet they persisted with further and further consultations in the hope of an improvement, each series of tests producing exactly the same verdict – "Your son will become totally deaf, and should take lessons in lip reading while he still has some hearing left." In the early 1930s he lectured at the Glasgow Society for the Deaf, but somehow never found the time necessary to attend their lip reading classes himself, so perhaps the blame should be equally shared. Blame was laid by Ben on his parents in one related matter. He loved Glasgow High School, and was very proud of his connection with it in later years, remaining extremely bitter about being sent off to a school for the deaf in Norfolk at the age of sixteen. I found among his papers his last school report from the High School, showing him dux of the class, no mean achievement for a young boy with rapidly developing deafness. The words "Dux of Class" had been underlined, an indication of his feelings at that time.

BEWILDERING INSTINCT

How, then, did he survive with only the very simplest of lip reading skills? How did he manage to complete his dental training, to set himself up in practice as a dental radiologist, to be able to examine patients and take the appropriate radiographs while many of them remained oblivious to the fact that he was completely deaf? Alex Small visited his Berkeley Street rooms quite often, and noticed his routine:

"Certainly it was a fact that while he was engaged in Dental Radiology most of his patients were unaware that Ben was deaf. He had a set stock of conversational phrases that allowed him to proceed with his examination, and they usually left without suspecting that he hadn't heard a word of what they had said. His conspiratorial smile to any bystander as the patient departed was a shared triumph of innocent deception."

Ben's single-mindedness and determination enabled him to survive professionally, although it was inevitable that the deafness increasingly hampered his work. When the younger dentists in Glasgow all went off to war in 1939 he recalled that "lack of referrals resulted in the collapse of my practice". Few people knew that as late as 1953, when he was having financial problems, he applied for a position as consultant dental radiologist to the Western Regional Hospital Board. Happily for him, I believe, that application was unsuccessful.

Every one of his friends over the years found that his remarkable ability to grasp the flow of conversation, or the direction of a debate, gave them cause to doubt the fact that he was totally deaf. Bill Murray described his own doubts, and also gave the best account of Ben's vocal trademark – the trademark that none could forget:

"Even at the general meeting of any society or club, he could not only take part in debates, working from brief notes passed by his friends, but had the most bewildering instinct for knowing instantly what had been said in response, when he would jump to his feet to rout an opponent. This happened so often that I began to doubt his deafness, which I at last tested (out of doors) by blowing a police whistle behind his head – and Ben was indeed stone deaf . . .

". . . Ben's long-drawn aaaaaah was an habitual expression. By subtle inflexion of voice he could use it to signify equally well approval or censure, or to convey from the gamut of emotion any note he chose – delight, derision, admiration, contempt, laughter, scepticism, wonder, scandal, irony – all unaffectedly since he could hear nothing of his own tone, giving unerring expression to inward feeling. His eloquent aaaaaahs could communicate more than other men's innumerable words."

That bewildering instinct became for Ben a sixth sense, almost a gift for mental telepathy. Was this the gift of a seventh son,[14] with extra powers? Perhaps not, but his other senses developed in an extraordinary way in compensation for the deafness. Many of his friends recognised that the clever way he asked questions or made statements enabled him to deduce an enormous amount from a nod, a wink, or a smile. Alex Small explained it further:

"I discovered that it wasn't so much that Ben had to contend with his deafness, it was rather the other person who had to get his ideas or opinions over to him. He had already thought out so much of what he wanted to do or say that he dominated the dialogue, and reservations, changes or difficulties had to be urged on him by sign language and notes. In this respect I don't think that many of the friends I knew, or myself, had much trouble in conversing with him. A sort of mutual telepathy developed which allowed the interchange of facts, opinions and discussions, with only a minimal use of written notes on the part of the recipient of Ben's flood of talk.

"But it was at meetings that his ability to follow argument and debate was most surprising. Time and again he would intervene or comment in the most logical manner about some proposal or motion, affirming or contradicting with power and authority. How he achieved this was a complete mystery, but among his close friends it was a recognised absurdity that if you held a different view from Ben at a meeting you didn't whisper about it to anyone, but wrote it in a note, otherwise Ben would sense your opposition and attack you vehemently! Deafness wasn't a handicap to him. It concentrated his energies and single mindedness to make him the many sided personality he was."

I accepted Ben's deafness naturally as a child, and can never remember it causing me the slightest difficulty. I soon came to realise that there was little point in writing at any length in his notebook, unless on a subject that particularly interested him, for he might only glance briefly at what one had written before handing it back. George Scarborough, an Aviemore friend, recalled a long train journey with Ben, during which Ben did all the talking, George's part in the conversation being limited to occasionally jotting down comments in the notebook. As they neared their destination, it struck George that the other passengers in the compartment probably thought that he was the one who had the problem with communication!

While our own children were growing up, though they had less opportunity of contact with him after we came to Canada, I used to watch how they always seemed to be on the same wavelength, often skipping along happily at his side chattering away, with Ben somehow instinctively knowing the direction of their thoughts. His eyes missed nothing; hence when a child indicated something to him, he already knew what had caught their interest. He had the greatest camaraderie with them. All were greeted with his own special children's handshake, and the bond between them instantly sealed. One friend remarked that as a proverbial bachelor he must have been "Uncle Bennie" to countless children over the years, children who enjoyed many of his jokes better than most adults did!

THE HUMBLE KIPPER

Humour and dispute were seldom missing from Ben's life, the latter often long pursued. Hamish MacInnes recalled examples of both, referring also to that special way with children, a relationship which Bill Murray described as "a gift that all might envy":

"One of my most vivid memories is of a meeting at Red Cross HQ in Glasgow. Ben had a long time dislike of one member of the Scottish Mountaineering Club. He did not regard him as a climber, and felt he should not have been elected. To make matters worse, this individual was appointed SMC representative on the Committee meeting that day, the predecessor of the Mountain Rescue Committee of Scotland. At the start of the meeting he must have been feeling particularly difficult, for he threw a great sheaf of papers across the room, and stood and shouted as only Ben could, 'I refuse to attend a meeting with this man present – aaaaaah!'

"I also remember him for his great way with children and his vast arsenal of practical jokes. What was even funnier was his subsequent laugh when a joke was enacted.

"One time he was with my climbing course in Glencoe for some companionship on the hill. We had arranged to meet up at the late Ian Clough's house in Glencoe village, where Ben arrived before first light. We decided that day to climb in the Cairngorms, and Ben thought he had got into Ian Clough's car for the journey; however, he was in mine, which was modified and very fast. As we headed north at speed Ben kept jumping up and down in the seat saying with great glee . . . 'Hamish will never catch us up!' "

That story indicates how Ben's humour could almost be childlike at times, and also how his deafness could hamper him in situations which the hearing person takes for granted. In the half-light of dawn, unable to hear the voice from the driver's seat, Ben was quite unaware of his correct identity.

Writing about Ben in *The Scots Magazine* after his death, Tom Weir echoed Hamish's remembrance of the famous laugh:

". . . He had a gusto and a Puckish sense of humour, sometimes expressed in wild cackling laughter, infectious to everyone within earshot."

Despite this great sense of fun, however, like many practical jokers he could not always take a joke directed against himself, and the problems of a natural sensitivity were compounded by his deafness. The major flaw in Ben's character resulted from this touchiness, coupled with his innate stubbornness, for he could build a perceived minor slight into a major insult, brooding over a situation without the normal two-way recourse to the spoken word. It was a weakness not easily disguised, well illustrated by Bill Murray in recounting the story of the "Humble Kipper", an incident renowned in Scottish mountaineering circles prior to the Second World War:

"Disputes with Ben were frequent and long pursued. Nearly all trouble arose from some written notes. He kept a notebook for companions to write down their thoughts or replies. Ben's advantage then was this permanent record of everything that had been said, often in unwise haste. He could refer back and confound the man who had changed an opinion or a lightly given promise. But the real ground of trouble was that written words so often fail to convey the full meaning of words uttered – the tone of voice is absent. In speech one can often say without offence to a hearing person many things that written would arouse wrath. One may speak frankly if the tone is heard to be friendly, or concerned, or humorous. When young I would sometimes forget this in the heat of the moment when scribbling a note to Ben – as most people did sooner or later – forget too, since Ben himself was most outspoken, that he was far more sensitive to our adverse opinions than we to his, and Ben, misinterpreting, would then feel grossly insulted.

"My worst offence came when I was organizing in Glasgow a photographic exhibition for the Junior Mountaineering Club of Scotland. Archie MacAlpine submitted a print of Ben sitting outside his tent in Glen Brittle eating a kipper. He looked the picture of an old tramp and the entry was titled *The Humble Kipper*. It gave me delight – a riposte too for the similar feeling he had once exhibited whilst taking a photograph of a cow eating my pyjamas. When Ben came into the room and saw it, he ripped it off the wall. I asked for his notebook and wrote, 'Don't be a b-f-, please put it back.' His fury boiled over. He would neither speak to me nor see me again for nearly two years, in which time war had broken out. The next time we met was by chance in the summer of 1945 in Sauchiehall Street. He came up to me grinning. 'Three years in prison camps – aaaaaah! – maybe you've been punished enough,' and held out his hand, which I thankfully took."

Bill was not the only person impugned over the Humble Kipper, for Ben – never one for half measures – went so far as to demand an official apology from the President and Vice-President of the Club!

Not long after Ben's death his old friend Ian MacPhail wrote to me at length about the many sides to his complex character: his loyalty as a companion; his individualistic and sometimes risqué sense of humour; his obstinacy and downright stubbornness; and his ready forgiveness of friends when an opinion was subsequently proved wrong. The facets of that character are inseparable from his deafness:

"He had at times rather extravagant ideas of jokes, and from time to time would call into Tam Sheppard's joke shop in Queen Street, Glasgow, later producing in his friend's houses props such as a hinged

teaspoon or a floating lump of sugar, which would always highly enter-
tain any children present. Perhaps his favourite prop was a very realistic
'specimen' which he would lay on the carpet of a house where there
was a dog, causing much embarrassment to the host or hostess as they
tried to dispose of it before any guests became aware of their pet's
apparent uncharacteristic lapse. On one occasion, I think at Glenaffric
Hotel, he almost lost his toy when the porter, seeing it near the fire, was
only prevented from committing it to the flames by what must have been
one of the loudest and longest of his famous shouts!

"Although a very keen photographer, he never liked being photographed himself. We were climbing from Lochgilphead on a very warm
day with Jim McKinney, a PT instructor, and all stripped for a swim in
a small loch. Bennie suspected he might be photographed and went off
on his own along the loch, but I managed to distract his attention long
enough for Jim to obtain a picture, only to provoke his wrath. Two years
later, however, when it was shown at a slide show at McKinney's house,
he joined the company in howls of laughter.

"The different sides to his character, exemplified by the sudden and
spontaneous shouts of joy, and the equally sudden anger that could
consume him, are well illustrated by the manner of my joining, and
leaving, the Scottish Mountaineering Club. At the end of the war, Bennie
suggested I join the SMC, of which he had become a member in 1936.
I just missed the 1946 election, but applied in 1947. I had climbed over
seventy 'Munros',[15] many of them alone, many in snow and ice, and had
done a great deal of rock-climbing, and Bennie had no doubt I would
be elected. When I told him I'd climbed Lochnagar in 1939 with a party
of schoolboys from the King's Camp at Balmoral along with the King
himself, George VI, he gave a great roar – 'You must put him down as
your companion' (and indeed applicants for admission were asked to
name companions) 'it will be the first time in the club's history that will
have happened, aaaaaah!' Needless to say, with Bennie as sponsor, and
such a distinguished person for a fellow climber, I was admitted.

"Over the years I attended many SMC AGMs as interpreter for
Bennie, who often raised serious and sensible objections to the way things
were run. I myself, although I am still climbing, gradually lost interest
in the Club's activities, and about 1973, when reviewing my list of
subscriptions to various clubs and societies, I decided to resign. What a
telling off I got from Bennie! He said he was 'shocked, nay, disgusted',
as my original sponsor, to learn what I had done. No one left the Club
he said, except for reasons of death or poverty, and neither applied to
me! Into the bargain, I was still climbing. My resignation, which

prompted his indignant reaction, was actually quite normal to a person like myself with varied interests and a fairly limited income, but it took Bennie a long time to accept that fact. In the end he forgave me, but it took many months. That was his way."

Stories from other friends echoed Ian's remarks regarding arguments, and I can remember many heated family disputes between my parents and Ben. They always ended in the same manner, with his refusal to read their written comments at the height of the disagreement, pushing the notebook away every time another brief remark was added. How can one continue an argument with someone who cannot hear, but who knows well what has been written, who at the same time refuses to recognise the only method of communication? In her younger days my mother regarded him as being very selfish, of having his own mother wait on him hand and foot during the years they lived together at Comely Bank. I am sure, that like most of our family at that time, she appreciated neither the full extent of Ben's outdoor activities nor the tremendous physical and mental energy he consumed, still less the countless hours and weeks of totally voluntary work he undertook. It is not easy for the hearing person to imagine what it must be like to survive in a world which seems at times to ignore the needs of the deaf. If Ben's deafness required him to look out for his own interests on occasions, it is hardly surprising.

Among his papers I came across a short, unpublished article about his deafness, written when he was living in Arrochar, and revised soon after he moved to Aviemore. Some of these feelings he had briefly described in print during the early 1930s; years later they still preoccupied him. The title is his own:

A DEAF MAN SPEAKS

Is total deafness the greater affliction than blindness? The late Helen Keller seemed to think so. Speak to a blind man and he immediately forgets his blindness in eager conversation. Speak to a deaf man and you remind him of his deafness. Always the blind receive sympathy, always there is someone there to help them cross the road – it is an instinctive reaction. On the other hand, the deaf are most often regarded as a nuisance, and left out of things. Folk who hear just cannot understand what total deafness means; they know what blindness means, for everyone is blind in the dark.

Try this. Disconnect the doorbell, disconnect the telephone, stuff cotton wool in your ears, and tie a large bandage around them. Stay in your house all day, hearing nothing, and speaking to no one. That would give you some idea of what it all means, as I have lived alone for many years, and had many days like that. Always it is worse in the winter when one's sense of loneliness increases.

The gossip of every day passes me by. Radio, the song of the birds and all of nature's sounds have been unknown to me since my childhood. Of music, singing and the theatre I know nothing. Books are the only solace, reading the only time when one can fully forget deafness. The world of today is perhaps harsher for the totally deaf than in former years. Much joy went out of my life when silent films gave place to the talkies. I seldom go now, for musicals are sheer boredom, and much of the rest is violence. In years gone by I greatly enjoyed weekly games of auction bridge with friends, but now they cannot be drawn from their television sets. I only managed to get one quite recently, and must confess that while it helps, I do not use it much. Almost every night endless violence, shooting, murders, all often impossible to follow. The nightly news and sports are my chief interest.

With understanding friends the deaf can manage quite well, for we are all lip readers to some extent. But when a third person joins in, all pleasure goes for inevitably the two hearing folk talk to each other and the deaf person is neglected. Moustaches and beards often conceal mouth movement, making it more difficult for those who lip read. One notices this on TV also: in almost every play or feature the telephone is used, and this totally conceals lip movement. A highlight for me was one occasion when good friends obtained the complete script of a play for me. I read it previously, then had it with me, and I could follow everything. That, alas, is seldom possible except for amateur plays.

There are problems too when travelling alone. I have lost trains because of loud speakers announcing change of platforms at short notice, and cannot hear any announcement when travelling by air. Perhaps the worst feature is when making enquiries in shops and offices. I say I am stone deaf, and can hear nothing. The usual result is a loud shout, which just makes things worse, and causes annoyance to those around. Shouting is perhaps what the deaf dislike most, as it just reminds them of their affliction. Slow and quiet speech is what we need.

Were I asked what I miss most in life, I would reply the ability to use a telephone. I must at all times communicate by letter, and mail these days is often very slow. The art of letter writing is almost forgotten, and I am constantly left out of things because folks cannot phone me, and can't be bothered to write.

There are Hard of Hearing Clubs in the cities, but none for those of us in the countryside. In the country too, library services are very limited; our own small one only seems to get new books, or change of books, about once in six months. The National Institute for the Deaf does fine work, especially in sending out details of TV features, but the coverage is limited, and the Institute is not nearly as well financed as the National Institute for the Blind. The blind have an income tax allowance, and while the hard of hearing have hearing aids supplied by the National Health Service, the totally deaf have many extra expenses and problems to deal with, but get no allowance to help. The reason is said to be that one cannot tell the degree of deafness, but surely any aurist could certify total deafness?

Please don't think that I am always complaining. I have good health, and have led a full life – but oh how much more pleasant life would be were hearing folk to give to the deaf the understanding and sympathy they always extend to the blind.

In his book *Journey into Silence*,[16] former Labour MP Jack Ashley (now Lord Ashley) describes the calamity of his own sudden and almost complete loss of hearing. With hearing on one side unaltered following three stapedectomies, he was advised that near normal hearing could be restored to the other ear by repair of a perforated eardrum. Instead, complications following the operation left him with virtually no hearing at all, where there had been previously only a partially significant handicap. Almost overnight Ashley came to appreciate two of Ben's major concerns. Both caused great distress: the sudden loss of the telephone as a means of communication, and the manner in which hearing people unthinkingly exclude the deaf from a place in conversation. It is sad to realise that if Ben had lived longer he could have made full use of closed captions in television programming (he once remarked on how easy that should be, long before it became a practical reality). Sad too, perhaps, to realise that modern telecommunications have now made the telephone available to the deaf, yet not so to remember how he overcame the challenge of his deafness.

Just how did he survive, and even thrive, in the face of total deafness, maintaining several seemingly full time occupations at the same time, and making unique pioneering contributions in a wide variety of unrelated fields? We found the answers to these questions in three places. Firstly in his writings, and what they told of his life; then in the contents of his Aviemore home after his death; and lastly, most importantly, in the story of his discovery of a new voice, one which spoke to all of his remaining senses.

3

EILEAN A' CHEÒ[17]

THE VOICE OF THE HILLS

There is another voice the deaf can hear as well as any other person – the voice of the hills. Some will hear it in their youth, while others will regret they did not hear it until a later age, and ever bemoan the lost years. Once the call comes clearly and one begins to understand these grand hills of ours, their spell cannot be broken and will last through life itself.

Ben wrote those words for an article entitled "The Deaf Can Hear", which was published in a magazine for the deaf in 1934. Five years earlier, setting off with George McKay on a walking tour of Skye, he had known little of the hills, and had no real thought of climbing. In daily letters to his parents he described in great detail their progress round the island, and these letters remain as a lasting record of the blossoming of his love affair with the Cuillin.

He began from Broadford by telling of the steerage passengers' discomfort on the MacBrayne steamer from Mallaig to Kyle of Lochalsh, forced to stand in cattle pens between decks, and then of Skye's typical welcome . . . "You ask my first impressions of Skye? It's a mist! . . . We shall soon see the hills, perhaps!" Blaven and the Red Cuillin did emerge from the mist on the second day, however, so instead of going on to Sligachan as intended, the two trampers stopped for the night at the little village of Sconser. Here, quite by chance, they found as their host the famous Cuillin mountaineering guide, John Mackenzie. In the small Sconser cottage that evening Ben found his footsteps being redirected, away from the road and onto the hills.

Second day, Sconser, 12 July 1929:
    Well, Father, here we are, sixteen miles today and still going strong, enthusiasm unabated, blisters commencing! We were very lucky to get in here, for the owner John Mackenzie is the only resident professional guide for mountaineering in Skye. The cottage is just a but and ben, and we are sleeping in the loft. Mackenzie

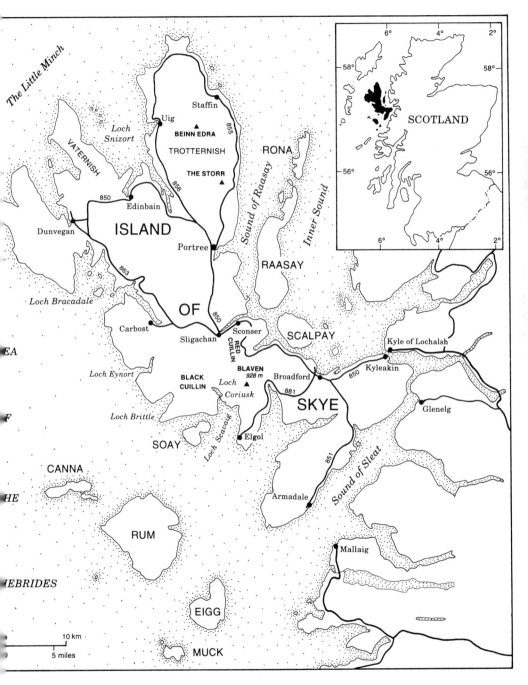

The Isle of Skye.

is a wonderful old veteran. No living man knows the Skye mountains better, for he has spent a lifetime among them. He is well
over seventy, but still acts as a guide and goes daily with climbing
parties to the top of some peak or other – and it is real climbing!
It is absolutely necessary to be roped together. He gave us many
good tips, and showed us many of his climbing treasures, including
a map of the Cuillin which had been presented to him (four inches
to the mile).

Sixth day, Staffin, Tuesday 16 July 1929:

I was much too tired to write last night, but we are feeling "gey
proud o' ourselves." Let me tell you.

We left Portree at 8.30 a.m. yesterday morning. Our bill for two
nights' lodging amounted to thirteen shillings each – not bad?? Look
at the map you have. We followed the Staffin road to Loch Fada,
about three miles out. This is apparently the most famous trout loch
on the island. At 10 a.m. we left the road where John Mackenzie
suggested, and climbed up onto the mountain ridge above Bealach
Mor, then had a weary three mile climb along to the top of the
Storr (2,360 feet), the highest peak on the north part of Skye.

The gods were kind, for it was a glorious hot day. It took us three
hours to reach the summit, where we were richly rewarded. The
blue sky overhead showed no trace of mist, and every peak stood
out startlingly clear. The whole panorama of the north-west lay before
us, with the sea island studded, as dazzlingly blue as any tropical
lagoon. To the north was the ridge of hills stretching up to Trotternish
Point. We could follow the whole length of the Outer Hebrides to
the north-west. South and North Uist were quite clear, with the
outline of Lewis hidden in a misty haze. Away to the north-east was
a promontory we took to be Cape Wrath, and we could follow the
coastline of the mainland right down to Gairloch and Loch Torridon,
with the Torridon and Applecross hills showing hundreds of peaks.

To the west lay the crystal clearness of Loch Snizort and Loch
Bracadale, enclosing between them the whole Vaternish peninsula,
and then to the south the full majesty of the mountains, every peak
standing out as if in a fine etching. It was the first time we had seen
the whole jagged range of the Cuillin, peak after peak reared up,
tumbling masses of sheer black rock, so clear that we could make
out every pinnacle and crag. Fittingly they are described as the greatest
mountain range between the Alps and Norway.

Were we not fortunate? Such a day does not often occur on Skye.
Our jackets and shirts were soaked with sweat, and for two hours

we lay on a long flat area of sheep-cropped grass on the summit of the Storr. There was scarce a breath of wind, and we were well above the midges and their clan.

But back to our story. You will see on the map that the Storr is further east than the rest of the ridge. We climbed down into the valley and then up to the top of Bealach Hartaval (1,566 feet), and from there followed the ridge the whole way to Staffin. Up and down, and ever up and down, we climbed in all I think nine peaks. It was as though we were walking along the very top of the world. We left the Storr at 2.30 p.m., and got to Ben Edra at 7.30. As the crow flies it is about six miles, but I reckon we covered twelve or thirteen. From Ben Edra we scrambled down and followed a burn to Kilmartin River, about three miles over peat bogs and marshes. Often we were in up to our knees.

At last, weary, oh how weary, we got to the water's edge about 9 p.m. For ten hours we had met no one; only sheep, hares, rabbits, and the gulls above had shared our ramble. It was a long day, but worth it! Worth it a thousand times! Sheriff Nicolson, the Skye poet, has said ". . . to ascend the Storr and follow the ridge the whole way to Staffin is the grandest promenade on Skye; he who would do so must have a long summer's day before him, and must be strong hearted and strong of foot." Dr MacCulloch in his book questions if Nicolson ever did it himself, and says that it is a walk attempted by few and accomplished by still fewer, so you see we have placed ourselves among the immortals!

P.S. You might keep these letters for me. I may do something with them later.

Ben concluded the day's story in *Tramping in Skye*:

Another two miles took us to Staffin. The long trek left us both very weary, and we were in despair when two houses refused us lodging. But about 9 p.m., at a wee farm, we were made welcome, and regaled like the Prodigal Son. Our feet were in a sorry mess, and I laugh when I remember how, in the dusk, we sat in the farmyard with our feet immersed in tubs of hot water, the whole household listening to our tale. Then supper – a hearty Skye supper – and we were as giants refreshed.

Douglas Scott, just leaving school at that time and not yet a climber, met Ben as he came off the hills at Staffin. He looked back fifty years to the encounter in his contribution to Ben's obituary in the *Scottish Mountaineering Club Journal*:

"It had been a blazing hot day and his face was shining to match the setting sun. He had just come down from the Storr ridge after doing all the tops, and his glowing account filled me with envy."

In the exhilaration of his tale Ben failed to notice that more than his feet had become casualties. He later laughingly described to his parents how he had been forced to return by bus to Portree to purchase another pair of second hand boots, his own having disintegrated totally following the trudge through the peat bogs below Ben Edra – less than a week after setting out from Kyleakin! When they headed out again, west across the island, the Skye weather had changed with a vengeance, but it relented once more by the time they arrived at Glen Brittle.

Tenth day, Dunvegan, 20 July 1929:

What a change! Up till now Nature has shown us all her smiles, but today she is in a very different angry mood. We are storm bound. As I write this I am sitting in an arm chair close drawn to a big peat fire, whilst outside the wind is howling and the trees swaying wildly. It has been raining continuously for over twenty-four hours, so we will stay here till Monday, and hope that the storm has blown over by then.

We left Edinbain Hotel this morning about 11.30 a.m. Mist hung over the hills and only the near mainland was visible, with the Cuillin retreated into a grey blackness. The road crosses over the Vaternish peninsula to the Fairy Bridge, where we took the south fork towards Dunvegan. By then it was raining heavily, and there was no shelter for miles, no trees at all, just the moorland and peat bogs. The road palled us so we took to a cart track to the right to Loch Dunvegan. This wandered across the moorland for a mile or two, then led through McLeod's estates to Dunvegan Castle. Were we wet by the time we reached the Castle?? Like a pair of drookit craws!

Fourteenth day, Glen Brittle, 24 July 1929

George and I are in the heart of the Cuillin at last. This is best of all. We came from Carbost yesterday afternoon, and we are staying right on the edge of the loch, looking up towards the southern range of the Cuillin, hardly half a mile away. It is now 10 p.m., and we returned less than an hour ago after a glorious day in the mountains. We have been away since 11 a.m., and we climbed the highest one!

We went by the guide book, and by John Mackenzie's advice, and took the easy way, so please don't think that we did anything rash. The peaks look terrible, but they are not half as bad as they seem. Look at the map. From Glen Brittle we followed the Lagan Burn up the corrie to the little lochan which lies imprisoned between Sgurr Dearg and Sgurr Alasdair. It's hardly more than two feet deep, and the water is crystal clear. The mountains around it have no touch of greenery, nothing but black rock and grey stone. I never thought that we had anything like this in Britain.

We did the climb by what is known as "the great stone shoot", which runs between Sgurr Alasdair and Sgurr Thearlaich. It is very steep, and consists wholly of loose stone, but is quite safe going as the stones are so many layers thick. It took us a while though, but from the top to the cairn at the summit was not too bad. The top consists of a small cairn, the peak itself being so steep and slender that only one person at a time can stand beside the cairn.

The view was glorious. We could see all the peaks in Skye. The Cuillin, Black and Red, and the Red Hills, with the Storr away to the north beyond Portree. The islands were all around us – the outer Hebrides, then Soay, Canna, Rum and Muck – while the mainland hills were very clear. We were again lucky, for it was the first decent climbing day for a week, with no mist or chance for any, and there were many parties among the mountains. The thing to do is to climb right along the ridges from one mountain to another till you have been on six or seven summits! The ridges for the most part are very narrow, practically knife edge, reared into pinnacles every now and then. Needless to say we did not attempt anything like that, for a rope is absolutely necessary.

While we were on the top we watched three parties – all roped together – climbing along the ridges. It was hair raising, and quite as good as a movie show! There were ladies in two of the parties, all wearing short trousers. But it is not as difficult as it looks, for the rock is full of footholds and one can always get a good grip (you have to!) The danger is loose stones, of which there are a great number, so that it is necessary first to test every grip and foothold, making progress very slow.

After leaving the summit, we scrambled down the other side of Sgurr Alasdair to another corrie, and followed that down to Soay Sound, then had a moor walk of four miles back here. We have just had a glorious sunset, perfect after a perfect day, our first in the high Cuillin. I will never forget it!

The scramble down the other side of Sgurr Alasdair was not quite as Ben reported, as he explained for readers other than his parents at a later time:

For an hour we stayed on the summit in brilliant sunshine, then

McKay scared me by insisting that we return by a different route, while I, ever cautious, thought we had better go back the way we had come. I should explain here that I was wearing boots with a few hobnails, while he had ordinary walking shoes with rubber soles, and both of us wore shorts.

We followed the ridge a short distance towards Sgurr Sgumain then descended direct to Loch Coir' a' Ghrunnda. George started down the Ghrunnda face, and I lost sight of him but had to follow. That descent is just a confused memory to me and we were lucky to get down safely. It was only when we found a copy of the SMC Guide to Skye at Mrs Chisholm's that evening that we appreciated how foolish we had been. We could not locate our route among the Ghrunnda face climbs described in the guide, and though I have been there many times since then, I have not been able to pick it out. Most certainly it is not a route for unroped novices and beginner's luck must have been with us.

Of that holiday such was our only climb in the Cuillin. George McKay had the makings of a first rate rock climber. He chose matrimony and an anxious wife instead, and never climbed again.

Most of Ben's letters were written on the same day as the events they described, with their details indicating frequent reference to maps and to other books on Skye. This regular discipline is typical of him, often completed late in the evening after a very strenuous day. The postscript added to the exuberant account from Staffin clearly indicates the early direction of his thoughts. *Tramping in Skye*,[18] which was published four years later in 1933, reflected the growing excitement of his original letters. One of the reviewers of the book, almost certainly ignorant of Ben's deafness, chastised him for his interpretation of sounds, but then went on, perhaps unwittingly, to capture something of the spirit that motivated him:

". . . some of the hints on Gaelic pronunciation are enough to make a Gaelic speaking person ill. But when Mr Humble climbs a mountain he is a fine companion. Every page registers an enthusiasm or an ecstasy, with what Mr Joseph Chamberlain called 'the madness of walking' inducing in Mr Humble's case a vanity that is really delightful, since the author seems quite unaware of it."

All of Ben's writings contain that vanity, which is simply the reflection of the infectious enthusiasm with which he faced most of life, part of his defence against the isolation of his deafness, an enthusiasm for the hills that would now lead him into a second career as an author, journalist, and photographer of the Scottish outdoors. On his return to Glasgow, he sent a photograph from the holiday to Douglas Scott, who later suggested they climb together. ("He seemed to think I was a great climber", Ben wrote.)

In the closing lines of "The Deaf Can Hear", Ben looked back to the early days when he and Douglas gained experience together:

> The hill-goer's memories are many and varied, and can never fade: of winter climbing when in the morning the tops are bathed in the rose flush of dawn; of the climb and maybe the hearty labour of step cutting; of gaining the summit and gazing around on a sea of snow capped peaks sparkling in brilliant sunshine; of the descent and exhilaration of the long glissade. Memories too of wild stormy days and the fierce joy of battle through the wind, the rain, and the mist, and of perfect summer days and bivouacs high up in the mountains.
>
> And the sunsets! After a long day on the hills there comes a pleasing sense of well-being and fitness, and the hill-goer appreciates the more those glorious West Highland sunsets. The lovely peaceful sunsets over Jura from the hills of Knapdale, the stormy sunsets over the mountains of Rum from Mallaig, and – above all – the sunsets in Eilean a' Cheò. To see the mighty steel blue range of the Cuillin, splintered peaks against a crimson sky, is unutterably splendid.
>
> These are just a few of the rewards of those who hear and answer the call of the hills.

THREE CLIMBING GIANTS

Ben's whole life turned on the 1929 Skye holiday. He was twenty-six, newly trained in dental radiology, and already full of ideas for professional research. His already keen senses were increasing in acuity in response to the growing deafness, and this blended easily with a natural affinity for the outdoors. He also had a compelling urge to write. At the end of the first day's walk from Kyleakin, he found a second hand copy of MacCulloch's classic, *The Misty Isle of Skye*, in a Broadford shop, and began to read about the island. Providence then gave him a rare privilege – that of meeting, and lodging with, one of the climbing giants of Skye. It was a pivotal event in his life, the portrayal he left equally memorable:

> Later, as we sat outside, a man came up from the road towards the croft. And what a man! He was an old man, yet he walked easily and his eyes were clear. That grand white beard would have made him notable in any company. He wore an ancient suit of plus

fours, big heavy boots, a deer-stalker cap and carried some trout. We were invited into the kitchen and sat round the fire in the gloaming. The old man's interest was aroused when we told him we hoped to climb one of the Cuillin peaks the following week. Obviously he knew them well, for, instead of talking of danger and difficulty as most folks would have done, he said that Sgurr Alasdair, the highest of them all, was "just a walk, . . . just a walk". He showed us many old photographs of rock climbing, and a series of stereoscopic views. There seemed to be nothing about the Cuillin that he did not know.

We had gathered by this time that he himself was a guide to the Cuillin, and that he had spent the day fishing in Loch Fada with a Professor Collie. The names Mackenzie and Collie did not signify anything to us, for we knew nothing of mountains and mountaineering. It was late when we went to bed, and though we were at breakfast by eight Mackenzie had already gone off for a day's fishing somewhere.[19]

We walked on to Portree, and it was that talk about the mountains that made us leave the road. If an old man of seventy could walk to the highest Cuillin surely we could climb the Storr, which looked quite easy. We did more than that. We walked from Portree to Staffin via the Storr and the intervening hills. For tyros with big packs who knew nothing of hill walking that is quite a hefty undertaking.

As he lay on the summit of the Storr with the Hebridean panorama spread out before him, Ben read the Skye poet Nicolson's eloquent description of the ridge walk to Staffin. The differing phrases which he used to describe their reception at the end of the day show just how his imagination was fired; they give evidence also of the "vanity" referred to by the reviewer of *Tramping in Skye*:

> So you see, we have placed ourselves among the immortals!
> We were treated like heroes.
> We were regaled like the Prodigal Son.
> We were as giants refreshed.

After the first glimpse of climbers in action from the summit of Sgurr Alasdair, Ben took his growing excitement home at the conclusion of the holiday, and began to read further. Almost immediately, he discovered three things: the full story of John Mackenzie's role in the history of mountaineering in Skye – they had talked with a man whose name had been given to a Cuillin peak before the end of the previous century,[20] a man who had been described as the only mountain guide of Swiss calibre Britain had ever produced; his companion Collie's fame extended far beyond Skye – to the Alps, the Himalayas, and the Canadian Rockies; and Nicolson was not simply a poet, but one of the early explorers of the Cuillin, with many first ascents to his credit. Three climbing giants, whose names had been completely unknown to him two short weeks before, now suddenly became part of his discovery of a whole new world. The impact on the impressionable Ben was enormous.

Tramping in Skye was the first product of that discovery. An early draft manuscript was turned down by a publisher as being too short, but he was encouraged to expand it, and did so after going back over his original route the following summer. He also increased the appeal of the book by weaving both legend and history into the final version, including details of the routes taken in Skye by the famous figures of the eighteenth century, Bonnie Prince Charlie, and the oddly mixed pair of Johnson and Boswell.

Under the influence of Nicolson's poems, and the search for short verses to head each chapter of his book, as was the fashion of the day, he then began to have ideas for a collection of songs and poems about the island. Nine publishers were not impressed, but Ben was never put off lightly.

> The tenth publisher shared my faith, and letters from readers around the world show that our faith was justified.

The Songs of Skye,[21] which was published the year after *Tramping in Skye*, was not simply a collection of verse, but rather a short history of the island presented through its legend and romance, illustrated by a total of sixty-seven songs and poems. In the last section, songs of mountain and moorland, Ben included a brief tribute to the man whose quiet encouragement had much to do with the early development of his own love for the hills:

JOHN MACKENZIE
(D. F. Rankine)

> Sing the praise of doughty John,
> Lord of crag and boulder,
> Peak and gully, slab and scree,
> Pinnacle and shoulder;
> Sure of foot and keen of eye,
> Cheery words to hail us;
> Ready still with rope and hand
> When the footholds fail us.

No book on Skye, whether prose or verse, would be complete without mention of the late John Mackenzie of Sconser. John died in 1934 after fifty years of climbing among the Cuillin. He was with the Pilkington brothers when they made the first ascent of the Inaccessible Pinnacle and was the first man to set foot on A'Cioch in Coire Lagan, that remarkable rock which has almost become a mecca of British climbers.

Sligachan Inn will never be quite the same without John. Professor Collie, another of the pioneers of Skye climbing, wrote of him: "As a companion on a long summer day he was perfect. Always cheerful, keenly alive to everything – the wild birds, the deer on the hillside, the fish in the rivers and all natural things. There is no one who can take his place. Those who knew him will remember him as a perfect gentleman who never offended by word or deed. He has left a gap that cannot be filled. There was only one John, simple minded, most lovable, and without guile. May he rest quietly in the little graveyard at Struan!"

Ben described Sheriff Nicolson as "The Great Explorer" in Cuillin history. Although born two decades after Nicolson's death, he was greatly influenced by him, and wrote of his exploits almost as much as he later did about Clement Wragge, the meteorologist of Ben Nevis. Nicolson's descent of Sgurr Dubh in the dark was the subject of several of Ben's stories, his use of a plaid rug (as a forerunner of the modern climber's rope) always figuring prominently.

Nicolson opened the door wide; he was the first real mountaineer and explorer among the Cuillin. His descent of the Coruisk face of Sgurr Dubh in darkness was the finest thing done in climbing in Britain up till that time, and might well be reckoned as notable as Whymper's first ascent of the Matterhorn.

He brought a new conception to the climbing game, and to his critics roundly declared: "The loss of life is a small thing compared with the full and free exercise of our powers, and the cultivation of a bold adventurous spirit; any nation which has ceased to think so is on the fair road to decay and degradation."

The Songs of Skye contained two of Nicolson's poems. One, *The Isle of Skye*, has a famous second stanza, the most recognisable of all his verses. The quotation was preceded by this introduction:

Skye has always had worthy singers; none more worthy than those who have sung of its mountains . . . Alexander Nicolson and Lawrence Pilkington – a Skyeman and an Englishman but of that mountain brotherhood who knows no country – were not content to worship the Cuillin from afar, but gained their utmost peaks very early in their climbing history. Sheriff Nicolson was one of the fathers of Scottish climbing and an early member of the Scottish Mountaineering Club. Before the birth of the club he climbed Blaven, Sgurr nan Gillean and Sgurr Dearg, and was the first to set his foot on the summit of the highest mountain in Skye, Sgurr Alasdair, which now commemorates his name. He is quoted as saying, "I would rather be remembered as the composer of one good song than as a writer of many respectable and superfluous books." So shall we remember him.

THE ISLE OF SKYE[22]
(Alexander Nicolson)

The beautiful isles of Greece
Full many a bard hath sung;
But the isles I love best lie far in the west,
Where men speak the Gaelic tongue.
Ithaca, Cyprus, and Rhodes
Are names to the Muses dear;
But sweeter still doth Icolmkill[23]
Fall on a Scotsman's ear.

Let them sing of the sunny South,
Where the blue Aegean smiles,
But give to me the Scottish sea,
That breaks round the Western Isles!
Jerusalem, Athens and Rome,
I would see them before I die,
But I'd rather not see any one of the three,
Than be exiled for ever from Skye!

Lawrence Pilkington, also a climber-poet, was recognised in the collection along with Nicolson, and Ben subsequently explained how he later came to know yet another of the great names of the Cuillin:

I found another link with the Golden Age in correspondence with Lawrence Pilkington during the last years of his life. He lived to the age of eighty-six, and his letters, in perfect copper-plate throughout, are full of love for the hills. He wrote of his last view of Skye, from the Mam Ratagan Road – "a glimpse of the promised land".

Norman Collie was the last of the distinguished climbers whom Ben had the privilege of coming across in his early years. Initially only a name mentioned casually by John Mackenzie, he never wrote of having talked with him, for by then Collie had become very reticent with strangers. But he was sufficiently impressed to describe his 1936 Skye holiday as being "blessed by a sight of the greatest Skye mountaineer of them all", and acknowledged Collie fully in the completed history of the Cuillin, including in it the last poignant picture by Richard Hillary,[24] a Battle of Britain pilot who was on leave in Skye in 1940:

"We were alone in the inn save for an old man who had returned there to die. His hair was white but his face and bearing were those of a mountaineer, though he must have been a great age. He never spoke, but appeared regularly at meals to take his place at a table tight pressed against the window, alone with his wine and memories. We thought him rather fine."

Having first come across Hillary's description of Collie in *The Cuillin of Skye*, W. C. Taylor wrote to Ben in 1971 while preparing his own fine biography of Collie, *The Snows of Yesteryear*.[25] He expressed pleasure, mixed with some awe, in the privilege of corresponding with one who had known both Collie and Mackenzie. That awe is perhaps a slight reflection of the feelings of respect which Ben held, right from the start, for all the early pioneers. The sense of history which he received from Mackenzie, Collie and Nicolson, before he had ever embarked on a proper climb, would lead him more than twenty years later to his last and best book.

THE CUILLIN OF SKYE

The mist hung low for the first two days, so that we had no far-off glimpse of the Black Cuillin, the wildest rock crags in all Britain. We had heard of them; we had seen photographs of them; no story or photograph could do justice to a first sight of those huge crags of black rock. At Sligachan Bridge we were almost surrounded by mountains – the Red Cuillin to the east, Ben Lee to the north and the Black Cuillin to the south. Mist still hung about the summit of Sgurr nan Gillean, then gradually lifted, and we could pick out its four pinnacles, one behind the other. To those who know only the smoother hills of the mainland it seems impossible that these mountains could be ascended, yet all have been climbed in hundreds of different ways . . . Such was the attraction of the Cuillin that we did much of the road backwards, turning around again and again for yet another glimpse of the mountains.

Those were Ben's earliest impressions of the Cuillin, thoughts he recorded after his first walk from Sconser to Portree. They were transcribed directly from one of his letters to his parents into the pages of *Tramping in Skye*, followed at a later date by this comment:

> The Cuillin will now ever be my Mecca, but are the more enjoyed because I did take the trouble – pleasure rather – of getting to know the lesser hills and hill routes first.

His history of the Cuillin, *The Cuillin of Skye*, was published in 1952. Its emergence from his thoughts in the years from 1929 can be traced through the countless articles on Skye that he produced in the intervening period, and from his first two books. The earliest short piece, "The Tramper's Paradise", appeared in the *Glasgow Bulletin* in 1930, followed by a longer one in *Chambers' Journal*, "Byways of Skye", addressed to the motorist who had taken pity on two drenched trampers on the road from Kyleakin to Broadford in 1929, and dwelling on the greater delights of the open road. Although he was quite an experienced climber by the time his first book was published in 1933, it contains only a few references to mountaineering and its history, being written primarily for the novice tramper or hill walker.

The history of climbing in Skye did find a small place in *The Songs of Skye*, through the references to Mackenzie, Nicolson, Collie and Pilkington. It ran into three editions, and a reprint edition, over a period of twenty-one years. As the author of two books on Skye Ben now came more into the public eye, and was given a somewhat unusual accolade:

> Strangest of all the results of that book was the appearance in Portree of a tea-room named after me! In 1934 people started writing to tell me about it, friends and strangers alike. On my first visit to Skye thereafter of course I had to go to "Humble's Tea Room" for tea – and was presented with the bill in the usual way.

(It is not difficult for Ben's friends to imagine him sitting in *his* tea-room,[26] taking perverse pleasure in being treated as just another customer!)

Despite the pressures of his professional career, which were greatest in the early 1930s, Ben somehow managed to spend every spare minute in the Glasgow libraries, delving into all manner of subjects, still searching through the literature on Skye. In a 1934 survey of all the important books ever written about the island, "Skye: A New Classic Required", itself part of his progress towards the history of the Cuillin, he could not resist the temptation to berate a well known English author:

> Once more it was an Englishman who gave us a record of a journey

in Skye. But Skye was worth a book on its own, Mr H. V. Morton, instead of just a chapter in your *In Search of Scotland*. What did you see of Skye? Like most other Englishmen, you came at the wrong time – in the autumn. You rushed from Portree to Sligachan in the dark, walked up Glen Sligachan, made a hurried visit to Dunvegan, and went off home again. And you had the impertinence to call the "Coolins" a "piffling name". It is no piffling name! When properly pronounced, not as an Englishman pronounces it, but with that lovable inflection which only a Highlander can give, it is a very splendid name – the only possible name. Look to your Lakeland, where mountains are called Gables and Pillars and Pikes, and burns are defaced with such names as becks and gills! Ah! No, Mr Morton, Skye is not to be treated in such a cavalier fashion. Go again, stay there a whole year, and perhaps even you might yet give us a new classic on Skye.

After a wonderful holiday in Skye in perfect June weather in 1936, Ben's ideas for further writing began to consolidate even more around the history of climbing, and a longer story called "The Rise of the Cuillin as Mountaineering Ground" discussed the subject fully. Alongside this particular article in his scrap book he pencilled in the words, "to be included in climbing book", so he was certainly thinking of at least one further book around that time. Those plans were interrupted by the beginning of the war in 1939, but even during the war years the Cuillin were never far from his thoughts. Writing to a friend in 1942, he said:

> Skye won't see us this year, but perhaps next summer we'll again camp in Glen Brittle, that delectable glen and cragsman's paradise. Mrs Chisholm, postmistress and hostess to generations of climbers, wrote to me recently and said, "The Cuillin are in grand condition, and there is no one to climb them." She, too, looks forward to that first summer. What a rush there will be then! Whatever may happen in Europe, the Cuillin are changeless, and they will welcome us all back – after the war.

That reply from Mrs Chisholm had been in response to an enquiry by Ben about a possible permit to visit the island while convalescing from an illness. Unsuccessful with the permit, he had to contain his growing impatience for a further five years. When the return to the Cuillin did come, it was not by the usual road.[27]

After such a long absence the approach to Glen Brittle had to be a novel one – by motor-boat from Mallaig. I had travelled north the day previously and spent the night at Morar. So stormy was it that we could not even go fishing on the inland Loch Morar, while next morning the Sound of Sleat was a mass of whitecaps. It looked as if we would have to take the prosaic route by ferry and bus.

Sandy, our fisherman, reassured us. Of course he would take all twelve of us to Loch Brittle! Out of the sheltered harbour we met Atlantic seas; now and then huge combers broke over and drenched the unlucky ones, but ours was a grand sea boat and held steadily on. Bright blue skies, masses of cumulus clouds, behind us the grape-black peaks of Knoydart and Kintail, on the port the white sands of Morar, ahead the Scuir of Eigg challenging the seas and the Cuillin of Rum standing out majestically.

Towards the Point of Sleat the waves became bigger and the seas rougher. Sandy, a tough old pirate, took us cannily round. Now the wind was behind us; with huge following seas we swept towards the mountains. Was there ever such an approach as this? There was the huge mass of Blaven. Coruisk lay in that dark hollow. The whole range of the Cuillin coming nearer every moment.

Confused seas again as we rounded Rubh' an Dunain into the home waters of Loch Brittle, the old hands among us busy pointing out and naming all the peaks. Ahead of us was the grandest of all the Cuillin corries, Coire Lagan, the hoary tops around it a climber's litany – Sgumain, Alasdair, Thearlaich, Mhic Coinnich and Dearg. By nine o'clock at night, after a seven instead of the expected four hours sail we landed by the River Brittle.

Next day, the rope, the hobnailed boots, the fingers tingling to the rasp of the gabbro – a Cuillin climb once more, and surely ours was the perfect return to the glen . . .

The preparation and publication of his book of mountain photographs, *On Scottish Hills*, took immediate precedence during the last years of the war, with the omission of any reference to Skye indicating to his friends that another book was sure to follow. Many other commitments kept him fully occupied also in the immediate post-war period, but by 1949 he was working in earnest on the Cuillin project, gathering together two decades of material. He helped advertise the first Skye Week in 1950 with numerous articles for papers and magazines across Scotland, the titles giving clear indication of their message: "Are You Going to Skye?", "Skye High!", "Skye Calls Her Exiles Back to the Hebrides", "The Call of Skye", and "Skye's Grand Old Man of the Mountains". These were soon followed by "The Conquest of the Cuillin" and "The Ascent of

Sgurr Dubh" (the story of Sheriff Nicolson), and the completed history was released by Hale in 1952, with his favourite photograph of A'Cioch forming a striking cover. Ian MacPhail, who helped him with some of the final preparations, recalled his memories of that time:

"Bennie's book on the Cuillin was – and is – a classic, and deserves reprinting. It was published at too dear a price, I think, and never sold quite as it should. I was involved in certain aspects, proof reading and checking the Gaelic names. His typing, which latterly became terrible, was not too bad then; indeed at that time he had a receptionist at Berkeley Street who typed from his manuscript. But enough errors reached the proof stage to make my job invidious. He would get into a bad humour over the number of errors I detected, and make out that he had noticed them all already, but in the end he would laugh and thank me. One of the chapters in the book was titled 'Norman and John', referring of course to Norman Collie and John Mackenzie. Those happen to be the names of our two boys, and he made much of that when he took them up the Cobbler on their first climb as youngsters.

"In 1951, at the King's Birthday holiday weekend in May, he took Donald Crabb and myself to Skye to check on various matters for his book. I wasn't keen to have that amount of travelling in a short weekend, but he promised that we would have climbing on three days, and I agreed to go. We left Clydebank on Friday afternoon, slept at Ardelve near Kyle of Lochalsh, and arrived at Sligachan at mid-day on Saturday, climbing Sgurr nan Gillean in fine weather. We went through the Sligachan Hotel visitors' book, which he borrowed, later publishing excerpts from it in his book. On Sunday we went over to Glen Brittle, and put up in Mary Campbell's house, where there was another visitors' book. Donald Crabb and I had a short climb on the Sunday, but that evening Bennie and I had a fearful row over my insistence on doing a short climb on Monday morning on the way back. The notebook I used for that conversation I kept for years, and I often laughed over the remarks I wrote down, such as 'Rubbish!', 'Never again', 'I'll bet you five pounds', etc. Bennie wanted to leave Sligachan by 12 noon, and argued that we would never manage Sgurr a' Mhadaidh (which I wanted to climb) en route to Sligachan. On the Monday morning we both looked grim, and never exchanged a word, except for me to write down, 'We'll be there by 12.' Well, it was hard going, I can tell you, and I practically ran the six miles back from the summit to Sligachan, to arrive there just after 11.30. Bennie was quite transformed, and when Donald came in twenty minutes later, he greeted him with great cheers, holding up his wrist watch as if it was a stop watch. This incident was typical of Bennie

– so certain he was right in a climbing matter, but generous and tolerant of the other person if he was wrong."

Although Ben said that it had only taken him three years to write *The Cuillin of Skye*,[28] it was in fact the product of more than twenty years of research, writing and climbing experience, and its pages clearly reveal his lasting affection for the mountains. The book was well received, Ben mentioning that he was able to buy his first new car around this time. By the early 1970s second hand copies were changing hands for more than fifteen times the original price, and he was very keen to have a second edition. I have a letter from him, dated June 1972, telling me of his hopes:

> I have a copy of *The Cuillin of Skye* with a publisher in England just now, together with a note of the extra chapters I can put in to bring it up to date, including reference to mountain rescue. Possibly about a 5 to 1 chance of them taking it up, but still hope. Should know any time. If they accept, then a new edition next year.

To Ben's sorrow nothing concrete ever came of this, or from approaches to other publishers, including one with a facsimile reprint programme. In 1973 a suggestion for a reprint edition was made, not by Ben, to the Scottish Mountaineering Club Trust, and a subsequent report proposed that an amended second edition could be produced as "the first in a small series devoted to narrative climbing history in the Scottish mountains." This report also recommended many changes, including cutting out a quarter of the text and possibly altering the title to *The Black Cuillin*. Ben left no doubt as to what he thought of that!

> I take this report to be entirely wrong. The question at issue was not the re-writing of the book in a different way, but reprinting the book as it now stands. It is stated that the book conveys the attitude to climbing up till that date, and then goes on to say that things are quite different today, suggesting that it should be re-written according to today's attitude. This is absurd – the author of the report wishes to change history while saying at the same time that the history is correct. The book is regarded as a classic, and it is a great presumption to suggest re-writing. I would never agree. I have already indicated that a new chapter would be added bringing the story up to date, and this would give the changed attitude of today, thus adding great interest as the modern professionalism is so different.

As late as March 1977, he was still holding out some hope of a second edition, for Bill Murray refers to the subject on 5 April of that year at the end of a reply to an earlier letter from Ben:

"I was most interested to hear of your *Cuillin of Skye*, a most excellent book. I hate to think of some publisher cashing in on a reprint long after you're dead. There is <u>bound to be</u> a demand, for it stands alone as a history of the Cuillin."

Just eleven days after those words were written, Ben was dead. Nine years later the facsimile edition finally appeared, published by The Ernest Press, with Bill contributing a splendid foreword. Ben would have felt vindicated by the reappearance of his book – exactly as he had written it. He would also have enjoyed the first official reproduction of the famous "Humble Kipper" photograph; the indignant first reaction long since forgotten, it would surely have been greeted by one of his great shouts of laughter.

Ben described *The Cuillin of Skye* as "the story of those who have gone to find the treasure of the Cuillin". One reviewer called it "the story of the Skye mountains and the spell they have cast on succeeding genera-tions". In its later pages Ben tells something of how "one of the most ordinary of climbers" was affected by that spell. A short selection from those pages gives glimpses of him on the Cuillin which illustrate well the many different sides of his personality:

ONE MAN'S TREASURE

A book like this must inevitably deal with the great figures of our sport, those bold spirits who seek out new climbs and venture on untrodden rock. Yet a vast number of climbers do not seek to be the first to pass; the climbing and the mountains count more than the actual climb. It is the fascination of the Cuillin that they hold untold delights for such as these. The story of the tigers has already been told; let that be the excuse for some stories of one of the most ordinary of climbers . . .

Once I tried to take an ancient car all the way to Glen Brittle. After a complete breakdown on the Mallaig road I left it behind me and continued by train, ferry and bus to Sligachan. At 9.30 p.m. I started over the Bealach a' Mhaim with a 50lb load. I had left home at 5 a.m. and was very tired. Every time I sat down to rest I fell off to sleep – and I sat down very often.

At midnight I reached the road, lay down in the heather and slept for an hour before continuing to Glen Brittle. My friends were camp-ing there but I did not wish to disturb anyone in the middle of the night and, being too tired to pitch my own tent, just spread out my

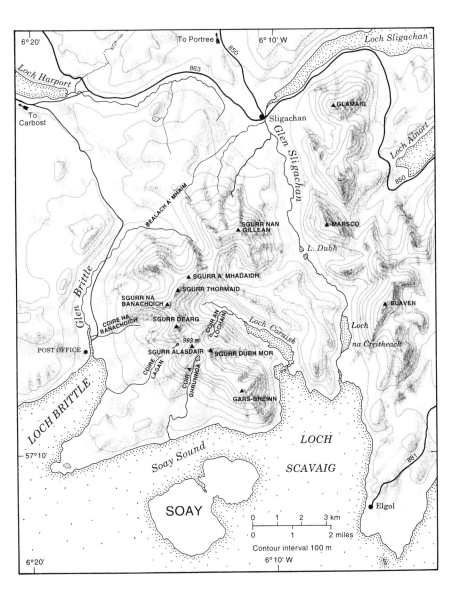

The Cuillin of Skye.

waterproof sheet halfway between two encampments, got into my sleeping bag and fell off to sleep at once.

A moment or two later – though it was really hours – I was awakened by someone tugging at the end of my sleeping bag. Without opening my eyes I knew it was daylight and thought my friends had found me and were having a game. I kept quiet till the tugs became vicious. I opened my eyes. A big white horse was chewing at the end of my sleeping bag – and my feet were inside! I shooed it away. No good! The colour seemed to attract it and it always returned. I got up and ran to the nearest tent. It was empty. I grabbed my kit, bundled everything in and went off to sleep again, too tired to puzzle over the problem of an empty tent (it was 5 a.m.), but not too tired to note from stray garments that it was obviously a woman's tent. Later I discovered that its owner had gone up to Coire Lagan to see the sunrise . . .

"One Skye holiday stands out beyond all others," Ben wrote of June 1936. Had he forgotten July 1929 so soon? For that moment perhaps, but a Skye heat wave is a rare event.

Come with me to Skye in June – the best month of all the year. At four o'clock on a Friday evening Ian Maitland and I left Glasgow, the car loaded to the roof and the weather set fair. I had been climbing at least every second weekend since the beginning of the year and always in the West Highlands, so that almost every mountain had its own memories.

Looking back from Tyndrum the Crianlarich mountains were fairer than I had ever seen them – that dusky blue colour which is the forerunner of good weather. On we sped over the Black Mount road, to be welcomed in Glencoe by Buachaille Etive Mor, now bright and sunny and contrasting strongly with the dark and towering mountain where rain had washed away our camp a few weeks previously. Nearing Clachaig, just a glimpse of the twin summit buttresses of Bidean nam Bian, the highest peak in Argyllshire, then on to Ballachulish ferry, from where Gars-bheinn of Ardgour appeared dim and dreamy in a heat haze. Now by Loch Linnhe and through Fort William; beyond the town that magnificent view of Allt a' Mhuillinn with the ridges of Ben Nevis showing up clearly.

Crossing from Spean Bridge to Inverlochy, the whole moorland was alive with colour, acres and acres of rhododendrons, then a blaze of gorse. Only when we crossed the Great Glen were we truly on "The Road to the Isles", and while I think the route from Fort

William to Mallaig the finer of the alternative train journeys, I place that by Glen Garry as the finest for a car. By the quiet Loch Garry grand old fir trees were reflected in its clear waters. We passed a car facing south and saw some climbers sitting by the lochside. "Poor devils", we thought – probably returning from Skye and reluctant to go back to civilisation on such a wondrous night.

From Tomdoun a hill road led us over to Cluanie and soon we sighted the peaks of Kintail. Then a rush down Glen Sheil with the peak of the Saddle dominating the scene. Up again, up and up, by the twisting Mam Ratagan road. It was nearing sunset now and we could look over the feathery tops of the nearer fir trees to Loch Duich lying far below, with the Five Sisters of Kintail beyond.

Then downhill through Glenelg and on to the ferry. It was 10.30 p.m. All was quiet. We saw no one, yet there by the shoreside was a brazier of coals glowing faintly. We questioned not the reason, just pumped the bellows and had some soup heating in a moment. Maybe the wee folk in green had arranged all this knowing that we would be too late for the ferry?

On a little headland above the ferry slip we found a perfect place to spend the night – a sheltered hollow of deep luxurious heather twenty feet above the sea and within half a mile of Skye. When the workmen repairing the ferry slip arrived at 8 a.m. they found their brazier already in use – our breakfast was cooking! We crossed by the first ferry, remembering that this was the route Samuel Johnson took on the famous journey. We did not dally, like him, at Broadford, but rushed on to Sligachan where the Cuillin were awaiting us.

A training walk being indicated after so much motoring, we climbed Sgurr nan Gillean by the tourist route. Even if classified as such it is always interesting to follow the route by which a great mountain was first climbed, and this way has the merit that the tourist does not see anything of the Cuillin till reaching the actual ridge; then the whole wild immensity of them bursts into view. And that section from the ridge to the summit of Sgurr nan Gillean is harder for the tourist than many of the other less known Cuillin peaks. Perhaps the shattered West Ridge, like a jerry-built wall, makes many decide that Sgurr nan Gillean will be their first and last Cuillin peak.

The best part of that day was a bathe in a crystal clear pool in the Red Burn on the way back to Sligachan. Just as we were leaving the hotel a car drove up and an old man stepped out. Tall he was and upright, a notable figure in any company; and that nose was unmistakable. It was Professor Collie! So was our holiday blessed with a glimpse of the greatest Cuillin climber of them all.

In Glen Brittle we found Bill Murray's party camping at a fine site by the river and soon had our tent up nearby. Our warm welcome was mainly because we carried a good supply of oil of citronella with which to fight the midges – the curse of Skye. That oil is an efficient preventive in most places, but the Skye midges seemed to feed on it, then started to feed on us. Midges were everywhere. We ate boiled midges, fried midges, stewed midges and drowned midges! Not till after the war and the appearance of the newer midge-preventives was the curse really removed.

Even in later years, however, the midge remained a curse. One of his friends wrote to me of a time when they had stayed at Rose Cottage in Arrochar while Ben was on holiday:

"Ben returned shortly before we were to go home. We had opened a window to let air into the children's bedroom as it was a very humid evening. A light had been left on. Ben went into the room, and let out a fearsome yell. On looking up he had seen the ceiling covered in midges and other insects. The children woke up and stared in amazement as Ben went to work with a huge spray, literally soaking the ceiling. We had to evacuate the children from the thick atmosphere; the ceiling was dripping and there were dying insects everywhere. 'You don't need to drown them,' I pleaded, but he loathed midges indoors – any death would do!"

Ben loathed midges *anywhere*, and never hesitated to castigate them in print, but they had no more mention on this holiday. The delights of the Cuillin soon banished them from thought:

> Next day the heat wave turned on and remained with us for the rest of our stay . . . In the evening the others went off to camp while I climbed Sgurr Alasdair once more to see the sunset. At 9 p.m. the whole range of the Cuillin were in shadow and quite dark, with the Red Hills and Blaven quite clear and beyond the faint outline of the Kintail peaks, a rosy haze above them fading into a light blue sky. The sun was now sinking just over Neist Point with its last rays lighting up Loch Bracadale and silhouetting MacLeod's Maidens. In the afternoon there had been many parties on the ridges; now I seemed to have the whole range to myself. Had I not been expected back at camp I would surely have stayed on Sgurr Alasdair all night.
>
> Time matters little in June, for darkness exists only for an hour or so. One may climb at any time of day or night. The usual programme

was a long substantial breakfast and seldom were we off before
11 a.m., returning eight to twelve hours later according to the state
of our appetite. One day it would be the Window Buttress and the
Inaccessible, another the ridges north of Sgurr na Banachdich or
the rock-climbing playground of Sron na Ciche. Variety is endless
and days may be easy or strenuous.

Of the ridge walks in Skye I shall always prefer the traverse of
the five peaks which circle round Coire Lagan. In such weather our
round was a most leisurely one, involving hours of bathing in the
lochans on the way up and countless stops for photography. The
Cioch is a perfect place for lunch, and the East Gully leads from
there to the summit ridge. Then one works slowly round – Sgurr
Sgumain, Sgurr Alasdair, Sgurr Thearlaich, to enjoy a bit of harder
rock climbing in King's Chimney of Sgurr Mhic Coinnich. Just un-
couth names to the Philistines, a thousand delights to the devout.
We must have made a record for slowness that day, for I remember
as I neared the top of the long side of the Inaccessible an orb of
bronze suddenly came into view; the sun was sinking in the west.

Sometimes we were very late in making for the hills. One morning
we seemed quite unable to climb, perhaps because of a large breakfast.
It was after six o'clock at night when Bill Murray and I left for a
farewell visit to the Cioch. Mist was down in Coire Lagan and things
did not promise well. The Cuillin had yet another surprise for us.
As we climbed up we found ourselves emerging from dense, dirty
mist on to the top of lovely white clouds with a normal sky-scape
above and the sun sinking in the west. The tip of the Cioch rose in
sunshine above the cloud level, which stretched out for many miles.

If there be such a thing as photographic ecstasy I knew it that
night. If I could capture that effect it would be the photograph of
a lifetime. I posed Bill on the summit, unroped, and climbed quickly
along the knife-edge to get a stance. I had no tripod, no lens hood,
no exposure meter. It was after 9 p.m. and the photo had to be
taken dead against the sun. There was but one thing to do – expose
for the clouds and leave the rock in silhouette. I held the camera
upside down so that the extending baseboard acted as a lens hood,
and took three photographs in rapid succession, each at 1/50 second,
but varying the aperture, and of course I had a filter permanently
fitted behind the lens. "Sunset from A'Cioch" was the result.

"I found Ben's photography a sore trial to my patience," Bill Murray
remembers of that same holiday . . . "He was so keen, his eye constantly
given to the endless search for dramatic stances, unusual lighting, right

composition, revealing effects, that hours would seem to go while we dilly-dallied. I learned more patience when I viewed the results. Perhaps the best reward we had, since it yielded his best-known and favourite picture, came from one trying hour in June 1936, spent posing me on the Cioch pinnacle. The time was 9 p.m. and broad daylight with a cloud-sea below, yet by judicious stopping of the camera he created a splendid sunset photograph, in which Nature was lent a helping hand, yet all was true to the Cuillin at their best. To me that seemed good art, and justified."

Ten years after that memorable holiday, after the emotional return to the Cuillin by sea, Ben described how his party's plans for the first day on the mountains were interrupted by a climbing accident:

The Window Buttress of Sgurr Dearg and the Inaccessible was the chosen climb for our first day. I remember best watching the ladies of the Lomond Club descending the steep side of the Inaccessible with grace and celerity. John and Jenny Nimlin were introducing their daughter to the Cuillin. They made for a climb on the Cioch, leaving me to look after the baby. Dorothy, fortunately, was used to this sort of thing, as she had been camped out since she was three months old. She gave no trouble, so that I was able to spend the time collecting and identifying all the flowers in the upper corrie. To the casual glance there appears to be nothing but grey rock, boulders and scree. On the far side of the lochan, at a height of about nineteen hundred feet, there is sparse greenery with minute flowers one might well walk over without noticing. I noted clumps of rose root, carpets of wild thyme, Alpine lady's mantle, lots of tormentil, bog asphodel, dog violet and common butterwort, together with various saxifrages, still another proof that countless writers have erred in denying the Cuillin any vegetation.

Our day was not destined to end so happily. Scarcely had John and Jenny returned when a climber came towards us from the direction of the Sgurr Alasdair Stone Shoot, his very appearance indicating that something was seriously wrong. He explained that he and his companion, a Polish soldier, had been traversing Sgurr Mhic Coinnich unroped when a loose stone was dislodged. This hit the Pole, who was knocked off his balance and fell away down out of sight on the Coruisk side. From the account given, and our knowledge of the ground, we were of the opinion that the unfortunate man must have been killed, but this fact had to be ascertained at once.

We contacted the remainder of the Lomonds, who were still climbing on the Cioch. A strong party of five of them undertook to make for the scene of the accident in an effort to locate the body that night. They took the climber with them, and arranged to split up and send word to us with all possible speed should the Pole be alive. They had been climbing all day and had finished all their food, so that further rations were their greatest need should the search be prolonged. Nimlin and I arranged to go down to Glen Brittle with the ladies and the kiddie, get further help in case of need, and return up the mountain with food. Thus we parted and hurried down the glen. Glen Brittle House and hostel were warned and after a short time a stretcher-party turned out and started off up the hill. We had a quick meal, loaded up with a big supply of food, flasks, primus stove etc., prepared for a night out.

About 10.30 p.m. we met the Lomonds at the mouth of Coire Lagan. They had ascended the Sgumain Stone Shoot, traversed to Bealach Coir' an Lochain, worked round rock and then seen the man lying clear on the screes below. One of them descended the rock and ascertained that he was dead. He had fallen about five hundred feet, struck rock, bounded off, and landed on scree, receiving multiple injuries. Death must have been instantaneous. The speed of this party cannot be too highly commended. The fact of their locating the body before darkness saved most of us a night out and an anxious and dangerous search. All of us returned to Glen Brittle.

Fourteen volunteers, including Ben, had to struggle hard the following day to retrieve the body by stretcher, not getting back to Glen Brittle until the late evening. His story continues . . .

A sergeant and a constable had come over from Portree to make enquiries. As I had not been in Portree since the war, and as supplies were rather short at the hostel, I got a lift back in the police car. At half-past eleven on the Wednesday of Glasgow Fair week we got to Portree – a very dark night, raining hard and Portree packed to the roof. As I did not fancy hunting for accommodation at that time of night the sergeant very obligingly put me in a cell at the police station! I was surprised at such a modern prison up there. The cell was all stone, had a high arched roof, a small barred window high up, a peep-hole in the door, light controlled from outside, while even the blankets had red arrows on them.

I was dead tired after two full days on the hills and remember nothing more till the sergeant came in at half past nine the next morning with a mug of tea and a big slice of bread and jam. It was still raining. To get back to Glen Brittle I'd have had to take the bus to Sligachan, then walk for nine miles over Bealach a' Mhaim. Still rather tired and with a big load to carry, such a prospect did not attract me, so I asked the sergeant if he knew of any vehicle going to Glen Brittle that day (for few cars venture on that awful road). He replied that a Portree man was going for the body and that I could go with him.

I went off to do my shopping, bought a dozen pair of kippers and much other stuff, and then located my man. What a shock I got! I had thought of a van or a truck, but here was a full-size hearse complete with coffin. I travelled the thirty odd miles back to Glen Brittle sitting inside the hearse, bouncing around on the bad road, holding on to the coffin with one hand and holding a dozen pair of kippers in the other, which must indeed be something of the ultimate in hitch-hiking.

A postscript was recalled by many of Ben's friends. As the hearse set off down Portree Main Street, Ben sat up to see what was going on. A number of local worthies, showing the traditional Highland respect for the dead, had stopped in their tracks as the hearse passed and doffed their caps in a last salute. Their solemn faces gaped as the "corpse" doffed its cap in reply! Ben's glee in the consternation he caused can be well imagined, so he repeated the performance before the hearse left the town. The undertaker was not amused, and threatened to evict him.

The Cuillin of Skye concludes with an Envoi – the author's last words. In it Ben talks briefly of how Skye had prospered in the years following the war, and of the brilliant success of "the brave experiment of Skye Week in 1950", a week to which he made a significant contribution. After then describing the discovery of many new routes in the post-war years, with climbing standards being pushed higher and higher, he drew his story to an end by looking towards the future:

> Must progress in climbing always be reckoned in new climbs? Should it not be judged by the increasing numbers who are able to look after themselves on the hills?
>
> I close my eyes and imagine myself on the hillside near Glen Brittle post office. There is a blaze of gorse by the river, cattle are browsing in lush green fields; beyond the brown moor rises up to the lighter scree and the black brown peaks. A moving trail winds up the hillside. Old and young, male and female, wearing big boots and old clothes and carrying ropes, cameras and food, they disappear from the lower world till darkness and hunger brings them home at night. The beginners take the easy way or picnic in the corries, the more

experienced make for the ridges, while the tigers test nerve and sinew on the hardest routes. From Sligachan, too, there will be a similar trail.

Where once there were but a few pilgrims, now thousands seek – and find – the Treasure of the Cuillin.

4

WAYFARING AROUND SCOTLAND

"Skye is an island of inspiration", wrote Lauchlan MacLean Watt in the Introduction to *The Songs of Skye*. Skye certainly inspired Ben to begin his writing career, and his climbing life had its initiation there. In the years that followed he became a constant wayfarer, one who travels from place to place on foot. Although forced in the end to accept the colloquial term hiking, he much preferred the older words with medieval roots, wayfaring or tramping. As if to emphasise his disdain of the new idiom, he used both these expressions in titles for his books, and adopted "Wayfarer" or "The Wayfarers" as pen-names when his writing output began to increase. *Wayfaring Around Scotland*,[29] his third major publication, appeared in 1936; its pages contained the story of a very modest personal beginning:

> A tramp round Loch Lomond was my first walking tour, so it is a particularly vivid memory. It was in July, in days before hikers were known. We left on a Tuesday morning, and planned to take four days for the tramp. We were complete novices. Our packs contained only water-proof sheets and what we thought would be sufficient food, while I had a small billy-can. We carried neither coats nor blankets, knew nothing about sleeping bags, and I seriously thought of taking an umbrella!

Several hard lessons were learned during the walk from Dumbarton to Balloch, and then along the east side of the loch to Rowardennan. Their food supply lasted only one day, midges ruined the first evening, and cold dampened their enthusiasm for camping the first night, forcing them up before dawn. By the time they reached Inversnaid later that morning the pair were famished, so a waiting steamer was gladly boarded for the short sail across to Ardlui:

> There we had a meal at the hotel. A plain tea it was called – 1s. 6d. – eat what you like. I can still remember the look of amazement on the waiter's face when he saw we had cleared absolutely everything from the table! So fortified we continued to Luss, but as my companion could walk at four miles an hour while I could do but three, I only saw him at Tarbet where we had tea and again at Luss at nine in the evening. My friend braved the lochside and was nearly driven mad by

70

the midges. I retreated to the hotel and got the loan of a needle with which to burst the blisters on my feet. Next morning we tramped home, and our folk refused to believe that we had been round the loch, saying that we must have taken the boat all the way back from Ardlui!

Ben dedicated *Wayfaring Around Scotland* to the memory of Alan Fothergill, the moving spirit behind the formation of the Scottish Youth Hostels Association. It was a practical book, meant for the hiker's pack. All the main hiking areas of the Highlands were covered in detail, by way of the author's own visits to many of the early hostels, each section giving a selection of walking routes between the chain of hostels. Varied additional information on accommodation, Ordnance Survey maps, and even Gaelic place names, increased its usefulness for the hiker.

This book was not Ben's only contribution to the growing hostel movement. Starting in 1934, he had begun to promote it throughout Britain with articles in such diverse publications as the *Spectator*, the *Scottish Field, Chambers' Journal, John O' London's Weekly,* and the *Christian Science Monitor*. For six summer months each year from 1935 to 1939 he had a regular weekly 1500 word article in the Glasgow *Evening Times* on some aspect of the "tramping game", as he called it. He received the princely sum of two pounds for each of these stories, which involved him in much time-consuming travel and research; in every case he seems to be writing for young people, trying to convey to them something of his own love for the open country.

When a somewhat tongue-in-cheek article critical of the youth hostels appeared in 1937, one of the founders of the movement issued a mild rebuttal, calling the author "a silly blether". Ben was more forthright. "Tramp Royal" had accused the hostels of pampering those who used them, advocating the minimum of equipment for camping on the hills. Entering the offending piece in his scrap book, covered with question marks, exclamation marks, "rot", "rubbish" and similar comments, Ben retaliated in his own vintage manner:

> Tramp Royal gives "expert" advice on the subject of packs and hiking. I can only say, "Heaven help the novice who follows his advice." It is obvious he knows very little of the Youth Hostel movement. I disagree with almost everything he says! . . . He says that some hostels which have been built are so comfortable that many motorists prefer them to certified hotels. The statement is absurd. Let him sleep in a wooden hostel in the depth of winter when the temperature is below zero, and the common room, with its big windows, like an ice-house in

the morning. He would see no resemblance to a hotel, and he would require much more than the one blanket which he carries!

. . . I'd like to see him climb up to the half-way lochan on Ben Nevis in the month of March, when there may be snow on the ground and the loch frozen. Let him put down his groundsheet, wrap himself in his one blanket, protect himself from the raging wind, sleet or snow with his second groundsheet, and find fuel and get a fire going. There is no natural shelter up there! His top sheet would probably be blown away in no time. He'd be mighty glad to seek shelter in the tent of one of the hikers who camp there at Easter time, and glad to have the use of a primus for a hot meal! . . .

Some of the subsequent prolonged correspondence was highly entertaining, especially one letter from "Colonel Blimp":

"I have just returned from the rigours of a weekend at Hoddam Castle Youth Hostel. While shaking out my napkin preparatory to attacking with gusto my dish of pâté de foie gras, prepared by the Warden himself, my eye chanced to alight on Tramp Royal's searing letter.

"I read it. I was staggered! Yes, by gad, I was positively staggered! My napkin fell from nerveless fingers, my jaw dropped, my monocle was lost in the deep pile of the carpet. I was so shaken I couldn't hold my patent collapsible hiker's hot water bottle steady, and poured the water over the floor instead. Then I tottered to my dorm, and lay down on my sprung mattress wrapped in my new superdown sleeping bag.

"Gad, Sir! Tramp Royal is right. The hostels are pampering our tramps. I make the suggestion to the SYHA that they should build a new type of hostel, under Royal patronage, to be called the 'Tramp-Royal Hikers' Hostel'! It should not have doors and windows. The roof should be pleasantly open to the sky. Access to the interior would be gained through one of the many holes in the walls, and of course there would be no sanitation.

"Two sticks would be provided to rub together for fire lighting purposes, all modern conveniences such as matches being eschewed. And who would be the Warden of this hostel? None other than the patron of the art of hardy hiking – 'Tramp Royal' himself."

Perhaps Ben could not have written that particular type of reply, and his name is unlikely to appear in any history of the early years of the SYHA, for he was never in any way officially connected with the Association. It is nevertheless doubtful if anyone in Scotland did more in the pre-war years to encourage youth to take to the open road. In the first article of a 25-week series entitled "The Open Road", published in the *Evening Times* in the winter of 1935–36, he began with these words:

You who are now facing the adventure of the open road little know how fortunate you are. The last generation of ramblers had to confine their walks to the vicinity of cities; the greater part of the Highlands was a closed book to them because of prohibitive hotel charges and many restrictions. For you it is different. You come into a fine heritage, for the Scottish Youth Hostels Association have opened up to you glens, moorlands, hills – the loveliest regions of our country – previously almost inaccessible. Some day perhaps we shall hear the whole story, for the 45 hostels did not appear on the map as if by magic. It will be a story worth telling!

He had himself given a brief summary of that story in an article in *Chambers' Journal* the previous year, one that is worth looking back at now as an early picture of the SYHA:

BRAVE YOUTH — AND THE OPEN ROAD

I

"It is just a craze. It will not last." So said the critics three years ago when youth, in increasing numbers, took to the Open Road. But the tramping movement has continued to prosper mightily. It now has its own magazines, its own place in newspapers; it has become well organised, and has built its own rest-houses, and is assured for all time of a very definite role in the recreation of youth.

Five years ago I tramped round Skye in mid-July, and – in a fortnight – met but two other walkers. Now Skye is the trampers' Mecca, and they have even penetrated into the fastness of the Cuillin and have a hostel in Glen Brittle, so long a climbers' sanctuary. Five years ago rambling clubs were few and their membership was small. Now thousands spend the week-ends tramping the roads and moorlands, while the railway companies run special trains so that these enthusiasts may start well away from the city.

Much as I detest the word, it must be admitted that the introduction of hike into our current speech coincided with this return to the countryside. The newspapers were ever picturing hikers of both sexes with a pack on back and stick in hand. Though the idea was as old as the hills themselves, youth seized on it, seeing something adventurous in a hike. The rambler was one who went off for a Saturday afternoon with some sandwiches in his pocket; the hiker donned a well-laden pack and made longer excursions. Soon the afternoon jaunt developed into a week-end walk. The problem of accommodation for the night was thus introduced, and the now familiar sign, "Supper, Bed and Breakfast" appeared outside countless cottages. The movement continued to expand, and the question of cheap lodgings at week-ends and when on holiday tramps became urgent. Hikers who had ventured abroad were enthusiastic in their praise of the rest-houses for walkers in Germany, so these were introduced into Britain.

II

Scotland was first in the field. Five years ago the Rucksack Club was born, and built a hut to accommodate eight members at Kinlochard. They builded better than they knew. Never could they have imagined that from that small beginning would grow up the Scottish Youth Hostels Association of today, with its chain of rest-houses throughout Scotland and a membership approaching ten thousand.

At first trampers were content to keep to the roads and paths; now they are more venturesome. The true tramper takes to the hills whenever possible, and is fast discovering a new Scotland, a Scotland the ordinary tourist never sees, a Scotland of moorlands and hill-paths and great mountains. Many there are who are summer trampers only, but an increasing number know that the game can be carried out at all seasons. Some of the hostels are open the year round, and witness many a cheery gathering on winter evenings. There is more winter climbing in Scotland now than ever before, and at the hostels near the mountains, like Arrochar, there is often a brave show of ice-axes and ropes.

Few outside the movement have any idea of its manifold activities. That its members may appreciate their journeyings the more the Scottish Ramblers' Federation organised winter classes – in Archaeology, Botany, Geology, Map-reading, and Nature-Lore. Both the Federation and the Hostels Association have well equipped enquiry bureaus. The tramper has only to give the length of his holiday and the area he or she wishes to visit to receive a suggested itinerary with information as to hill-paths, ferries, accommodation, etc. There are ferries in outlandish places unmarked on any map, and you will be told exactly where they are and the sign that will bring the ferryman over from the other side. It is foreigners mostly who make use of such services, and some of their requests are not easy to carry out.

There are hustlers among trampers as well as among motorists, and those who want to see Scotland in a fortnight are firmly disillusioned. Most difficult it is to explain to a German with little knowledge of English that, though there is a railway at Mallaig and a railway at Kyle of Lochalsh – 20 miles away – to travel between them by rail would mean a tour of several hundred miles over the half of Scotland!

The ramblers' leaders, too, have been the means of restoring to the public forgotten rights-of-way and keeping open many a known one when its closure was threatened. They have ever waged war on the litter fiends and the thoughtless and brainless folk who knock down fences and trample over crops. The farmer is beginning to realise now that the trampers' clubs are his very good friends, and that his worst enemies are the bus and train picnic parties, who have no rules and generally think of themselves alone, giving no thought to the preservation of the countryside.

III

The Scottish Youth Hostels Association is now a thriving infant three years old. It has direct control of thirty-five hostels throughout Scotland. A hostel may be a new timber building, a stone cottage, a forestry hut, a converted school-house or boat-house, but the services are uniform. Members are provided with three blankets and a bed or palliasse, and facilities to cook their own meals. That means free oil, coal and wood, and use of a big stove – all for a shilling a night, and a yearly subscription of two-and-six if under twenty-five, and five shillings if over that age. Other than an initial grant from the Carnegie Trustees and the gift of a cottage up by Gairloch, the Association has had little outside assistance. Great enthusiasm, wise leadership, much hard work, freely and voluntarily given, were necessary to overcome the many difficulties and achieve such a result with but small financial resources. In the future, hostelling will play an important part in the life of Scottish Youth – aye, and some of those who are no longer youths.

"Come with me now round some of our hostels," Ben continued, taking his readers on a tour of the West Highland chain, as far as the then northern outpost in Wester Ross. There he named the hostel the finest of all – Carn Dearg on Gairloch – titling a photograph appropriately 'At the sign of the cleft birch pole'.[30]

If you would pass into fairyland, take the road to Carn Dearg in the late evening when the sky in the west is ablaze in glory, for when silhouetted against the sky on the edge of the loch, the hostel seems a veritable land's end. After one has danced outside by moonlight and picnicked on Longa Island, one becomes one of the elect.

"Brave Youth and the Open Road" ended with what may have been one of the earliest assessments of the youth hostel movement. Perhaps it is too idealistic, but it is interesting to compare Ben's philosophy with the words of the late Frank Smythe:[31]

If it all be regarded as a great game, surely it is the best of all? Football, cricket, tennis – all fine games – giving physical fitness and engendering the team spirit, but bringing knowledge only of the game itself. The tramping game, to which so many other hobbies can be added, brings much more. The tramper who explores the countryside at all seasons will learn something of hillcraft, much of nature lore, will be more adventurous, capable of greater endurance, more appreciative of beauty, and, above all, have a much greater knowledge and love of country than the average mere player of games.

It can truly be said of hostels, "Abandon rank all ye who enter here". The student, the apprentice, the clerk, the teacher, even the professor – all meet together for interchange of ideas and understanding of each other's problems. There is much good talk in the hostels of evenings – many a friendship formed. Nor is the talk always of great tramps accomplished, of great tramps still to come. There is much serious discussion, for youth of today is very critical of its elders.

The newly opened Edinburgh hostel is especially becoming a meeting-place for the Youth of Europe. Although the numbers of foreigners were few, English, Welsh, Dutch, German, American, French, Canadian, and Austrian trampers have passed through last year, and many of them went on to visit other hostels. Look to the future! That trickle will surely become a steady flow, and as the movement spreads throughout Europe – and it is doing so – British Youth will take to tramping abroad.

It is no idle dream. Soon the youth of the nations will meet together in such a way, will talk together, and make lasting friendships. Will the men of the future who have such memories behind them ever think of going to war with each other? Will they, when they come to take part in their national life, do other than cement more closely the friendships thus formed? May not Youth, in its own quiet fashion, be thus on its way to solve the problems overshadowing the world today – the menace of another war?

DUMBARTON CASTLE WAKES UP

When Ben started to write in earnest, it wasn't long before he turned to local topics, the town and Castle of Dumbarton becoming regular subjects for his articles. It was always his complaint that Dumbarton neglected its history, his hope one day that this might not be so. As in virtually every arena he entered, here again Ben was ahead in his thinking. Consider the wording of the literature made available today to visitors by the Dumbarton District Tourist Association:

VISIT DUMBARTON, ANCIENT CAPITAL OF STRATHCLYDE
Got a Break? Take part in Dumbarton
ANCIENT CAPITAL OF AN ANCIENT KINGDOM

"The Castle Rock, fortress of the ancient Britons and capital of the Kingdom of Strathclyde, has one of the most spectacular settings in Scotland. Gun emplacements and batteries overlook the rivers Leven and Clyde and command the road north by the beautiful Vale of Leven. An energetic climb to the cliff-top flagpole is rewarded by uninterrupted views of the Firth of Clyde and the surrounding mountain ranges.

"Dumbarton Rock is one of the oldest fortified sites in Britain, with various figures both legendary and historical claiming associations with the Castle, from King Arthur's wizard Merlin to the infant Mary, Queen of Scots, who stayed there for safety some months before sailing for the lavish French court to marry the Dauphin."

Dumbarton and its Castle Rock were not always promoted in this way. Almost sixty years ago, many years before the town began to take a proper interest in its own history, Ben's pen first began to draw attention to the complete absence of any such promotion:

I stood by the ruins of the watch tower on the summit of Dumbarton Castle. It was a week day, and I seemed to have the whole Castle to myself. Even at weekends very few of the tourists who pass through Dumbarton give a thought to that ancient fortress. It seems strange that Edinburgh and Stirling Castles should attract so many visitors and Dumbarton be almost neglected – Dumbarton for hundreds of years capital of a Kingdom, a town whose story is so closely inter-woven with the history of Scotland.

There are no signs indicating the route to its entrance. The passing motorist cannot tell on which side of the river the Castle is situated, owing to the curve of the Leven as it enters the Clyde. Compare Dumbarton with Stirling. The population is about the same, around

22,000. Both are county towns. Both have ancient castles. Stirling Castle is advertised on posters at every railway station. Dumbarton is never mentioned. A visit to Stirling Castle is included in most organised tours to Scotland. Dumbarton Castle sees no such tourists . . . There is no finer view in all the West than from its summit. Some local folk know that. Strangers don't. Dumbarton must wake up – she must tell the world!

Signs should be placed at the entrance to the town indicating the route to the Castle, and describing its historical interest. The Town Council should see to it that the Castle is mentioned in the literature of all the bus and railway companies, and travel agencies. Have attractive tearooms nearby. Publish an attractive booklet (Stirling will show you how). Arrange for guides to conduct parties around . . . Why not tell the world?

For over thirty years Ben did exactly that, telling anyone who would listen that Dumbarton had a lot to brag about, reacting fiercely to any criticism he came across, and constantly reminding the local Council of their neglect of Dumbarton's Royal history. One long article[32] discussed the whole history of the town, the Castle and the shipyards. Visitors to the town today could still use his words to bring the past alive, and to guide them with increased interest round the Castle ramparts.

Although Dumbarton seemed to ignore its own history for so long, the town used to awaken from its slumber briefly on the occasions of Royal visits, two of which Ben witnessed. An earlier one, by Queen Victoria and Prince Albert in 1847, was made special for him because of Victoria's obvious love for Scotland. A Queen who could gain the summits of Lochnagar, Beinn a' Bhuird and Ben Macdhui, and trek by pony through lonely Glen Tilt – she really was a Queen worth writing about, the first Royal Mountaineer. He wrote many "Royal" articles based on the Queen's Highland Journals, including a radio play, and many more on the 1847 Dumbarton visit which coincided with the first Royal Cruise. When Royalty came to Dumbarton Castle in 1937 and 1953 his pen was at work again, comparing each occasion with the preceding ones, honouring the Royal visitors, yet wondering out loud why the Castle should not stay awake in the intervening years, instead of lapsing back – Rip van Winkle-like – into comparative obscurity. The headlines over some of the articles reflect his involvement: "When the First Queen Came", "The First Royal Cruise", "What a Row When Queen Victoria Went to Dumbarton", "The Queen's Visit prompts Ben Humble's plea: Restore Wallace's Sword to Dumbarton" and simply, "Royal Dumbarton".

There was great excitement in Dumbarton at the beginning of August 1847, when it was rumoured that Queen Victoria would visit Dumbarton Castle during a voyage to the Western Highlands. The Provost only got definite word on the 12th and she was expected on the 16th. Only four days and so much to be done! A landing stage had to be built near the Castle, a platform put up for the local gentry, precautions taken to prevent crowding of boats on the River Leven, and, of course, a loyal address prepared.

Everything was ready for the 16th. Crowds gathered. Hours went by. Then at last word came that the Royal squadron had been delayed, and would anchor in Loch Ryan that evening, reaching Dumbarton the next day. Crowds were even larger on the 17th, and right on time the *Fairy* – the tender to which the Queen and Prince Albert had transferred from the *Victoria and Albert* – appeared, followed it seemed by almost every steamship on the Clyde. Excitement grew as two boats were let down. Lord Grey was in the first, and in the second were the Queen, Prince Albert and their two eldest children.

The Queen was greeted at Victoria Wharf by Sir John Colquhoun, Lord Lieutenant of Dumbartonshire, while Lord Grey immediately asked for the Lord Provost of Glasgow, whom he seemed to think was in charge of arrangements. Dumbarton's magistrates were incensed at being ignored, and were trying to discover the reason when a salvo of guns boomed out from the castle, startling the Queen and causing the horses of the waiting carriages to become restive. Lord Grey gave orders to silence the guns, and the royal party drove through decorative triumphal arches to the Castle, with an escort of Dragoon Guards.

They stopped in front of the Governor of the Castle's house, where an immense concourse of people awaited them, and Lord Grey told the Lord Provost of Glasgow to get his address ready for presentation to the Queen. The Sheriff of Dumbartonshire objected strongly, saying that as they were in his County then the loyal address from Dumbartonshire should come first. Lord Grey blandly agreed, but pointed out that the Glasgow magistrates had sailed all the way to Loch Ryan the previous day and arranged about their address, and that as the first party to make arrangements, they must have priority.

The procession then continued upwards, the Queen finding the long stairway rather tiring. At last they got to the Argyll Battery, overlooking the Leven and the town. The Lord Provost of Glasgow and the Sheriff stepped forward with their addresses and were presented to the Queen. All this time the Provost of Dumbarton had been ready with the town's address, but was never allowed to present it, and none of the local magistrates were presented. All the Provost could do was to hand the address to Lord Grey, who promised "to lay it before Her Majesty that evening".

Dumbarton's folk were angry. They bitterly resented Glasgow's butting in, and a contemporary account reads: "The Glasgow authorities attempted to throw our local magistrates in the shade and treat them as if we had been inhabitants of a conquered province, or suburb of their big town."

Later the Queen was taken to see the view from the heights of the Castle, but when the official party reached the top of the stairs they discovered to their consternation that it was so cloudy that little could be seen, Ben Lomond being hidden in mist. However at the conclusion of the ceremonies, the royal party returned to the *Fairy*, and in it they sailed up Loch Long to Arrochar, the Queen and Prince Albert being entranced by the magnificent scenery.

The conventional story of Victoria's 1847 visit was not the only one retold by Ben when King George VI and Queen Elizabeth came to Dumbarton in 1937. He frequently wrote under the name Alan Hume, and a certain *"Aileen* Hume" now appeared in the Woman's Viewpoint section of the *Glasgow Herald*, giving a detailed discussion of the dresses of the ladies in the 1847 Royal party! Other articles illustrate just how determined he was in promoting Dumbarton's Royal history, and how stubborn he was in the matter of the Castle's oldest treasure:

At one end of the Square are the ruins of Wallace's Tower. Wallace's sword was once found in this tower, and its story is an interesting one. It is first mentioned in the books of the Lord Treasurer for December 8th, 1505, at which time James IV was at Dumbarton. The entry reads: "For bynding of ane riding sword and rappayer and bynding of Wallas's sword with cordis of silk and new hilt and plumet, new skabbard and new belt to the said sword XXVI sh." In 1644, Provost Semphill of Dumbarton made an inventory and found in the Wallace Tower "ane auld twa handed sword without a scabbard". It is impossible to say if this was the same one as mentioned in the Lord Treasurer's books. At any rate, the Wallace sword was exhibited at the Castle for many years. After an examination at the Tower of London in 1825, experts pronounced it of a later date than Wallace's time. The sword was returned to Dumbarton and again exhibited at the Castle. Records do not show who actually removed Dumbarton's treasure,[33] but it was quietly spirited away to

Stirling, and in 1888 openly gifted by the War Office to authorities there, where it may yet be seen.

A decline in the fortunes of the Castle coincided with the loss of the sword. Troops were withdrawn, and the Ministry of War seemed to lose their interest at the same time. In 1894, an English MP (oh, where were the Scottish Nationalists then??) with the delightful name of Alpheus Cleophus Morton brought the matter up in the House of Commons, accusing the War Minister (a Scotsman, Sir Henry Campbell Bannerman) of neglecting the Castle. The Minister replied that he, Morton, could have the Castle if he would look after it, or he would transfer custody to the Corporation of Glasgow or the Clyde Trust.

Now the Castle is within the bounds of the Burgh of Dumbarton, and the local Town Council were astounded at being ignored once more. Dumbarton wired immediately to Morton and Sir Henry offering to take the Castle over, but the War Office authorities had changed their minds. Fourteen years later they relegated care of the buildings to HM Office of Works. Dumbarton protested at the loss of military status, but the War Office replied that it was of no use to them – though troops were to be barracked there during both world wars in this century.

All this time Dumbarton resented the Wallace sword being exhibited in Stirling. In November 1936, four masked men, after locking the curator in a room, stole the sword from the Wallace Monument. Dumbarton hoped that the sword would come back to the Castle at last. Again questions were raised in Parliament and the authorities were forced to admit that, in spite of a prolonged and very thorough search, no trace could be found of the culprits or the sword.

The sword was later found in the grounds of the Covenanters' Monument at Bothwell Bridge, and was returned to the Wallace Monument in 1941. That Monument[34] is no ancient building. Dumbarton Castle has been a fortress and a strength since the beginning of time, enshrining the whole history of Scotland. It is the sword's rightful home.

Ben brought up the subject of the sword once again when Queen Elizabeth visited Dumbarton before her Coronation in 1953, pointing out that with television and newsreel cameras there to see Her Majesty receive the Keys of the Castle from its keeper, the attention of the whole country would be focused on the town. Despite his best efforts, however, the "captured" relic has never been returned, and I suspect that the authorities in Stirling would be quite astonished were its presence at the Wallace Monument to be questioned today.

But Dumbarton no longer neglects its history. Looking at the colourful leaflet which now promotes the town, the Castle Rock and the surrounding countryside, Ben would remark that he had told them to do this more than fifty years ago. Told that Dumbarton Castle had 16,000 visitors in 1991, that it is floodlit at night, and that it has a detailed entry in *Chamber's Guide to the Castles of Scotland*, he would most certainly say: "Dumbarton Castle has woken up at last, aaaaaah!"

HUGH CLIMBS THE COBBLER

Ben was never idle for a moment during the thirties, collecting material for "Chronicles of the Wayfarers", "In the Footsteps of Hugh Macdonald", "Mountain Indicators of Scotland", "Wayfaring Around The Firth", and "Viewpoints of Scotland", five separate series which followed "The Open Road" articles. It would take a book in itself to include all the stories he wrote in these years. Every one was part of his celebration of the Scottish outdoor scene. In hundreds of miles of walking he neglected little of Scotland, seeing things that few others did, seeing things that some still miss today. What a wonderful guide he would have been, given normal hearing, one is tempted to think. What a wonderful guide he was without it, with the gift of special perception added to his naturally enquiring mind!

One year saw him taking time off from regular weekend climbing for a few months, spending most Saturdays and Sundays exploring the Glasgow environs, following the rambles of Hugh Macdonald, trying to find what was left of the Glasgow of 1850. In his classic book,[35] Macdonald described twenty-one tramps within a radius of ten miles around the city. Ben followed them all, making what he called "a pleasant pilgrimage, which involved some adventures in trespassing" – tracing the windings of the Clyde up river and down, and on both banks; walking by the Kelvin, the Luggie, the White Cart, the Black Cart, and the Earn; visiting every village and town within ten miles of Glasgow, seeing all the by-roads and glens, all the best viewpoints. At every stage Macdonald's writings reminded him of the historical, legendary and antiquarian lore of each district, and he revelled in his mid-nineteenth century descriptive prose . . . "It is sheer delight, for Hugh never uses one word when five will do instead!" How many Glaswegians today could claim to have even thought of attempting such a pilgrimage?

As Ben was by this time an experienced climber, it was natural that he found a special interest in a reference to an early ascent of the Cobbler. "Hugh Climbs the Cobbler" was published towards the end of the Hugh Macdonald series, following the review of all his sojourns around Glasgow; it is presented in Ben's usual personal style, a commentary on the climbers of the nineteenth century:

Macdonald was not content with the countryside immediately surrounding Glasgow, and set off to explore the sea lochs and hills of the west. Arrochar was his first destination, and he sailed to Garelochhead. Today's Sunday excursions are no new thing. The first one to Garelochhead was organised about 1850. Macdonald tells the story of it.

The cottages by the lochside were owned by comparatively wealthy folk, and they and their laird resented the intrusion. When the first ship arrived a band of gillies held the pier. They threw off the mooring ropes and threatened violence to anyone who landed. The excursionists replied with a volley of lemonade bottles and potatoes, and a landing party armed with sticks made their way ashore, routing the gillies. There was no interference after that.

Hugh walked up to Whistlefield and entered the inn, where he found he could obtain "beverages varying from the pungent blood of the barley to the wholesome produce of the animals that browse on the neighbouring pastures". In other words, he had the choice of whisky or milk – and he did not drink milk! He tramped the eight miles to Arrochar, and said that the walk was preferable to the sail. Arrochar was then "a quiet and secluded hamlet at the head of the loch". It was neither quiet nor secluded the last time I was there. Cars and buses were racing through, dozens more parked outside each hotel, discharging their occupants by the lochside – campers, trampers, cyclists and would-be climbers.

The hills, the everlasting attraction of Arrochar, remain the same. Hugh talks of the Cobbler, and of the resemblance of the hill to a shoemaker at work. I have yet to see that resemblance, and prefer the explanation that Cobbler was an Englishman's attempt to pronounce Gobhlach, the proper Gaelic name of the hill.

Macdonald determined to climb the mountain, and ferried across to Ardgartan, "a plain but neat mansion". Now Ardgartan is a youth hostel in the centre of a dream come true – the Scottish National Forest Park. To those of us who know the Cobbler well, Hugh's description of the ascent makes delightful reading, and is full of the exaggerations inseparable from descriptions of mountains in the old

days. To begin with, he took the route by the ridge instead of the
much easier journey following the course of the Buttermilk Burn,
where there is now a well marked path. "We zigzag along, now
scrambling through a dense forest of bracken, now leaping from one
tuft of green to another, and anon climbing almost on our hands
and knees over some swelling and precipitous acclivity."

He thought of turning back, but did not like to say so to his companions because, "In ancient times no individual, whatever his claims
of blood may have been, was reckoned personally qualified to succeed
to the chieftainship of the Clan Campbell until he had demonstrated
his prowess or strength of limb by putting his foot upon the cowl of
the Cobbler." Could a Macdonald give up when a Campbell had
gone on?

Hugh arrives at a mountain spring. ". . . how immense our libations
– native from the hillside, or dashed with a slight modicum of the
soul inspiring dew." They met no one on the way. Nowadays it is
impossible to ascend the Cobbler at weekends without meeting dozens
of climbers, either hill walkers or cragsmen intent on the various
rock climbs. As Hugh neared the summit, ". . . the grandeur of the
scene became awful, and huge masses of embattled rock threatened
to crush the aspiring climber." Come now, Hugh, it is scarcely as
bad as that! By dint of ". . . scrambling, crawling and gliding" he
eventually got to the cairn. Most of us have seen photographs of the
actual summit of the Cobbler. Listen to Hugh: "One scraggy and
precipitous projection seems ready to topple over, and we almost
tremble as we approach it for the purpose of taking a look through
a rift in its sides called Argyll's Eye-glass, lest our touch should send
it thundering down. There are cliffs all around of immense depth
and the most harsh and jagged features, while projections of gnarled
repulsiveness shoot out on every side."

Who would recognise the summit of the Cobbler from that description? If Hugh were to go there to-day he would find boys and
girls crawling through the "eye-glass", walking along the narrow ledge
on the other side and climbing up to the summit rock which he
considered unattainable. I have seen a dozen folk on that boulder
at the same time, and it showed no tendency to topple over. Had
he seen modern rock climbers at work on the Cobbler, language
would have failed him. The South Peak, once thought inaccessible,
is now climbed in many different ways, while the Centre Peak arête
and buttress and the crags of the North Peak offer dozens of routes.
The overall outlook towards the Scottish mountains has also entirely

changed since Hugh's times of around 1850. Then they were regarded
with awe, the heights of many of them were unknown, and the climbs
were all "terrific and full of danger." The ordinary man – if he
considered them at all – considered the hills a nuisance, something
to be avoided. Now we fully appreciate their grandeur, in a way
that Hugh and his companions never imagined, and we know that
the climbing game is the best in the world. Though all the mountains
are well known, and all the great climbs fully explored, the bolder
spirits can yet find new routes to test nerve and sinew to the very
utmost. Long may the good old Cobbler be a training ground!

THE TOWER OF EMPIRE

Only a few can have duplicated the manner of Ben's wayfaring, which
included journeys to all the Mountain Indicators and notable viewpoints
of Scotland – some well known, others neglected. Time and vandalism
may have weathered many of those indicators, but the viewpoints remain, nowadays constantly thronged by tourists. One indicator he visited
– and one view – is missing, for it existed only for little better than a
year. With Ben as our guide we can still relive a few highlights of its
long forgotten panorama.

The 1938 Empire Exhibition at Bellahouston Park, Glasgow will be
remembered today only by an older generation. The marvel of the
promenades, the huge golden figures guarding the United Kingdom
pavilion and the Tower of Empire are still clear memories of mine as
an eight-year-old. Over twelve million people attended the Exhibition.
Almost all must have ascended the elevator of the Tower of Empire, yet
how many saw what Ben saw? How many climbed the Tower before
the opening of the Exhibition, how many stayed on till dark, how many
wrote as he did of that Glasgow and of that Clydeside, urging our visitors
to go and see for themselves the distant places they had glimpsed?

> The biggest thrill was the first ascent of the Empire Tower before
> the opening and before the lifts were working. It is strange to think
> that I had the upper balcony to myself for several evenings. Have
> you been up the Tower? Did you get a good view? Thousands of
> visitors from England and overseas will obtain their first glimpse of
> Clydeside from the Tower. Here is the panorama that will be unfolded
> for them and for us . . .
>
> Look down at the grounds first. Trees to the east and trees to the
> west. You'd scarcely know you were in the middle of an Exhibition.

Remember that no trees were cut down. It's only to the south that there is any suggestion of a formal lay-out on the Wembley[36] lines. Visitors know the Clyde as the place where the biggest ships in the world are built. They can hardly be seen! Just huge cranes here and there and a forest of masts and coloured funnels sticking up among tenements and chimneys. If you look very carefully you'll see a little water in the canting basin at Prince's Dock. The great new Cunarder[37] itself? It's easily visible looking down from the north-west corner.

Ben then took his readers on a circular tour round the four balconies, describing in detail the sights of Glasgow in the foreground, using the opportunity to enthuse about the delights of the encompassing and distant hills. His final images of the Bellahouston Exhibition are memorable:

You do not know the Tower of Empire till you have been there by day, at sunset, and at night. That north-west corner is the best stance. I watched the sunset the other night. A pall of fog hid all views to the north, east and south. I could not even see to the river, but 30 miles away to the west the hills of Argyll were silhouetted sharply against an orange-red sky. The last rays of the sun tinted the silvered metal of the Tower. Then the western skies were ablaze in glory, with the intense glow dimming the far hills as the sun sank lower. As it disappeared lights sprung up in all the Pavilions. The grand stairway became a flowing cascade of ever changing hues, and the fountains started to play. Only from the top of the Tower do you get the full effect of all the coloured fountains and floodlighting. The climax comes when the Tower itself is illuminated.

After seeing this wonderful panorama from the top of the Tower, a panorama that can thrill and captivate, the gateway to the Romantic North Country, surely your visitors will want to go and see those distant places. At least I hope so!

The Tower of Empire was close to home for Ben, but he was prepared to travel the length and breadth of Scotland in search of material. These were still the early years of motoring, and of limited travel. Many of the locations he described were comparatively inaccessible to ordinary folk, but his countless stories on the Scottish outdoors were available to – and aimed towards – average readers of daily newspapers, with every outing capable of being duplicated by the non-climber. The opening up of Scotland during the 1930s was the natural consequence of social progress. Ben understood the process as it was actually happening, and made a significant individual contribution through his constant writing, another diverse chapter in his fascinating story. He drew his long cycle of articles to a close in the following way:

. . . My pilgrimage to viewpoints and view indicators has ended. It involved a few strenuous journeys, in good weather and in bad. Some were easier jaunts, while other visits were no more than afternoon walks. Together they gave vistas of every phase of Scottish scenery – the rugged mountains and wild corries of the North, the deep sea lochs, the lonely hill lochans, the isles and seas of the West, the bare moorlands, the plains and smoother hills of the Lowlands, the Forth and Clyde from their source to the sea, and a much better knowledge of Edinburgh and Glasgow.

So what is the best viewpoint in Scotland? Let each decide for themself; association and history, and knowledge of the near-by country, will have much to do with your own choice. The most magnificent evening I had this summer was when I stayed by the Lyle Hill indicator above Gourock Bay for an hour and watched the sunset over the Argyllshire hills, with the Tail of the Bank [38] a grand foreground. But my own favourite (I do not say the best) is the summit of Dumbarton Castle. How could it be otherwise for a Son of the Rock? [39]

5

ON SCOTTISH HILLS

Only a hill: yes, looked at from below:
    facing the sea, the frequent west.
Tighten the muscle, feel the blood flow,
    and set your foot upon the utmost crest!
There, where the realms of thought and effort cease,
wakes on your heart a world of dreams and peace.
Geoffrey Winthrop Young [40]

Fortune favoured Ben in his birthplace, for the town of Dumbarton lies just to the south of the Highland Line. The benefits thus provided an aspiring climber may best be explained in John Buchan's words:[41]

"The Highland Line of the Scottish mainland has been fixed by nature with sufficient clearness. The true battlement of the hills runs with a north-easterly slant from Argyll through the shire of Dumbarton, and then turns northwards so as to enclose the wide carselands of the Tay. Beyond it lie the tumbled wildernesses stretching with scarcely a break to Cape Wrath."

It was not far from Dumbarton to the beginning of that line of hills, as Ben discovered soon after his return from Skye in 1929. In time he came to know almost every peak from Dunbartonshire to Sutherland-shire, and this became his real world, the professional life in Glasgow mostly something which had to be endured until the weekend escape to the hills. Cycling at first to Arrochar[42] and later further afield by rail and then by road, he and his companions unknowingly took part in the beginnings of the modern era of climbing in Scotland.

In *On Scottish Hills*,[43] Ben looked back at the highlights and vagaries of those early days, presenting at the same time a chosen seventy-five from over a thousand mountain photographs taken during the ten years prior to the Second World War; there was no mention of Skye, for which by then he had other plans. Several verses from Geoffrey Winthrop Young were included, their author noting in the foreword that this was the first collection of Scottish mountain views to be produced by a mountaineer who was also a native of Scotland. A further comment provides an appropriate introduction to extracts from Ben's book:

"They are not merely a series of views or panoramas arranged to make a logical revelation of the best of Scottish hill scenery. They seem rather to be suggesting the inner experience, the personal reactions of a sympathetic mind wandering at will with like thinking friends, through good country, for sheer love of all which that country has to say, to our idle hours no less than to our strenuous hours."

No stories are here of great new climbs and hairbreadth escapes, just of happy hill days when the photographs were taken. To describe only good weather days would give an entirely wrong impression of Scottish climbing, so, to keep the balance, I have described also certain climbs when photography was impossible. There is no need to try to answer that age-old question as to why we climb. Enough, that to many of us, in these years, climbing became a regular weekend sport like golf or tennis – a sport in which we took part at all times of the year. For only those who go to the mountains at all seasons, in summer and winter, in sunshine and rain, in hail, and snow, by night and day – only those may know the true heart of the mountains.

AVALANCHE ON BEN LUI

When the West Highland Railway started Sunday excursions to Mallaig in winter we jumped at the chance of getting beyond Arrochar. For, without a car, Arrochar was till then the most distant base for a Sunday climb. Afterwards we got snow climbs from Crianlarich, Tyndrum and Bridge of Orchy, and have many cheery memories of drying out round waiting-room fires before the arrival of the evening train.

One year, when snow lingered long on the hills, it was the end of May when we rallied for the last snow climb of the season. Strange it was to play tennis in brilliant summer weather in Dumbarton, and then spend Sunday on a snow slope. Ben Lui was our choice, and as we approached the mountain we could see a great deal of avalanche debris at the foot of the central gully. We had never seen an avalanche, and thought all snow likely to fall down had already fallen. There might be a little more, but we could easily withstand it! One member of our party had just been reading George Finch's book, *The Making of a Mountaineer,* and comforted us with that expert's assurance that avalanches did not occur on Scottish mountains.

We roped up and climbed leisurely up the narrow, sunless, centre gully to the sunshine of the wide upper snowfield. Quite a respectable cornice still remained, and the leader tunnelled through it. A quiet half hour by the cairn revelling in the panorama of mountain and moorland; then, one by one, the other three slipped through the hole in the cornice and started downwards. I gave a last look round and followed. Our plan was to keep on the rope till we reached the top of the centre gully, then to unrope and glissade down singly. Suddenly the whole upper snow slope avalanched and poured like a cataract down the funnel of the gully. Down we went with it! The first two men got the full force, and went head first now and then. One likened it to swooping round corners like dirt-track racers, another to a glorified helter-skelter. My own memory is of fighting hard to keep my feet first, grimly hanging on to my ice-axe and keeping the shaft in the snow behind me.

The snow was in huge chunks; we went down at a terrific rate for over a thousand feet, and finally stopped well below the foot of the gully, none of us any the worse, but one man lacking pack and ice-axe. These were buried under many feet of snow and it was hopeless to look for them; anyway, we had a train to catch. The mountains gave us best that day. Since then we have been chary of climbing gullies late in the season, and have always accepted the plain warning shown by avalanche debris. Since then also, we have questioned if even Himalayan climbers can write with authority on Scottish snow conditions, or was that not an avalanche, Mr Finch?

Ben was well known for his life-long advocacy of the ice-axe as an essential piece of equipment for the winter climber in Scotland, and of the necessity for adequate training in its correct use. No word other than life-long would be appropriate, for his very last public communications concerned the ice-axe. Tom Weir remembers well an early remonstration on the subject:

"Let me flash back a wheen o' years to myself as a teenager with two other lads on an icy April day beneath the snow-filled central gully of Ben Lui. Watching us was a baleful looking, balaclava helmeted, bespectacled but well equipped solitary climber, who did not respond to the cheery 'Aye-ayes' we gave him. 'A Scottish Mountaineering Club snob,' we thought him.

"We soon forgot him as the slope quickly steepened and became ice-hard where the gully walls narrow to a cleft. Above, we were having to kick harder with our nailed boots to make the tiniest toe-scrapes. I used a house key to cut hand-holds and tried to shut my mind to the consequences of a slip. Then we made a fearful decision to traverse out right to the ridge, hands numb and heart pounding. Joy to get up.

"On the following Friday evening we knew who the 'snobbish' climber had been when we read an *Evening Times* article by B.H. Humble describing an encounter with three novices, none with ice-axes, and only one wearing gloves in hard winter conditions on a classic mountaineering route. I was the one with the gloves, which were so full of holes that I was frost-bitten on the fingers like the others.

"We chortled when we read Ben's account, and laughed heartily on a later occasion when we heard that the safety conscious Ben had been swept down that same gully when roped to three friends. All were unhurt, but not all held on to their ice-axes like Ben. You don't become experienced without sticking your neck out.

"Our laughter at Ben's slide was not malicious, since by that time we knew why he had not responded to our greeting in the gully. He was stone deaf. I love the story of him ski-ing down a snowy hill-road with a lorry honking behind him to get out of the way, and Ben sliding unaware until the slope ran out! He was in kinks of laughter as he told the story against himself."

THE ROAD

They are planning to make a great new road, they say, planning to iron out all its twists and turnings so that our Loch Lomond road will become a great modern boulevard. In pre-war times that road was often condemned as dangerously congested. We climbers never found it so, and we used it every weekend throughout the year. For us it was a friendly road, luring us to the mountains and speeding us home at night.

"The climber who really intends to climb, and not just to dawdle on the hills, must make an early start. Hence we were on our way when the city was still abed. That is the best time to appreciate Loch Lomond, when all is quiet, when you may meet scarcely any traffic for the long length of it. That first grand glimpse, the Ben, in all its majesty, from the Cameron shore, the islands at Bandry Bay in their idyllic setting, Luss still asleep, Inverbeg, and the hills drawing closer; Tarbet, and the blood quickening of the sight of the well loved peaks. Arrochar was often our journey's end, but often too we went farther north, by Ardlui to Glen Falloch. We knew just what peak every bend in the road would bring into view; every corrie and burn was known. On to Crianlarich and then – eastwards to Ben Lawers, westwards to Ben Cruachan, or northwards to Glencoe? Glencoe was our usual choice. We rushed over the Black Mount till the tremendous bulk of Buachaille Etive Mor came into view, then turned down Glen Etive to Coupal Bridge.

In winter the road really became a road of adventure. We never knew what to expect, for conditions were different every weekend. If there was even a little snow on the south face of Ben Lomond there would be a good deal farther north. If the Ben was covered below the shoulder Arrochar would give us snow climbing, the conditions would be fine at Crianlarich, while snow would be down to the road in Glencoe. How grand to turn north at Tyndrum with a thin layer of snow on the road, and yours the first car to make tracks on it that day

STUCK FAST IN GLENCOE

George Maskell had come from England and was anxious to climb Glencoe in snow. We set off on a Saturday afternoon. There had been heavy snowfalls and rumours of blocked roads, so we carried ice-axes and spades. In Glen Falloch it was ominous to see returning cars with snow on their running boards, and sticking to their wheels and wings. At Crianlarich we met a lorry driver who had turned back beyond Tyndrum, and were told that some vans had gone on, but that private cars were giving up. At Tyndrum there was a ray of hope. "The worst part is between here and Bridge of Orchy. There's only black ice on the Black Mount. You can go round by the back road." We went on to Dalmally and took that "back road" to Glencoe – through Glen Orchy. Here it was spring like, but when we spoke to a shepherd he told of five cars being snowed up. There must be snow somewhere!

At Bridge of Orchy there was no snow on the road, so we stormed the Black Mount in the dark. Then we got the snow – too much of it. A blizzard raged up there! Snow blew hard against the windscreen and across the road; at times we were uncertain whether we were on the road or on the moor. On we went slowly through knee deep ruts in the snow or over icy stretches where the road had been blown quite clear. We were almost on the top of the hill – twenty minutes would see us at Kingshouse.

Twenty minutes – sixteen hours! We ran right into a drift. Five minutes' work with the shovels had us almost all out. A lorry came along from Glencoe and squeezed past. Now was our chance! If we could get on to its tracks we were safe. We cut up our climbing rope and tied it round the rear wheels, cleared the way, and then – the engine went dead. MacBrayne's bus came along, so we jumped into it, for the bus would surely get us to Glencoe! But new drifts were piling up every moment. It was a case of running into a drift, all turning out for furious work with the shovels, helping to push the bus back for some distance, then charging the drift again. So we went, gaining a few yards at a time; the blizzard became worse, and after about half a mile the bus stopped for good. Much snow had drifted inside and was piled up on the seats. We had been floundering about outside, slipping and falling down, so were more or less soaked through.

I'll pay tribute to the crew of that bus – especially the driver. His bus wasn't going to be snowed up and abandoned! We tried to get some sleep, but he worked all night, keeping the engine going – digging – reversing – gaining an inch or two. The work at least kept him warm. Our coats were covered with frozen snow, and it was still there in the morning. That shows the overnight temperature in the bus.

The dawn came slowly, and a strange one it was, for we were exactly at the highest point of the Black Mount Road with a waste of snow all around. At about 7 a.m. the driver's work was rewarded, and the bus lurched forward. For a mile it progressed drunkenly, then we were all thrown off our feet – deep in another drift! Shovel drill again, but this time it was quite hopeless. In front the road was completely blocked for thirty yards, and the snow was six feet deep. We went back to hunt for our car. New drifts had blown up overnight, and there was still a raging wind. The poor car looked quite derelict, and how did so much snow get inside when we had left windows and doors tightly closed? Snow was piled up under the bonnet, and we had to chip ice off the radiator. Wonder of wonders! – the car started within half an hour. Back we went to the bus. An Argyll County Council road gang appeared on the scene. "We'll dig out the bus and dig on back to your car," said the foreman, "but if the road is blocked beyond you'll have to go back by Ballachulish and Oban." The prospect appalled us, especially the ten shilling charge to cross the Connel Bridge!

The gang set to it with a will. We left them to it, and trudged through the snow to Kingshouse Inn three miles away. The landlord was surprised to see us, but what a meal he set down. We did full justice to it, having had only a cup of tea since noon the previous day. While the others dozed off I went out on the hunt for photographs. For a short time the sun came out, and the snow slopes of Clachlet and the Buachaille sparkled brilliantly. I was rewarded with one view of Buachaille Etive Mor through the trees, well worth that night in the bus.

In the afternoon we got back to our car, and had to use our ice-axes to break through six inches of ice over a pool to find water for the radiator. But at last we got off, and made it back to Tyndrum without running into new drifts. There we stopped for petrol, and informed our guide of Saturday that there was not only ice on the Black Mount, but also a few dozen cubic miles of snow!

Yet such an experience was nothing compared with the difficulties of the pioneer climbers of the Glencoe Hills. Impossible for them to motor from Glasgow in the morning, climb the Buachaille and return that night. They travelled by train to Bridge of Orchy and walked, cycled or drove in a open trap for the next thirteen miles. The cyclists and walkers were sure of arriving, but the trap could not be relied on. Often it never appeared. Often, too, they were turned off the hills, for the whole area was a carefully preserved deer forest. "The modern rifle is very silent, and has a range of two miles." Such was the grim notice once exhibited in the Glencoe Post Office.

Now the Glencoe hills are free to all who would wander there. Tourists by the thousand rush through this glen in cars; comparatively few explore its surroundings. Soon, maybe, they will realise that the district offers much to hill walkers and ramblers as well as to expert climbers. Now the twenty-two square miles round the most historic, if not the grandest glen in all Scotland is now the chief possession of the still young Scottish National Trust, and the region is one of the three major rock climbing centres in Scotland, the other two being Ben Nevis and the Isle of Skye.

Ben's comment that one photograph was "well worth the night on the bus" is typical. Also typical is his use of a personal escapade to draw a parallel for his readers between the problems faced by the Glencoe pioneers and the opportunities now open to those prepared to leave the hurried tourist trail. Still favouring historical connotations, the reminiscences of the Buachaille from *On Scottish Hills* continue with the story of a first ascent:

A LAZE ON THE CURVED RIDGE

Enthusiasts will tell you of the classic Crowberry Ridge, the great precipice of the Rannoch Wall, and the fearful Chasm which will test the stoutest cragsman. Dare I confess that my favourite climb on the Buachaille is the easiest of them all – the Curved Ridge? There is a spot half-way up where I like to laze. From there one August afternoon I watched the first ascent of that magnificent climb, Agag's Groove. It came about this way. For a decade the Crowberry Ridge was regarded as the finest climb on the mountain, and no one thought that the precipice which bordered it to the east could be climbed. At last some-one noticed a crack running up that precipice and expressed an opin-ion that it might be climbable. Others heard of the discovery, with the result that, on one August day, two rival parties trekked across the moor, each intent of having the honour of making a new climb.

Rightly the discoverers were the first arrivals, so I settled myself down on the Curved Ridge and developed a crick in the neck watch-ing that pioneer effort. Only those of us who saw that first ascent realise fully how well named was the climb. Agag, you remember, was the Biblical character who trod delicately. J. A. Hamilton led magnificently, and the great quantity of loose stuff sent down by the last man showed how delicately his leader must have trod. I recom-mend the stance I took that day for a laze on a busy day on the Buachaille. To one side a party may be struggling with the intricacies of the shadowed Rannoch Wall, while another party will be silhou-etted against the clouds as they climb up D. Gully Buttress.

Of many visits to the summit of the Buachaille, one day stands out. We had climbed up by the North Buttress. There was no wind. White clouds trailed in all the valleys and the mountain tops rose above them. To the south-west a glimpse of the shapely Starav and his satellites above dense rolling clouds; beyond him, to the west, the hills of Benderloch and Appin, and near at hand, Etive Beag and the peaks of Bidean nam Bian. There was the notched ridge of Aonach Eagach, a glimmer of Loch Leven, and afar off, more hills – the hills of Ardgour – with dainty fair weather cumulus clouds above them. Below, in the valley, the straight new road and the twisted old one – as twisted as the river; green pastures around Altnafeadh, clouds from a thousand to two thousand feet, and countless mountain tops towering over them with Ben Nevis and the great Tower Ridge easily distinguishable.

Excelsior! Nearing the summit of Buachaille Etive Beag. Photo: Ben Humble.

Those were the good weather days, but it is not always good weather in Glencoe! Sometimes dense, dark mist will hide the mountains, the rain will lash down, the rivers will be in spate and every burn a foaming torrent. It was like that when we camped at Coupal Bridge, raining continuously for two days and two nights till our tent was in a sea of mud. My companion got into his sleeping bag, and then into a huge canvas cover which seemed to be for either a grand piano or a horse. The whole contraption took up three-quarters of the tent, leaving the remainder for me. What else he took to bed with him I do not know, but he cooked two meals without moving out of that sleeping bag! Next day we climbed Buachaille Etive Beag, a mountain almost neglected because of the fame of its twin shepherd. Near the summit we came upon a steep slope of wind-furrowed snow, with the furrows perfectly parallel like a ploughed field. Never had I seen such an effect as that – the discomfort of the tent became just a distant memory.

To the outsider it would seem that Ben's deafness must have been a major hindrance when climbing. Alex Small, who along with Rob Anderson drew sketch maps and diagrams for his early publications, described the code of rope-tugs used when they were out of sight of each other, signalling to Ben either to stop or to climb up. Inevitably the signals were misconstrued on occasions, when Ben might start climbing when his companion was in an airy position with no belay; the only resort then was frantically to pull the rope so tightly that it nearly jerked him off his hold, or to throw a stone down near him as a warning. Tom MacKinnon also remembers having a prolonged wait on a cold cramped ledge in an exposed situation, and of descending round a holdless corner to meet Ben face to face coming up! It is a tribute to his climbing that many friends felt safe in his company, despite these occasional difficulties.

THE LONG WAY BY LOCH LEVEN

Everyone who passes through Glencoe is acquainted with that rampart which blocks the Pass to the north. Two miles long is that Aonach Eagach ridge, the narrowest main ridge outside of Skye. On a certain day of snow and ice and sunshine I stayed at home while two friends made their first traverse of that ridge. Afterwards one of them told me he was disappointed because it was not so difficult as he had expected. He ought to have been mighty thankful. I would give much for perfect conditions on that ridge. I have traversed it four times in snow, but never has the weather kept up from end to end. And I, too, like many another climber, have been benighted there. For once started, one cannot descend to Glencoe till the far end is reached. Hence when conditions are difficult, darkness may come and cause a long descent northwards to Loch Leven, where fortunately the slopes are easy.

A late start, much new snow on the rocks and a large party (eight on two ropes) caused us to be only nearing the third of the four tops one day with but a short time of daylight left. On this mountain the ridge is so very definite that there may be a cornice only on certain sections of it. Towards the third top I was leading the first party and was walking slowly up a gentle slope about five feet from the edge. Suddenly I dropped out of the world – or so it seemed. One second I was on top of the ridge; the next, I very definitely was not. I had no sensation of falling.

The second party, some way behind and lower, heard a loud noise and saw a huge mass of snow crash down the gully ahead of them. Actually I had been just at the junction of the cornice and the ridge when the snow split beneath my feet. The main mass hurtled down the slopes while I dropped neatly into a double lip about eight feet below. I did not "come on the rope", and retained my ice-axe. Even if I had gone farther I would have been held, for Bill Mackenzie, behind me, was well placed and instantly ready.

A grinning face peered over. I was promptly hauled back, relegated to the rear, and we continued. This little adventure delayed us, and darkness came some way farther on. At first we tried a descent to Glencoe by a steep and unknown gully, till halted by a rockfall which we could not negotiate in the dark. We climbed to the ridge again, our torches flashing the while. One man's wife had ferried the cars from the eastern to the western end of Glencoe, and now we could see the headlights as she cruised backwards and forwards. She could see our torches, and must have been wondering what was wrong. Her worthy husband kept muttering: "Blast the wife, wasting petrol all night at one-and-sixpence the gallon!" No more rocks for us! It had to be the long descent to Loch Leven, first by gradual snow slopes, then slipping and falling among deep heather, and finally floundering through a young plantation which seemed to abound in unsuspected ditches.

Towards midnight we reached the road. That much maligned lady had understood what we were up to, and we did not have to walk far. One o'clock on the Monday morning found us sitting down to a mixture of supper and breakfast at Kingshouse, and at five we crawled into Glasgow with a thimbleful of petrol in the tank.

Those matter of fact words, ". . . at five we crawled into Glasgow with a thimbleful of petrol in the tank", belie the reality that by 9 a.m. on a Monday morning Ben had to be back in harness in his professional practice. How on earth did he keep it all up? Pure climbing forays aside, how did he find the time in those years of the mid to late 1930s to visit Youth Hostels across the length and breadth of Scotland, to tramp the hills and glens around and between them; to walk or climb to the top of most of Scotland's famous viewpoints and mountain view indicators; to explore the little used paths and byways up and down the Clyde estuary from Ayrshire to Cowal and Bute; to follow Hugh Macdonald's rambles in and around Glasgow every weekend for six months; to visit countless ancient castles, abbeys and cathedrals, exploring their environs and history; and to write of all these journeys, constantly urging both local and visitor alike to step aside from the beaten track and find the real Scotland? All this, yet still a practising dentist, still in those same years producing more scientific papers, reporting unusual dental cases, producing lengthy reviews of books on dental radiology, writing letters to the dental and medical journals when topics interested him – the list goes on and on. Bill Murray summed up this extraordinary capacity for work:

"Ben roused in me, and all who knew him, wonder and admiration. We could not imagine how he made the time or kept the pace. One thing is certain, he was driven, positively driven by deafness into a need for constant communication and perpetual involvement in affairs."

Every now and then, Ben would come home to the house he shared with his mother in Dumbarton, and abandon himself to sleep for twenty-four hours and more. As a youngster, and even into my University days, often when I visited my grandmother she would say to me, "Go and wake Bennie. I can't get him up." Usually this would be in the afternoon, sometimes much later. I would always find him in the same position, dead to the world, totally curled up and hidden under the blankets with not an inch of his bald head showing. I always thought it a position liable to induce instant suffocation, but then I had never spent a night out on the hills! He was almost impossible to rouse, for with his deafness he slept the sleep of the dead. After minutes of repeated shaking, there might be some response, but I had always to stand around for a while before being forced to make other attempts. It was never long, however, before he was off again, either to the much loved Cobbler,[44] or further north beyond Glencoe and the Buachaille to Ben Nevis.

BEN NEVIS WAS SPOILED BY THE ENGLISH

In terms of volume Ben wrote as much about Ben Nevis as he did of any other mountain, and the Nevis chapter in *On Scottish Hills* included some of his best winter photographs in snow. During the 1950s, after much preliminary correspondence, he submitted a proposal and synopsis for an extensive history of Britain's highest peak to his publishers, Robert Hale. They replied in enthusiastic terms, but the letters suddenly stop at that point, with no subsequent indication from either side as to why the book was not proceeded with. More than ten years later he produced a four part article for *The Scots Magazine*, called simply "The Nevis Story", which followed the order laid out in his original synopsis.

The subject of Ben Nevis provides another example of Ben's vulnerability to tongue in cheek writing. "Brush up Ben Nevis – an Englishman's plea for climbing comfort", ran a 1938 headline, over a story in which F. Washington Flatt asked the Scots if they were oblivious to the bounties bestowed upon them by nature, and claimed that Ben Nevis was a standing reproach to Scotland. Wanting a smooth macadam path to the top instead of "the present miserable mule path", Mr Flatt advocated a cable railway and a hotel on the summit. "Can we be surprised that visitors are going to the Swiss mountains in increasing numbers each year?" he asked.

One reader suggested that perhaps Mr Flatt might feel disposed the following year to have a go at breaking the record time for the Ben Nevis Hill Race, or even spurn the beaten track in preference for negotiating the climb by the crags on the northern and eastern faces. There were no such subtleties in Ben's reply. Stung by the combined slights to the mountain and to Scots in general, he roared to the attack in his own typical style under his pen name Alan Hume, proclaiming, "Ben Nevis was spoiled by the English":

> Mr Flatt wants a good road up Ben Nevis and a building on the summit where one can put up for the night. Once Ben Nevis had just such amenities, and it was Mr Flatt's compatriots who let them go to rack and ruin!
>
> Once, Mr Flatt, when very little was known about the mountain, the people of Scotland – rich and poor – contributed £4,000 and built on the highest point of Britain a completely equipped observatory, and a good road from Glen Nevis to the summit. The road was six feet wide with a gradient nowhere exceeding one in five.

A motorist could drive to the top where a small hotel provided supper, bed and breakfast for 10 shillings.

This lonely scientific post was Scotland's contribution to the Empire's and the World's knowledge of Meteorology. It was built by Scotsmen and maintained almost entirely by Scotsmen, though the results went out to all the world. The Royal Societies of London and Edinburgh thought so much of the work that they spent £1,500 in printing and tabulating the results . . . For 21 years, day and night, hourly observations were made at the high level station coincident with similar observations at Fort William. At 9 p.m. each night a summary of the meteorological results for the day was telegraphed to the Press.

Visitors from over the Border made full use of that splendid road and the buildings on the summit. Did they help in any way towards the heavy cost of the work, or the upkeep? Not a bit of it! . . . When the Directors asked for an increased Government grant (from the initial miserly sum of £350), every single Scottish MP supported them. The Government refused to increase their grant by a single pound, the then Chancellor of the Exchequer expressing surprise at "such a demand". With decreasing annual subscriptions and no hope of a higher grant the directors had to close down the Observatory in 1904, and dismiss their loyal staff . . .

To sum up, Scotland built the road and the Observatory for the use and good of Britain, bore 90% of the expense for 21 years, then asked England to play the game and help run the scheme. England refused. Is there any need for an Englishman to tell us what to do with Ben Nevis?? Scafell and Great Gable are favourite mountains. Have the English yet constructed roads to these summits for the use of the Scots and others?

Mr Flatt did not respond to such a telling off! The reference to the Ben Nevis Observatory, however, had much more meaning than readers of the riposte may have imagined. Ben loved to climb Ben Nevis, particularly in its winter grandeur, but his exhaustive delving into the mountain's literature also left him held spellbound by the story of the Australian meteorologist Clement Wragge, whose research led to the founding of the Observatory in 1883. He found something of a kindred spirit in Wragge, a man who thought nothing of expending enormous amounts of time and energy in obtaining the smallest scientific detail, almost losing his life in pursuit of daily observations during one of the worst ever Nevis storms. Ben wrote countless versions of Wragge's story, including a radio play, and devoted the second part of his short history to the founding of the Observatory. Included in this were his early impressions on the man Fort William folk dubbed "Inclement Wragge":

> "The Scottish Mountaineering Club may well hold his name in honour as a pioneer who first became acquainted with our beloved Ben Nevis in all its aspects of storm and stress." More years ago than I care to admit, after a first climb on Ben Nevis, on reading the SMC guide to the mountain, that phrase attracted my attention, and I wanted to know more about that remarkable character, Clement Wragge, who once ascended the mountain every day during the summer of two successive years and established a temporary observatory on the summit.
>
> The more I learned about him the more he became the great hero of Ben Nevis, amply justifying the phrase in the guide book . . . What records had been kept by Wragge? Where were they to be found? At last, I located his diaries. I still remember the thrill that summer day when dozens of volumes were placed before me – volumes that had lain dust covered for nigh on sixty years . . .

If the story of Clement Wragge contains echoes of Ben's determination of purpose, another tale confirms the uniqueness of his own personal story. His account of 100 years of Coronation festivities on the summit of Ben Nevis goes on to describe how he and a companion, two from among hundreds of millions of citizens of the Empire, held their own private celebration of the Coronation of King George VI and Queen Elizabeth in 1937:

A TALE OF TWO FLAGS

There have been many ceremonies on the summit of our highest mountain, the first of them well over one hundred years ago, shortly after Ben Nevis had been declared to be the highest point in Britain, and at a time when mountaineering was unknown. This was to celebrate the young Queen Victoria's first tour throughout Scotland.

A contemporary account records that . . . "many were the fires which blazed on the auspicious occasion over all parts of Scotland. But the most aspiring of all was that erected and ignited by the inhabitants of Fort William, who with incalculable labour and perseverance, carried an immense quantity of fuel and a great many tar barrels to the summit of Ben Nevis. Salutes were fired from the ancient Castle of Inverlochy. While the booming of the guns awoke echoes of Locheil, Ardgour, Glen Nevis, and other wild passes of the neighbourhood, the passing clouds of mist on the mountain occasionally veiled the blazing beacon: and ever and anon, as the breeze cleared away, it burst forth with a Vesuvian splendour, and shed a red glow on every mountain top around."

For about forty years after that there were comparatively few ascents of the mountain until interest was aroused by the building of the Observatory in 1883. From then there was a constant stream of visitors to the summit during the summer months, and, of course, something had to be done on Ben Nevis on the occasion of Queen Victoria's Diamond Jubilee in June 1897.

Alas, Nevis was on its worst behaviour – snow fell heavily in the forenoon and there was rain in the afternoon and the evening. Nevertheless, during the day a contingent of Cameron Highlanders in full highland costume marched bravely up the mountain and announced their arrival by firing off a rocket from the highest point in the land, after which the regimental piper played the National Anthem. The gallant soldiers were hard put to it, for they were standing in two feet of snow, and shivering under blasts of icy sleet. A photographer fixed up his tripod and big plate camera, but the whole thing was blown down, and he did not manage to take a single photograph. Fortunately for them, there was a small hotel on the summit at that time and the whole company promptly adjourned there, having "an excellent dinner washed down by a goodly supply of the Brew of Ben Nevis".

As darkness came, a bonfire was ignited, like many others on vantage points of lesser heights. Had it been clear, all the blazes, with perhaps a glimpse of a huge fire away over in Northern Ireland, would have been a magnificent sight. Alas, rain, thick clammy mist and sleet spoiled it all, and the bonfire could hardly be made out from the hotel door a hundred yards away! Most of the company departed for Fort William, leaving a few stalwarts to hold high revel in the hotel till early morning.

In spite of this disappointment, the local folk planned an even bigger bonfire to mark the coronation of King Edward VII in August 1902. For months beforehand, material was taken up on pony-back, once again under difficult snow conditions. On the great day, mist, sleet and snow swept the mountain once more. Nevertheless, visitors from all parts of Scotland, including the whole Town Council of Fort William, struggled up to the summit. The large company gathered round the cairn and the Provost delivered a loyal address. A telegram was sent off to the King, but it is doubtful if he would have been able to read it as it was written in Gaelic!

The new King's health was then pledged with full Highland honours and an abundant supply of whisky. On the same day, the Masons of Fort William made history by holding a Masonic ceremony on the highest point in Britain, initiating several candidates into the mystic order of Freemasonry, and finishing up with a convivial banquet in the hotel. They, too, sent off a telegram to the King. At nine in the evening the bonfire was ignited. The mist obstinately refused to lift, rain started to fall, and little could be seen of the blaze or fireworks which followed, and once more the company retired to the hotel to forget their disappointment.

The bad weather on these two occasions dulled local enthusiasm, and there was no ceremony at all on Ben Nevis to mark the coronation of King George V in 1911. Probably the main reason was that both the hotel and the Observatory had been closed down by this time, and there was no possibility of the grand banquets of previous years. Nor did Fort William folk make any plans for celebration on the summit on Coronation Day in May 1937.

But as that 1937 Coronation Day approached, I sounded a half dozen of my friends in the Scottish Mountaineering Club, the general idea being to have a bonfire and firework display on the summit of Nevis at midnight. All were enthusiastic, but as the day grew near, they called off one by one, preferring the softer pleasures of the town, till only two of us remained, appropriately enough an Englishman, George Maskell, and myself, a Scot.

We left Glasgow on Coronation Eve. He wanted to carry up a Union Jack. I wanted the Scottish Standard. We bought a Union Jack without difficulty, but found shop after shop had long since sold out of Standards. It was the same story wherever we tried, all the way to Dumbarton – hundreds of Union Jacks but no Scottish flags. One patriotic shopkeeper refused to take down the Standard decorating his doorway even though we offered a black market price! At last, on the outskirts of Dumbarton, we saw a lady starting to decorate her house, and induced her to sell us her one and only Standard. It required a good bit of argument, and was hardly a sale, for we had to promise to return it.

After a fast run north we got to Fort William about 10.30 p.m., and enjoyed a fish and chip supper before facing the journey up the mountain. It was very dark when we set off an hour later, laden with thirty pound packs, and carrying flags, fireworks, ice-axes and ropes, and a tripod for our cameras. We hadn't gone very far before we discovered that neither of us had any matches. The prospect of no hot meals for two days appalled us, so we retraced our steps; how the night watchman at the Ben Nevis Distillery laughed when he supplied our want!

We often lost the path and climbed very slowly – maybe we had consumed too many chips – and about 2 a.m., when folk were beginning to gather in the London streets, we reached the Alpine Hut, which stands at a height of 2,500 feet under the shadow of the great cliffs. Before we stumbled into bed, that whole range of cliffs was clear in the ghostly light of the hours before the dawn. Later on Coronation Day we climbed the Ben. Encumbered with large flags – awkward things to carry – and a battery of cameras, we chose the easiest of the many rock climbs, the Castle Ridge. When the Coronation procession was on route, we had the whole north-east face of Nevis – the mightiest range of cliffs in Britain – all to ourselves. It was the sort of day the beacon builders of earlier years had been denied, with brilliant blue skies, a tropical sun, and magnificent views. What a contrast, too, dreamy blue Hebridean Isles, glittering lochs and western seas, yet snow and ice-clad rocks around us.

At last we reached the plateau, where snow lay many feet deep, and walked on to the summit. The Lion Rampant flag was lashed to an ice-axe and stuck on what was once the tower of the Observatory. The Union Jack we fixed on the new Ordnance Survey cairn so that it flew higher, as was its right. Then, on the highest point in Britain, we toasted the health of the new King and Queen. No banquet or Dew of Ben Nevis for us, merely tea from a thermos flask.

Afterwards, we had two hours of sun-bathing on the summit, stirring ourselves now and then to take photographs or to admire the widespread views. We saw no glamorous procession, no glittering coaches and regal figures. But, as we identified peak after peak, there passed between us a procession of memories of long happy days on their ridges, gullies and summits. In the late afternoon we descended No 3 Gully to Coire na Ciste in the very heart of the mountain. After roping down over the cornice we kicked steps in the steep upper portion, then glissaded in a glorious rush, right down to the tiny lochan. After a much required tea we rested for an hour or two, before setting off again, heavily laden with our supply of fireworks and much extra clothing. We ascended by the same gully, where our glissade tracks of the afternoon were quite icy, and we had to cut steps with our ice-axes. At 11 p.m. we approached the cornice, and as I got over I saw at once a sickle moon in the sky, and a huge bonfire by the shores of Loch Linnhe. We hurried to the summit; it was by now very dark and terribly cold.

I fixed up camera and tripod, set the shutter for time and left it open; then we got busy with the fireworks. It was a dramatic moment as our first rocket soared up and sparkling stars fell over the precipices to the valley two thousand feet below. Quickly we went through our whole supply, for it was too cold to linger. Our best and biggest rocket we reserved to the last. It soared to a tremendous height, higher than fireworks had ever gone in Britain before. Did they see our show from Fort William, we wonder? Or did they think of shooting stars?

The beacon by Loch Linnhe died down. All was still. The moon disappeared, and it became darker and colder. After midnight we sought our steps leading to the gully by torchlight, and roped down over the cornice once more. The great cliffs on either side were ghostly again, and a canopy of stars sparkled frostily. It was an eerie journey down the gully in darkness, and we were glad to get below the snow and reach the haven of our hut.

Thus was the 1937 Coronation celebrated on the summit of Ben Nevis. Returning reluctantly to civilisation, we were amazed to read of fog and rain in London – while we had perfect weather. In the words of A.D. Godley, we had indeed been in "the higher purer air".

THE ROAD'S END

Whatever our destination in those years, we were always late in returning – and the road was ours again. Drugged by content after a day on the mountains, the miles flew by. At all hours we returned; sometimes, when hard conditions in Glencoe had caused delay, towards midnight; sometimes, after a weekend on Nevis, at dawn on the Monday morning, fighting hard to keep awake. Perhaps that road would not hold such a treasure store of memories for our small group were it not for the white house of Glen Falloch. Almost always we stopped there when returning; often we rushed up there late on a winter Saturday night and made it our base for the morrow's climb. It became a second home to some of us – always the same cheery welcome, always those great log fires.

Then came the war and that small band was scattered to the ends of the earth. On leave, in Britain, they came to the white house.

From there they bade farewell to Scottish hills before again faring overseas. But they continued to climb.

Two – the luckiest ones – climbed in the Rockies, in Alaska, and in Iceland; one climbed in South Africa, one made a new route up the Great Pyramid, one climbed in Madagascar and in Italy; one reached the foothills of the Himalayas, while one kept spirit alive during weary years in prison camp, re-living days of glory on the hills; and one – good comrade – gained the Ultimate Heights – that we might climb again.

6

INTERLUDE

MY WAR

ARP MEN FAINT AT `H´ FILM

A HORROR FILM THAT MAKES FRANKENSTEIN AND BELLA LUGOSI
THRILLERS SEEM FIT FOR THE NURSERY HAS BEEN PRODUCED BY
MILD MR B.H. HUMBLE, A GLASGOW DENTIST

So ran the headlines of the *Scottish Sunday Express* for 28 June 1942. The story continued . . .

"Hundreds in his audience have fainted. One victim, a Paisley man, took half an hour to revive, while a high Scottish police official had to be removed by ambulance. The film has been made in colour for teaching Air Raid Personnel[45] in the Glasgow Casualty Service, but now doctors all over Britain are clamouring for copies.

"Cameraman Humble joined the Casualty service as a first aid man, but when his talent was discovered he was encouraged to devote all his time to film making. Realistic wound faking with plasticine and liquid 'blood' has been perfected by Dr A. G. Mearns, a lecturer at Glasgow University. Such realistic effects are produced that many doctors have been unable to distinguish between real and imitation wounds. Shots include rescues from blazing debris after a mock air raid. It is all horribly real, and intended to be so. Such sights help to harden Civil Defence workers, who might otherwise be overcome when faced by the real thing.

"First experiments were made on the initiative of Dr John Dunlop, the chief of Glasgow Casualty Service. He told me yesterday . . . 'The Medical Officer of Health Sir Alexander MacGregor and the Glasgow Emergency Committee have lent enthusiastic support. The films will be shown in city parks during the Glasgow Fair fortnight, when we shall be calling for 2,000 casualty service volunteers.' "

That brief Press item from the Second World War must have caught the attention of many Glaswegians. It underlines Ben's uncanny ability to move effortlessly into new fields of endeavour, leaving his own individual stamp on each. He presented the film *A Bomb Fell* to more than two hundred audiences, travelling up and down Britain during the times of the London and Clydebank blitzes, and in the process finding himself in such unlikely places as the top of the highest fire-escape ladder in Glasgow and the inside of a police van – detained on a charge of unauthorised wartime photography.

He left an amusing account of this voluntary civil defence work, calling it simply "My War". Not previously published, his story gives a picture of Glasgow which is almost impossible to imagine today:

My war was centred around the City Chambers in George Square. It came about in this way. When war came doctors were allocated to all the First Aid Posts, but there were no jobs for dentists. Dr John Dunlop, an East-end general practitioner who became Medical Officer for Civil Defence, put up the idea that dentists should man the central First Aid Post at the City Chambers, with added fire watching duties in the event of an air raid. All the Glasgow dental surgeons co-operated. We were divided into groups of four, each group having to be available on the same night each week. Rooms were adapted in the Public Health Department, one as a post, and another two as dormitories, and we worked with a permanent staff consisting of a Sister, a nurse, and one orderly. For over three years my own group would check in at the Cochrane Street entrance at 8 p.m., and after a cup of tea sneak up through long-deserted corridors to the members' smoking room, where we would play bridge for hours. Then to bed, up at 7.30 a.m., with our breakfast provided, and off to work again at 9 a.m.

There were giants in Glasgow's Local Government in those days. Sir Patrick Dollan was Lord Provost, Sir Percy Sillitoe Chief Constable, Sir Alexander MacGregor Medical Officer of Health, with James Robertson – later Sir James and Chief Constable himself – in charge of all departments of Civil Defence. With all the chiefs located in George Square we saw much of the inner workings.

The chief problem in the beginning was the training of first aid workers, as massive air raids were expected. Dr Alex Mearns, then a young GP in Partick, was attached to Knightswood First Aid Post. He had much experience in amateur theatricals, and faked wounds on the staff of his post, giving demonstrations to show the first aiders the types of wounds they might have to deal with. His faking was wonderfully realistic, but it was of limited use because it took so much time for only an evening's demonstration each time. As I was a cine photographer with a first class cine camera and a battery of lenses, Mearns and I got together and conceived the idea of making a cine film. We staged a mock air raid, with wounded and bleeding victims being removed from blitzed buildings, with treatment on the spot, and then later at First Aid Posts. It is difficult now to realise the impact of that film. Colour movies were unknown, so injuries or bleeding had little impact on a black and white screen. Ours was in the early Kodachrome, with lots of blood, and we added actual injuries, so that a medical audience were unable to spot which were real and which were faked. Wound faking is common nowadays, and bleeding often seen in the cinemas, while the Red Cross and other organisations can supply kits of all types of injuries to be attached to "victims". But in the early 1940s it was unknown, and Alex Mearns has never received full credit for his pioneer work.

The authorities were delighted, so that in addition to the weekly stint at the City Chambers I had the job of screening the film, often three times a week, at First Aid Posts, Rescue Depots, and Warden's Posts, and had to give a commentary while it was running. After a week or two we had to cut out much of the blood, as there was fainting at every show, but even after that the fainting continued. I remember one night when I showed it to a good class of audience at Hillhead three men fainted, then the next night tough housewives at Bridgeton were not affected at all! There was often difficulty in wiring up in various types of buildings, and I had to carry much extra gear. At Govan Town Hall I put the projector on the balcony, started it up, told a chap to keep an eye on it, and went to the platform to give a talk. When the lights went up 400 feet of film was draped around a man on the floor below, and he was in no fit state to say anything!

Our fame spread. Big firms asked for a show to their employees, as well as other surrounding towns, and I often had eerie returns to Glasgow around midnight in the blackout with dimmed lights. London also asked for the film, and this gained for me my only wartime visit to the blitzed city. Alex and I had a technical article about the film and the wound faking published in *The Lancet*,[46] and this was reviewed favourably in the *British Medical Journal*. The *Daily Express* gave it a scare headline. Then the British Council became interested, and had copies made, some of which even went to South American countries. The different attitude of today is shown by the fact that folks usually just laugh when they see the film, although recently when I screened it in a private house, when the lights went up the room was full of smoke. A man had fainted, dropped his cigarette, and an armchair was smouldering.

The fear of gas attacks was another great concern, and the authorities asked if we could make an anti-gas film. So one Sunday we cleared a quiet street near Eglinton Toll, and staged a gas attack. Then the following week we filmed gas decontamination and gas cleansing at Pollokshields Baths. Here I almost became a casualty myself. The floor was running with water, my light standards were of metal, and when I tried to move them I received a fearful shock.

Army headquarters in Edinburgh asked to see the films. A Captain of the Army Cine Corps called for us in a rather ancient car. Dr Dunlop and his second were there as well as myself. Not far out of Glasgow the car started to go very poorly. I am no mechanic and didn't know what was wrong. We stopped at two garages, but there were no mechanics available. All the men were on service, and the garages were staffed by women who didn't know much either. At a third garage a minor repair was done, but someone forgot to screw back the radiator cap properly and it fell off. We stopped and walked back along the road looking, even searching ditches, but could find no sign of it. Then the car wouldn't start, and we had to push it up to the top of a slight rise and jump in. We were almost an hour late by this time, and the Captain drove hard, with water boiling out of the radiator constantly. In Edinburgh the Headquarters staff were all waiting, all red caps, a Major-General and no one under the rank of Colonel. John Dunlop was the cheeriest of individuals, got on well with everyone. He tried to laugh it off, but that was the only time I saw him put out. The atmosphere was icy for they had been waiting for over an hour. "Get on with it," they said. We started the film and the Sergeant operating the projector promptly fainted, so an Army girl had to take over. That night also a high ranking police officer blacked out and had to be passed down from the back of the hall over a sea of hands! I didn't see the poor Captain afterwards, I hate to think what his superiors said to him.

When the Clydebank Blitz started, I was on duty at the City Chambers, and there was coming and going all night long, with all sorts of rumours. Next afternoon I started back for Dumbarton by bus. Beyond Yoker there was just a huge pall of smoke, with all the traffic stopped. It took me hours to walk round via Duntocher. My sister-in-law had arrived from London two days previously to get away from the bombing there, but that night a bomb fell on the road outside her parents' house and blew the front in, while others fell near my own house. The next day I cycled down to Cardross, and my chief memory is of horses and cattle lying dead in the fields, and of the clubhouse at Cardross Golf Club, the Church, and adjoining houses blitzed and still smouldering, for Cardross got some of the incendiary bombs meant for Greenock and Port Glasgow across the river. The folks around Dumbarton and Cardross were very amused when Lord Haw Haw[47] announced on the propaganda radio that the Port of Cardross had been heavily damaged, for there is hardly more than one small jetty at Cardross! On the return journey to Glasgow by bus an oil pipeline was still burning at Bowling, there was scarcely an unbroken window the whole way, and I saw the full extent of the destruction through Clydebank.

Dr Dunlop then said that we must have a full record of Civil Defence for the future. I don't think any of us realised the full magnitude of the task, for every single aspect of Civil Defence had to be included, and the film was taken at odd intervals over the next two years. The Heads of all Corporation departments were responsible for arranging what should be filmed, and provisional scripts were worked out with endless voluntary help. Photography was of course prohibited by law, and I had no official permit, but they just told me to go ahead. The police stopped me in Sauchiehall Street one day, put me in a Black Maria van and drove me away! I objected strongly, for after all I was providing all my own gear. After that word went out that I was not to be disturbed, and I was able to film wherever I wanted. Kodachrome was in short supply, so the main part had to be in black and white, though I did manage a few colour scenes. Apart from the outdoor filming there were long nights in the library of the Public Health Department, cutting, splicing, editing and titling. There was a good deal of talent available. A commercial artist, unfit for war service, drew some fine titles, and using single frame exposures we even managed cartoons.

Finally towards the end of the war the job was completed, the whole film running for almost two hours. It then was put into storage. Just recently I was given the opportunity of running that film again after almost thirty years. What a Glasgow that was! Had I really filmed all that? I could scarcely believe it. There was George Square with huge shelters, a water tank as big as a swimming pool, and tramcars passing by. There were scenes of Army divers going down the tanks and retrieving all sorts of things. Communal shelters in streets, strutted closes with baffle walls, shelters behind tenements,

Anderson shelters in back greens, and huge underground shelters all over Glasgow Green. Large round emergency water tanks in many places, with a big one right on the roof of Beattie's Bakery. Everyone carrying gas masks, and queues of people testing them in mobile gas vans. Evacuation scenes, with the Welfare Department looking after evacuees from Poland, and of Glasgow children being sent to the country. There were good stories of these children. I liked the one about the wee boy who had never been out of town in his life. On arrival at a farm he saw a duck swimming in a pond, so he threw a hen in as well. When the farmer's wife remonstrated with him he replied, "Wha wis ah tae ken that the silly auld thing coudna swum!"

There were also scenes of First Aiders practising bandaging and dealing with casualties, indoor shots showing how incidents were dealt with at Warden's Posts, with communication by boy messengers on bicycles in case other services might break down. One of these boys was killed during the blitz. Then stirrup pump drill and the work of the Auxiliary Fire Service. I remember that bit particularly, for they sent me to the top of what they said was the highest fire-escape ladder in Glasgow, much to my dismay! Scenes also of buses being decontaminated and washed down at the bus depots, and the City Analyst testing and classifying all types of war gases. The most exciting scenes were those of the tough men of the Rescue Depots. They used a blitzed building in Adelphi Street, knocked down walls, re-trieved a mock casualty from a tottering building three stories up, strapped him onto a stretcher and sent him down by involved pulley tactics which would astonish the Mountain Rescue teams of today. We also showed huge parades of Civil Defence personnel and in-spections, and even a close up of the King and Queen, although I have no memory now of taking it. At all times there was cheeriness and enthusiasm, everyone determined to play their part, indeed the whole impression was of a Glasgow entirely different from the city of today. It seemed that everyone contributed in their own way. Glasgow in the end got off lightly, and was never really tested, but we were all trained and ready to go.

Ben's contribution to the war effort was not limited to the making of *A Bomb Fell*, the film that could make strong men faint, and the subsequent Civil Defence films. Towards the end of 1939 he was asked for an article for the Scottish Mountaineering Club Journal on all the known Cobbler climbs. Here he joined forces with Jock Nimlin for the first time, and their rock climbing guide to the Cobbler was later published separately. It subsequently proved of great value in the training of the newly formed

Commando units, a branch of the forces which was to have considerable significance for him.

Travel was very limited in the war years owing to petrol restrictions, but Ben was sometimes able to get away to Arrochar on his own, and writes of lying for hours on a favourite spot, a sheltered ledge just below the summit of the South Peak of the Cobbler. He only gives details of one other snatched climbing weekend during the war, included in a later article, "Firstfooting the Munros":

> Once we managed further afield, and only then did I really feel away from the glaring headlines, the ARP and all that. In the afternoon of the 31st December we reached the mountaineers' hut at the foot of the cliffs of the great north-west face of Ben Nevis. In the late evening we strolled higher up the corrie to the foot of the Tower Ridge, returning to the hut as the New Year entered.
>
> Till we reached Fort William again on the evening of January 2nd we met no one. The two of us had the greatest snow peak in Britain all to ourselves. A panorama of mountain and loch, of island and sea for us alone. We did a gully climb from shadow to sunlight. We roamed the ridges and revelled in an enchanted land. The graceful curves of the windswept snow slope, the loveliness of those snow crystals, those icicles sparkling diamond-like as they caught the rays of the sun, that bluish-green sheen in the snowy hollows and the grandeur of the frosted cliffs! All beauty was ours. War could not be, war had never been in such a wondrous world. Small wonder that we lingered long, reluctant to return to the murk of Glen Nevis – to the murk of a warring world.

THE BEN HUMBLE COLLECTION

The filmed record of Ben's war forms the core of *The Ben Humble Collection* of silent 16mm cine films. Made intermittently from 1939 to 1966, the collection[48] of eighteen titles is stored permanently under the care of the Scottish Film Archive in Glasgow. Over 3,000 feet of film relate to different aspects of the war years. A number of reels were transposed onto video tape some years ago, including the classic *A Bomb Fell*, but the remainder were restricted until recently owing to the fragile condition of the originals. With the aid of a 1993 grant from the Imperial War Museum, the Civil Defence films are now being repaired and duplicated, preserving a priceless record of Glasgow during the 1939–1945 war. Ben was a good amateur cine-photographer, using mainly black and white film, and not always working in the best lighting conditions. The quality of the pictures reflects this fact in a few places, but does not diminish their value. His pioneering contribution lay in the willingness and enthusiasm he brought to their making, and in the countless hours he donated without financial reward. Had he not been there, quite simply there would be no photographic record of these times. His brother John, and his old school friend Campbell Brown, together with Archivist Janet McBain, deserve much credit for ensuring their survival.

Ben also made two historic climbing films, equally important in their own field. The first, *The Cragsman's Day*, shows Jock Nimlin, Harry Grant and Dave Easson climbing on the Cobbler. This solo photographic effort, which compares very favourably to those produced by today's film units, won a major prize at the 1948 Scottish Amateur Film Festival;[49] it has particular significance in view of the contributions made by both Jock and Ben. *In Days of Old* commemorated the 50th Anniversary of the Ladies' Scottish Climbing Club in 1958, depicting members of the Club climbing on the Campsies in 1908 Edwardian dress. After a simulated "sleep" at the completion of their climb, the old-time ladies offer appropriate surprise when awakening to the sight of others dressed in the very changed style of 1958; the inclusion of this scene would appeal to Ben's active imagination. A third climbing film on mountain rescue was shot in the Cairngorms in 1966.

Forum Frolics lends a lighter vein to the collection. A discussion group known as the Dumbarton Forum had been founded during the war by Hugh Davidson. Ian MacPhail told me that though Ben rarely attended its regular meetings, he seldom missed the annual Forum dinners, for which he often obtained speakers. From the start these dinners included the type of "high jinks" which were well suited to his extravagant brand of humour. A sketch which Ian particularly remembered was of a mock operation during which a "patient" was delivered of a baby doll and a pound of sausages, as well as having a plastic limb cut off. Ben was a trifle disappointed that he was not allowed, as the orderly in attendance, to squirt red ink over the floor of the dining room of the Dumbuck Hotel!

A highlight of one of the early dinners was the first showing of *Forum Frolics*. It consisted of a series of comic shots, starting with Ian MacPhail as an Edwardian athlete, dressed in long woollen pants and complete with handlebar moustache, training for the Olympic Games; trick photography[50] followed, showing other club members using a variety of props, the film concluding with sequences of Campbell Brown (Convener of the Housing Committee of Dumbarton Town Council at the time), seemingly building houses at a fantastic rate. Ian told me that at the dinners he used to write down for Ben a precis of the jokes told by the speakers, but he was never certain if he always got the correct drift. The interest in the Forum and the Forum Dinners was only one aspect of Ben's sociable character. Despite his deafness, he was an accomplished and witty after-dinner speaker in his own right. ("Though you may not believe it, I have quite a reputation as an after-dinner speaker," he told me in a letter in 1976.)

THE OPEN AIR IN SCOTLAND

The Second World War and the immediate post-war period form an interlude in Ben's story. Behind lay the years of his most active climbing, still ahead the times which were to be largely occupied by service to others. Knowing that the rush to the hills would resume soon after the cessation of hostilities, he had prepared himself accordingly, often developing ideas on the escapes to the Cobbler when bombs could be forgotten, and future opportunities properly considered. Most important was the groundwork for the production of Scotland's first magazine for hill-walkers, *The Open Air in Scotland* – no simple task in a completely new field, with many to be convinced by his enthusiasm. The chosen name relates as much to his own life as it did to the contents of the magazine, in which Ben used his position as editor to promulgate personal and forward-looking views.

"National Parks are surely coming," he wrote in an editorial in the first issue. This also contained an article[51] in which he outlined a dream for a 600 square mile National Park to the east of Loch Linnhe, bounded in the west by the coastline from Ballachulish to Connel Ferry, and contained by the main roads from thence to Kingshouse, Bridge of Orchy and Tyndrum in the east. In further essays,[52, 53, 54, 55] both at that time and in later years, he continued to press for the reality of National Parks for Scotland. Despite the efforts of many people, going back to the National Parks Committee set up by Tom Johnson in 1944, that vision remains unfulfilled today.

Although it only survived for four years, largely owing to failure to attract continuing advertising, *The Open Air in Scotland* provided an important outlet for dissemination of information about the rapidly increasing numbers of outdoor Associations, Clubs and Youth Hostels, as well as covering every type of outdoor activity through its articles. Many of the latter describe pioneering efforts, a typical example being "Pass

Storming by Cycle", by H. G. Haxton, which heralded in the late 1940s the exploits of today's mountain bikers. Long since largely forgotten, the magazine nevertheless deserves a permanent place in the story of the development of the Scottish outdoors.

Ben's next scheme involved the production of a series of pictorial guide books for the tourist market – *Sailing up Loch Lomond*, *The Three Lochs*, *Sailing Down The Clyde*, *The Burns Country*, *Through The Trossachs*, *Fort William and The Great Glen* (all of which ran to three editions), and *The Scottish Scene – A Pictorial Journey*. While these publications were taking shape he was also preparing the final draft of *On Scottish Hills*, as well as continuing work on the Cuillin history which had absorbed him since the mid 1930s. Despite the ease with which he pursued these multifarious projects, perhaps many of his ideas arrived too soon, and his choice of a publisher somewhat ill-advised, for Bill MacLellan was a charming man who proved less than successful in business at that particular time. In the event, MacLellan was forced out of business just when Ben felt they had the whole guide book market there for the taking. He described some of the financial and personal difficulties of that time in his final biographical notes:

The years immediately after the war when I was working on my two books were very trying for our family, and for me personally. It seemed as though every misfortune was quickly followed by another. The magazine I had edited for four years, *The Open Air in Scotland*, had to stop publication, although at one point we had achieved a circulation of over 6,000. Then in the winter of 1950, when I was away from Dumbarton, our neighbours failed to get any reply from my mother when they felt certain she must have been at home. My brother David and his son Roy, who was then a medical student, let themselves into our flat at Comely Bank, and found her unconscious on the floor of the bedroom, as cold as ice. Neither could detect a pulse, but David thought he heard a faint flicker of a heart beat and immediately gave an injection of a stimulant directly into her heart, before starting to re-warm her. She had suffered a slight stroke, and must have lain on the floor for hours before they found her. Astonishingly she regained consciousness later that day, with only a temporary slurring of speech to show for her ordeal. Undoubtedly saved from major harm by the hypothermia, she was up and about within a week.

However it was obvious she could not be safely left alone in any of my absences, as at that time I had already started to act as a voluntary instructor at Glenmore Lodge and was often away for

weeks at a time. Mother agreed to go and live with my brother Alec
and his wife at Thames Ditton in Surrey, but she had barely arrived
there when Alec suffered a major stroke and became bedridden, so
she had to move again to stay with my other brother John and his
wife a few miles away near Hampton Court. But the fates of those
years were not done with us yet, for David died very suddenly one
September, and then Alec too, both of them at a comparatively young
age. Then in her nineties, Mother had outlived five of her eight sons.
She died at Skelmorlie in her 95th year after being ill for only two
days, whilst visiting our Hutchison cousins – the family who had
shared Tayvallich with us those long years ago.

   Throughout this time I was trying to recover from another disaster.
I had written and produced pictorial guide books for the famous
tourist areas, but when we had sold up to 10,000 of these my publisher
messed everything up and had to go into liquidation. I lost everything,
over £2,000, and had to start anew, printing and publishing postcards
from my own photographs, but I lost out on that too when colour
cards became popular.

Misfortunes such as these were only temporary setbacks, quickly put
aside as he continued in a self-appointed role as unofficial ambassador
of the countryside. While many others may have contributed perhaps in
more concrete ways, few can have rivalled his diversity of commitment,
and none shared his individual style. Looking back at his scrap book of
published articles, his inexhaustible energy remains a source of
astonishment. Although every facet of outdoor life was covered, a gradual
change in the pattern of his presentations is apparent around this period.
Short pieces continued to predominate, including many different series
of climbing and hill walking tips, but more and more these single stories
were interspersed by thoughtful essays. Mountain rescue became a
recurrent theme, with the unique perception and years of experience
starting to shape the remainder of his life. At the same time, no
information was ever wasted. His habitual note-taking resulted in a
collection of interesting snippets concerning the origin of Scottish place
names, and he parleyed this into both a newspaper and a radio series;
to his disappointment he was failed in a BBC voice test, the producers
of the programme replacing him with his school friend John Bannerman.

   At the heart of his many individual articles is a constant delight in
his varied surroundings. So many still have special interest that it is
impossible to refer to them all, but some are made even more fascinating
by the passage of time. More than once he took a nostalgic look back
at the steamers which used to service our lochs and inland waterways –

"Our Inland Loch Sailings Were Unequalled", he proclaimed. How many now remember that steamers once regularly plied the waters of Loch Eck, Loch Tay, Loch Awe, Loch Maree, Loch Rannoch and Loch Earn? The very names of the ships are part of our history. Ben was one of the few who kept the subject to the fore, insisting that though the famous "Royal Route" from Glasgow to Fort William might still be so called, it held only a fraction of its former charm:

> Then, we sailed in the *Columba* from the Broomielaw to Ardrishaig, through the quiet waters of the Crinan Canal by the *Linnet*, from Crinan to Fort William – the finest coastal sail in all the west – by the *Chevalier*, and from Fort William to Inverness through the Caledonian Canal by the *Gondolier*.

Often, too, individual descriptive gems appear in unexpected places in his writing, leading us to places most never visit, by routes only a few have the opportunity to take, sometimes reminding us of characters now largely vanished from our lives. One such piece comes from "In The Far North", the simple story of a holiday. Setting off with a companion in July 1947 for John o' Groats and Dunnet Head, walking, camping and fishing lay ahead, with an added chance to explore the climbing possibilities of Ben Hope and Ben Loyal. Along the way they took a side trip:

> A rush back to camp, a bathe in the burn, then we moved on, and towards dusk found another perfect site by the white sands of Rispond Bay. Sunset there was a thing to remember, and next forenoon we had that glorious stretch of sands all to ourselves.
>
> After laying in provisions at Durness we made for Scourie. Why Scourie? Well, I had visited and photographed gannets on Bass Rock, and I had camped more than ten years before on the Isle of Noss, that famous sea-bird sanctuary in the Shetlands where the Arctic skua, a pirate of the air, is the most notable inhabitant; so I had to visit the best known sanctuary of the north-west coast – the Isle of Handa,[56] two miles out from Scourie.
>
> We enquired about a boat and were directed to a certain cottage. "Yes," said the good wife, her man had a boat but was working in the graveyard. Off we went to the graveyard and found the worthy. If he wasn't the local grave-digger he seemed to be that person's first assistant. He agreed at once to take us out to Handa, and said he would meet us at the harbour in half an hour. But time goes leisurely in the far north; it would be more than a full hour before he reappeared. Soon we were chugging out to sea in a most ancient of motor-boats.

The shoreward side of the Isle of Handa is flat with sandy bays, the ground rising to the seaward side where the great cliffs rise sheer from the Atlantic for four hundred feet. Luckily for us there was only a gentle swell that day, so it was possible to switch off the engine, use the oars, and take the boat right under the cliffs till we could almost touch them.

What a noise[57] and what a sight! Gulls wheeled all around, with the cliff ledges lined by sea birds of all types – puffins, gannets, kittiwakes, terns, guillemots, and a host of others. It was the solemn little puffins with their white owlish faces and big red bills which attracted us most.

Starting the engine again we went round to the shoreward side. Our boatman put us ashore by a sandy bay and went off home, arranging to come for us at 5 p.m. For four hours the freedom of Handa was ours. The first job was to cook and consume a substantial lunch, then we made our way across the island to the top of the cliffs. We traversed their length, photographing, exploring, and watching the birds through field glasses. Now we could more easily distinguish the many different types, and watch youngsters in the nests. The most interesting part was the Stack of Handa, a huge isolated stack with a flat top separated from the main cliffs, and an absolute sanctuary.

Too soon we had to cross the island again and join our fisherman cum grave-digger. We wanted to wait till later, but he said he had to be back at the village by six o'clock. We got back by six, and at seven saw him – now clad in postal uniform – delivering the mail! A man o' parts indeed.

After that a wild road led us out to Achiltibuie, but time did not permit a visit to the Summer Isles, made famous by Dr Fraser Darling. For contrast after island visiting and lazy shore days, we climbed the strange little Sutherland peaks and the much higher peaks of Kintail, dallying in Glencoe on the way home, and spending our last night canoeing on Loch Lomond.

The abiding impression is of that lovely northern coastline and the wonder of Handa. Sometime we will return – may we again have fourteen days of unbroken sunshine! Some day, too, when sections of the route are improved that road will form a part of a magnificent "Round Scotland" tourists' route, equal to anything to be found anywhere in Britain.

7

FROM ARROCHAR TO AVIEMORE

After the collapse of his publisher and loss of his growing guide book business in the late 1940s, Ben's financial position was bleak. Although he still had the rooms in Berkeley Street, his practice had all but disappeared during the war. For a time he considered a return to dental radiology on a salaried basis, but when that possibility was finally quashed his life became increasingly divided between Arrochar and visits to Glenmore Lodge. So many times did he take the road from Dumbarton and Arrochar to Aviemore, his old car must have been able to find the way by itself. As a result he gradually began to sever his residential and professional ties to Glasgow and his home town.

That he managed to survive financially, and even prospered modestly in following years, is evidence of his stubborn business skills. Apart from the few published books, his limited income came from countless articles and photographs, as well as from a myriad of small ventures including the sale of maps, postcards, and latterly even heather blooms. Most hours were spent in voluntary activities, for he was increasingly occupied in the 1950s and 1960s with Mountain Rescue affairs and Glenmore Lodge. These activities brought small honorariums only, while any royalties from his books were never very significant; he ruefully remarked to me once that some of his friends seemed to think that being an author brought untold wealth, adding that he had never really made any money from his books. He did acquire one final skill. Shrewd investment in the stock market resulted in some limited capital gains towards the later part of his life.

Fortunately it had long been agreed by his brothers that any small amount of capital left by their mother should go to him, including that resulting from the sale of their Dumbarton flat, so this allowed the purchase of Rose Cottage in Arrochar. With his special feeling for the Cobbler and the Arrochar Alps, it was a natural choice for a new home.

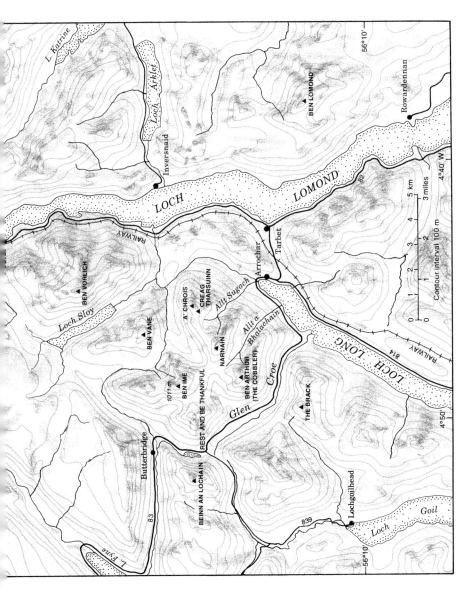

Arrochar and district.

THE COBBLER AND HIS WIFE

Situated on the shore of Loch Long, Rose Cottage looked out towards the peaks of the Cobbler. They made up a second family Ben came to know almost as well as his own, one which he enjoyed referring to in colloquial terms. Of two versions which appear in his writing, the first can be found in *Wayfaring Around Scotland* (1936), while the brief story which follows helped to enliven the last page of *Rock Climbs on the Cobbler* (1940):

> One story makes the Centre Peak a farmer, the North Peak his wife, and the South Peak a milkmaid, Jean. The farmer was carrying on a flirtation with the milkmaid when they were interrupted by his jealous wife. Jean, in confusion, overturned her milkpail so that the milk ran down the mountainside. And to this day, the burn which flows from the Cobbler to Loch Long is called Allt a' Bhalachain (the Buttermilk Burn). When you see it from Arrochar, turbulent after rain, you realise how appropriate the name.

> The soldier, billeted near Glasgow, managed to wangle a day off parades, telling his sergeant-major he had to visit "close relations in the West Highlands" – for surely the Cobbler and his wife can be so termed! When we were walking through Arrochar, the soldier in uniform, with a coil of rope over his shoulder, a little boy asked, "Is that rope fur tae hang Hitler?"

A splendid summary of the Arrochar years is contained in a presentation Ben called "Arrochar – the Early Days". We found it in Feithlinn along with every other one of his written stories. What a fascinating mixture is in that lecture: climbing experience, pioneering nostalgia, mountaineering history, humour and tribute – a mirror on almost four decades, back to the days when climbing in the Arrochar Alps had meant miles of cycling before it could even begin. Although neighbouring peaks received almost equal mention, whenever Ben talked of Arrochar, he usually reserved pride of place for his single favourite mountain:

> There must be something magnetic about the Cobbler. Many times I have gone up to Arrochar alone, meaning to climb Ben Vane, the Brack or one of the other tops, but early afternoon would instead find me nearing the summit of the Cobbler, whether ascending from Glencroe, by the burn, or along the ridge. Owing to the strange formation of its summit rocks it is one of the best known hills in Scotland, but even yet it never fails to thrill me when it bursts

into view at that bend of the road near Tarbet – in high summer, steel blue against a cloudless sky, or in mid-winter, majestic among the snows.

There are many stories about the Cobbler. I like best that one about the novice who was being taken over the South Peak in winter. And the South Peak in snow can be quite a test for a beginner. The novice did not like it. He did not like it at all! At one stage in the proceedings he suggested going back, and shouted up to the leader: "Remember I'm a married man!" But the leader was having none of it, and shouted back: "I don't care if you're a Mormon, you'll have to come on because I can't come back!"

I've never lacked for entertainment while climbing here. One June Sunday a good few years ago I reached the South Peak and found an English party, immaculately clad with new anoraks, with virgin nylon ropes, rope slings and all, starting off on the Jughandle route, one of the older climbs. The leader was some way up while his second, still on the ground, appeared quite anxious and called up, "Are you all right, old chap? A little bit further to your right I should think," and so on. All this in a perfect Oxford accent. Just round the corner some lads from Clydebank were on the first pitch of the Bow Crack, one of the new severe routes. The leader got up, but his second paused a long time at half-way, not at all sure of himself. The three others sitting below waiting subjected their companion to jeers and cat-calls. "Gawd, Wullie, there's a jug haundle stickin' oot in front o' yer nose!"[58]

At Easter 1936 I met Bill Murray when Mackenzie, MacKinnon and myself were trying to do all the Arrochar Munros in one day, and by June in that year I was climbing with Bill in Skye. One day in August 1937 he phoned me in my rooms in Glasgow, asking about the Recess Route of the Cobbler, and of its standard. I had never heard of it, but made prompt enquiries and found out about John Nimlin's Ptarmigan Club, and all his fine ascents. So Bill and I decided to try for all the known routes on the Cobbler in one day.

We camped out outside the Narnain Stone late on a Saturday on a wild and windy night. The rain continued on into the late Sunday forenoon, but then the sun came out and the rocks dried quickly. It was 1 p.m. before we roped up, and by 8 p.m. we had climbed sixteen of the twenty-four distinct routes on the mountain. The newer climbs were a revelation to us, giving us an altogether different conception of the Cobbler. Especially was this so with the Recess Route of the North Peak, for that climb takes you into the very heart of the mountain. It starts at the lowest point of the rocks, and after a first pitch of balance climbing, consists of a series of chimneys with a succession of cave stances, giving sensational outlooks.

Of the north face of the South Peak the old timers said that it was, ". . . so excessively difficult and forbidding that it has hitherto repelled all attempts to climb it. On that side at least the peak will remain unclimbed." We were delighted with Nimlin's direct route up the edge. When Murray and I got out onto the face we got quite a surprise, for the cliff which looks so sheer is really a succession of ledges with very steep sections of rock between them. The holds are very fine, and situations exposed, while the climb finishes dramatically at that well known semi-detached block on the summit.

Climbing was everything that day, both of us in tune with the rocks. Everything went easily, and nothing seemed difficult. With the Cobbler unfolding its new wonders to us, I never thought of taking a photograph. It was so grand to find my favourite mountain, whose climbing possibilities have often been dismissed so scathingly, offering sport of such a high standard after all those early years. The day left me with a very sincere respect for John Nimlin, who pioneered most of the new routes, and who has done so much for the younger mountaineering clubs which have grown up in the West of Scotland in recent years.

Bill Murray remembers well that same day, referring to it in a comment about Ben's climbing ability:

"Ben and I climbed often together in 1936 and 1937, but rarely on rock above very difficult standard. On severe rock his deafness affected balance, and communication became too chancy (unless on a short climb). For this reason he never led difficult routes. He was competent and never came off. In August 1937, he and I accounted for all the known Cobbler climbs in seven hours on wet rock, starting at 1 p.m. when the rain stopped. (In those days there were fewer than twenty routes.) In wider fields he was a thoroughly good mountaineer."

"Arrochar – the Early Years" documented an important period in the post-war years, when Ben and Jock Nimlin were asked to prepare a second guide with a complete listing of all the rock climbing routes in the area. While members of the Creagh Dhu Mountaineering Club helped cover the Cobbler, Ben and Jock, together with Dave Easson, between them spent almost every other weekend for two years at Arrochar, concentrating mainly on its other mountains, Beinn an Lochain, the Brack, Creag Tharsuinn, A'Chrois and Ben Ime.

Jock Nimlin pioneered many of the new climbs on the Cobbler in the

1930s, a time when rock climbing in Scotland as a whole was undergoing an early transformation with the discovery of outstanding new routes on the cliffs of Ben Nevis and Glencoe. The guide books he brought out with Ben,[59, 60] will always have a small but permanent place in the story of the first twenty-five years of the modern era of Scottish climbing. A new Arrochar guide[61] appeared in 1971. Sadly, neither of their names are included as joint editors, and it has to be said that this was largely Ben's own fault, another example of the major flaw in his character. When they failed to produce a long awaited revision, Jock having new job commitments and Ben being heavily involved at that time in the aftermath of the successful Mountain Safety Exhibition, the Scottish Mountaineering Club passed the editorial control over to J. R. Houston. With his great experience of the area, Ben was invited to continue his input, but he took offence at several imagined slights, only one of which (quite unrelated to the Arrochar guide and to the new editor) had any real validity. Hampered in full and easy communication by his deafness, and by his own stubbornness, small difficulties soon became major obstacles, and he demanded his name be withdrawn from the title page. It is clear from the correspondence (all of which Ben kept) that he did contribute significantly to the new guide, making it all the more unfortunate that his name had to be left out, although due acknowledgment to both previous authors was naturally made.

Ben's story would not be complete without mention of howffs[62] and howffing. Many of his friends wrote to me about his incessant search for these natural outdoor shelters, particularly among the Arrochar hills. He was prepared to go to great lengths to improve them, as Ian Brown recalled:

"On one weekend visit I went up the hill with him; below Narnain we navigated in the mist to a boulder set amongst many smaller ones. Under one side there was possible shelter for one, but for two it would have been inadequate. Ben wanted to dig out below it to give room for three at least. This was to be a hide-away for use on the next mountain rescue exercise. We laboured in the mist and rain for around four hours, longer than I would have lasted but for Ben's obvious determination to get the howff improved. I never got back to see the finished shelter. Ben himself made two more visits to complete his task, and it proved in snow and mist an almost impossible shelter to find."

Tales of howffs dominated the second half of the Arrochar lecture, but other memories are also worthy of inclusion here, particularly those of climbs on Narnain, of the naming of "Ben's Fault" on Ben Ime, and a brief reference to his mountain rescue involvement and an occasion

when he earned some temporary personal disrepute. The final tribute
to his companions was a sincere one:

> Days with Nimlin were always howffing days – with him you had
> to stay in a howff. We built wonderful ones on the banks of Allt
> Sugach, spent many nights and one New Year there, then dug for
> many weekends to get "Cobbler View" below the cliffs of the Brack
> in order. I was always proud of my own discovery of one howff.
> Nimlin had put out the thesis that any group of climbers should be
> able to go to any unknown high corrie, find or make a howff, and
> spend a comfortable night in it at any time of the year. From the
> main road at Butterbridge I had seen a mass of boulders just below
> Beinn an Lochain, and I made a bet with Ian Charleson that I could
> find a howff there. We started up in late afternoon one April. The
> first two casts were unsuccessful, but I noticed a deep shadow where
> two boulders overhung. This became "Sunset Arch". Later that eve-
> ning Jock arrived from Ben Donich, and found us by the spiralling
> smoke from our fire. "A rale guid howff!" he called it.

Howffs are only part of my many Arrochar memories – others of
the early days are legion. I remember Jock's disgust when we saw
no fewer than five pitons on the Ardgartan face of the South Peak
of the Cobbler (Porcupine Wall). He refused to go near them, and
later wrote an article for the *SMC Journal* advocating a club to de-piton
all climbs!

The Cobbler's fame has rather dwarfed his neighbour, though
Narnain is the higher mountain. Yet Narnain, until the newer Cobbler
routes were discovered, had the best climbs in the district. Though
the approach by Corrie Sugach is steeper, this is compensated by
the fact that there are finer bathing pools. Hence summer days on
Narnain often meant long halts by the burn and late arrivals at the
summit. Making for the Sugach Buttress first, the climb goes by steep
rock and a long sloping slab to finish with a perfect "knife-edge"
ridge, before moving on to the summit rock. There one has the
choice of the sound, clean rock of the Spearhead Arête or the deep
recesses of the Jamblock Chimney. Never was a climb so well named!
It is about 200 feet high and splits the rock from top to bottom.
Very seldom is it quite dry; usually it is clammy and wet. The first
two pitches are easy, the third more difficult, when one arrives at a
cavern about the size of a small room, with an exit in the roof high
up in one corner. Of that I have a particularly vivid recollection.
The leader wriggled through the chimney quickly. The second man,
of stouter girth, stuck tight, so that for a long time my upward vision

was of two legs waggling convulsively like a corpse on a gibbet, before he managed at last to squeeze his way up.

The Cobbler and Narnain were always the main attractions, but I have hundreds of memories of climbs and hill walking days, of the Brack and Beinn an Lochain, of Ben Vane, Ben Vorlich, and Ben Ime. Once on Ben Ime on the eastern face when I was prospecting alone, I managed to get into a crack about half way up the cliffs from the south, on the face of Fan Gully Buttress, and decided a complete climb was possible. Alas, I missed the train the following weekend, and Nimlin and Easson made the first ascent. I did not favour the name they gave to the climb, "Ben's Fault".[63] On that mountain, on its day, which is very seldom at Arrochar, the Fan Gully ice pitch can hold its own with the much more famous upper couloir of Stob Ghabhar in Black Mount.

Of more recent years the great day was one January when we had a Mountain Rescue Meet with the Leuchars and Kinloss RAF teams, the Police, the Arrochar Team and members of the SMC. Four parties used howffs built by us over ten years previously, and all had comfortable nights. One lot thought they knew all about it, and built their own. Here is the account from their journal:

"We would gladly murder Ben Humble, who urged us to try howffing. We four clung precariously to life in a bat infested dripping rock fissure 2,000 feet up on the south-east ridge of the Cobbler. As howffs go it was a fine one. We levelled the earth floor, excavating quantities of rock, and finally built a snow block wall against the entrance. The thaw which set in overnight brought this wall about our ears at 3 a.m., and if wetness was not enough, we were by then convinced that the roof was falling in on us."

That party evacuated early on, and were last seen waiting for the opening of the public bar at the village hotel! I saw their so called howff later. It had no decent roof at all, and would never have come up to the requirements we set. The Servicemen in the howffs and all others had to find their way to Narnain summit by noon on the Sunday. All got there, with about fifty on the summit. No dark rock could be seen; all was frosted with icy hard snow. I think I was the only one that day without crampons, which by that time had come into more general use.

I have never been much of a leader, usually second in line on anything like the harder routes. It has been a great privilege to climb behind such men as Bill Murray, Jock Nimlin, Tom Mac—Kinnon and Douglas Scott. All of them were magnificent leaders, and all free climbing – never did I know any of them to get into difficulties.

Another earlier tribute forms a fitting ending for Ben's Arrochar years:

> . . . Sooner or later the Scottish climber has the urge to try greater peaks. Years ago in July 1938 our party was at Riffelberg – the Riffelhaus of Alpine literature – 3,000 feet above Zermatt. From the Gornergrat at 10,000 feet we had that wondrous panorama – Monte Rosa, the peerless; Liskamm with its hanging glaciers; the Twins, Castor and Pollux; the great white dome of the Breithorn; the shapely Dent Blanche; and, lesser in height but dominating them all, the rocky cone of the Matterhorn.
>
> It captured us completely. Always it was with us, morning, noon and night. On the first morning when I looked out of the window the clouds hid Zermatt far below, while the Matterhorn towered up towards the heavens. On our first climb, from the Gorner glacier at dawn, it became a living thing of fire as the sun's rays shivered its summit. On a snow trudge to the Breithorn it loomed up on our right, immense in moonlight. On our last day we gained its summit . . .
>
> And, yet, all the way home, knowing that such holidays could be but few and far between, I had an uneasy sense of foreboding, fearing the homeland hills might have lost their attraction. Nearing Dumbarton I got the first glimpse of Ben Lomond. My heart sank! What had happened? It had shrunk in size, its once broad shoulders strangely insignificant. What of the Cobbler? Off we went to Arrochar that first weekend.
>
> It was typical Arrochar weather, with mist low down and a hint of rain. We saw nothing of the mountain till we were in the upper corrie, and then the huge beaks of the North Peak loomed out of the mist as grand as ever. We travelled the three peaks leisurely – lovingly. It was as good a day as I have ever had. I was delighted, delighted beyond all things that the Cobbler had not lost its appeal to me after greater peaks. It never will.

THE LENNOX QUESTION

Although the Cobbler itself is in Argyllshire, the village of Arrochar lies just inside the border of the County of Dumbarton, as Ben mentioned in one of his many local articles, "On the Fringes of Lennox", reiterating his strong preference for "Lennox" as the appropriate name for

Dumbartonshire (or Dunbartonshire). At one time or another he must have covered every square mile of his native county on foot. When *The Scots Magazine* ran a series called "My Town", Ben was asked to present a brief picture of Dumbarton. No more fitting local author could have been chosen, for his life-long commitment to both town and county never wavered, culminating in two final campaigns. The first was an attempt to persuade the County Council to re-adopt the original territorial name. One headline and story read as follows:

SPELL DUMBARTON – OR IS IT DUNBARTON?

DUM *vs* DUN

(B. H. Humble states the case for both sides)

Which is correct? Your guess is as good as mine. Each has a good argument . . . .When Scotland became a united whole, the name was changed to the Gaelic Dun Bretean, or Fort of the Britons. Through the centuries which followed that name appears in many different forms; there was no uniformity and each scribe had his own spelling. Thus we find such versions as: Dunbretane, Dunbrettan, Dunbertane, Dumbretane, Dunbertan, Dunbartane, Dunbarton, Dumbarton.

In earlier spelling the prefix is most usually Dun while in later times Dum is much more common. When the present shire came into being towards the end of the sixteenth century, the same spelling was used for both the burgh and the shire. At first it was Dumbartane. By the beginning of the eighteenth century the spelling Dumbarton was more or less universal, being applied to the Parliamentary constituency, the sheriffdom and the burgh, though certain historians and antiquarians still used the form Dun.

The confusion dated from 1889 when County Councils were formed, and the local one called itself the County Council of Dunbarton. That spelling appeared in all its documents, but the name appeared on maps as Dumbartonshire. Then in 1934 the County Council made representations to HM Ordnance Survey and the Scottish Office, with the result that the spelling was changed to Dunbartonshire on all maps, despite prolonged protests from the chief officials of the Town of Dumbarton. Finally the Parliamentary constituency which had previously been Dumbartonshire was divided and the new county divisions called Dunbartonshire (East) and Dunbartonshire (West).

The case for the county is that Dun is the earlier and more correct form, and that the Commissioners of Supply, predecessors of the county, used the form Dun. Against this the town points out that the county should take its name, and its spelling, from the ancient county town, and that if absolutely correct spelling is insisted on then it should be Dunbreatan or Dunbritton.

Since all attempts at uniformity of spelling between county and burgh have failed, it would appear that the way is certainly open to change the name of the County to Lennox, which was the ancient territorial name. The County Council has adopted as its crest the arms of the Earl of Lennox, with the name "Levenax" beneath.

This story appeared in the *Evening News* in 1953. Three years later the same arguments were more fully developed by Dumbarton historian Ian MacPhail in a long article published locally in the *Lennox Herald*. The persistent Ben had left no stones unturned in the intervening period. He sought the support of the counties of Angus and Moray (previously known as Forfarshire and Elginshire),[64] enquiring as to how they had been successful in their own reversion to ancient county designations, and forwarding the information he obtained to the local Council. Through more than thirty letters he also helped maintain the topic in the correspondence columns of the West of Scotland newspapers. One paper, at least, was persuaded for the change. Shortly before the County Council of Dunbarton was due to make a formal decision on the matter, "An Editorial Diary" in the *Glasgow Herald* presented all the relevant facts of the case, noted that the paper had always resisted official pressure to use the County's spelling, and gave the opinion: ". . . The only answer is Lennox, which is not a compromise, but a sound reversion to the oldest historical territorial name for the district."

Despite the support of the Lord Lieutenant of the county for the proposal, the local authorities were not convinced. Ben never quite gave up, for his letters on the subject cover a period of four years. Never short of ideas, he also sent letters to many more Scottish papers, inside and outside the county, advocating a "Lennox Week" along the lines of the highly successful Skye Week in which he had been involved. Despite significant public support and many private letters of encouragement, including numbers from Dumbartonians living abroad, nothing came of this proposal. He would have been very pleased, however, with the later re-emergence of Strathclyde as a regional designation.

The ultimately unsuccessful Lennox campaign was not quite the last local one in which Ben involved himself. When the Beeching[65] axe threatened the sailings on Loch Lomond in 1963 he took up his cudgel once again:

Surely no other county in all of Scotland has such contrasts as

Dunbartonshire or, as I like to call it, the Land of Lennox. Though almost surrounded by water, no seas touch it, just a land loch,[66] two sea lochs, and a great river . . . For almost 150 years a sail up that famous land loch has been the highlight of most tourists coming to Scotland, but now if Dr Beeching has his way, such Loch Lomond sailings will stop . . .

Ben went on, in "Sailing Up the Loch", to describe the history of sailings on Loch Lomond, which had enjoyed steadily increasing popularity to a high point of 124,000 passengers in the 1963 summer season, and since the Queen herself was planning such a sail, followed this with a sequel in a Glasgow paper. Dr Beeching probably never saw "Will the Queen Save the Maid?", but it is doubtful if he would have had any sympathy with the continually stubborn local author's sentiments. In the event it was to be thirty more years before the old *Maid of the Loch*, the last inland steam driven paddle-steamer built in Britain, would be finally "saved", purchased in the winter of 1992–93 by Dumbarton District Council with a view to its restoration in a non-sailing role at the head of Loch Lomond.

Ben's reaction to that particular idea may be easily predicted, but perhaps he will be left with the last word once again. One might even say that the paddle-wheel has come full circle, for under the heading "A Damsel in Distress", details were given in the *Herald* for 25 May 1994 of a feasibility study advising that the *Maid* could be successfully returned to a full pleasure sailing role on the Loch.

CAIRNGORM AMAZON!

If one were asked to choose one from among all of Ben's articles to illustrate best his enthusiasm for the hills, my vote would go to "Cairngorm Amazon!", the description of a single day's trek on the Cairngorms. It was made during the period between the Lennox and Loch Lomond campaigns, in his early days at Rose Cottage. The familiar drive north from Arrochar to Aviemore formed a necessary preliminary for the occasion. As the story unfolds it represents a bridge between the Arrochar years and his next major involvement in the Cairngorms:

> "Will you climb the four highest Cairngorms with me?" she said. "Sure," I replied, "and you'll do it easily!" Of course I took it as a joke, for the ascent of Cairngorm, Ben Macdhui, Cairntoul and Braeriach (all over 4,000 feet high) in one day is quite a considerable

proposition even for the strongest of male hill walkers, and she was just a slip of a girl.

I grew alarmed, therefore, when I found she was taking it seriously. My problem was how to withdraw without losing prestige, for one tends to take it rather easier on the hills at the age of fifty. I pointed out that the expedition included about 22 miles of very rough hill walking, plus just over 7,000 feet of ascent, and that while ladies had done the four in one day from end to end (a rather lesser trip), I did not think that many, if any at all, had done the round trip returning to one's starting point.

"That's just why I want to do it," she said. I then dilated on the suddenness and fury of the storms which sweep the plateaux of the Cairngorms, the most exposed place in all Britain, of the possibility of being lost in the thick mist, of the scarifying wind – but she knew all about that! She had been on the high tops in November, the worst month of all the year.

The next I heard was that she had arranged accommodation at a cottage, and fixed a date. I had to travel north. I found her busy preparing sandwiches for the morrow. Nothing but honey. "Didn't Hillary climb Everest on honey?" she said.

I slept badly, and was delighted when I looked out at 5.30 a.m. to see thick mist around 2,500 feet. I planned to ascend Cairngorm, then foresee a storm from the south and retreat downwards for a second breakfast. We got off at 6.30 a.m., and the thought of an early return wafted me up the mountain. One halt at the stile over the deer fence, then a steady plug to the summit. Over the last section I tried to outpace her, but she kept doggedly at my heels. It seemed a long time before the cairn loomed out of the mist.

The "Cairngorm Amazon", Elizabeth Lindsay,[67] remembers the start of that day quite differently, showing that like other authors, Ben was not above some manipulation of events – all in the interests of producing a good story!

"I know Ben made out that it was my idea, but he was really the one who was keen to do it. At that time I'd been trying to start my mountain guide service for hill walking, and Ben suggested that if I did the four tops it would prove my qualifications! I had taken a lot of parties out on the Cairngorms, and knew them well, as did Ben, so we were both aware of what a trek it was (nowadays, of course, there is a road and ski-lift up Cairngorm). We booked in at one of the Forestry houses with Bunty and Ginger Jamieson for bed and breakfast. Bunty made the sandwiches, not me, and whatever they were made of, it certainly wasn't honey (poetic licence on Ben's part, likely so that he could bring in the reference to Everest and Hillary). We were woken up at an unearthly hour, with breakfast ready. Ben took one look at the weather and changed his mind about going. I took one look at all the preparations Bunty had made, and said we'd better get going after all the work she had done. He grumbled all the way up Cairngorm in his typical fashion."

I looked at my watch. We were just under two hours on our way. The classic formula for hill walkers allows one hour for each three miles, plus half an hour for each thousand feet of ascent. Applying the formula our time should have been one hour and twenty minutes for distance, plus one and a half hours for height. Hence we were fifty minutes up on bogey[68] as it was.

For the first time I realised what I was up against. We were in thick mist, with visibility of about only twenty paces. Before I could counsel a retreat she got out her compass. "Bearing 227, the Yellow Loch, we'll do it in an hour," and off she went. Perforce I had to follow.

Not quite accurate once more. Elizabeth told me that it was actually the other way around! . . .

"Ben became enthusiastic at the top, and shot off into the mist over the plateau bawling at me to make for the cliffs. I rather think that he went one way to the Yellow Loch and I went another, with him making enough noise to scare off the ptarmigan, disappearing and reappearing in the mist like a mountain gnome!"

Up and down we went across the upper part of the corries which fall down to wild Loch Avon. We never glimpsed the Loch. Just as the hour was up we reached a burn emerging from a snow field, and traced it west to the lochan with its high banks of snow. This was at a height of 3,600 feet, the dividing point between Cairngorm and Macdhui.

I called a halt for our second breakfast. Never had honey tasted so delicious. Only ten minutes was allowed, then a new bearing on Macdhui, two degrees east of south it was. Easy going, a gradual ascent of six hundred feet and we hit the cairn dead on. Just over four hours out and still within the formula. But still that thick mist.

Cairngorm and Macdhui are divided from Cairntoul and Braeriach by the deep cleft of the Lairig Ghru, the longest, stoniest and toughest hill pass in all Scotland, which rises to 2,700 feet at its highest point. Our problem was to find the quickest and easiest way down to the

Lairig, losing the least possible height. We could have gone direct from the cairn by way of Tailor's Burn, an obvious route. Once before I had taken this route, and vowed never again, for a steep descent of 2,300 feet in one mile is mighty sore on the knees. We steered instead in a north-west direction, descending gradually.

Suddenly the mist lifted, and for the first time the lady showed signs of dismay. No wonder! We could not see the Lairig, so deep it lay below us, but we gazed right across to the immense corrie between Cairntoul and Braeriach where snow lingers for all the year. We noticed the huge mass of Braeriach and its seeming great distance from Cairntoul; particularly did our eyes focus on the steepness of Cairntoul – no easy way up there!

We had hit off a good route to the Lairig, anyway, and the descent went easily to strike it at about 2,300 feet. The infant Dee was in spate after several days' rain, but that did not stop the peak bagger. Off went her boots and stockings and she waded across. Icy cold from the melting snows, the water almost paralysed us and we had to jump about on the far side to restore the circulation in our feet.

A pleasant half hour for lunch, leaning back among the heather, and then we faced the sternest part of the day – 2,000 feet of ascent to the summit of Cairntoul. We could have gone down the Lairig to Corrour Bothy and followed an easy stalker's path to the summit, but that was too far out of our way. We knew that Lochan Uaine (the Green Loch)[69] lay almost a thousand feet below the summit of Cairntoul, and that a steep ridge would lead us from there to the cairn. To gain this lochan did not look easy, for the burn which issued from it to join the Dee fell down very steeply over slabby rock. We penetrated west into the great corrie, then found a way up by the far side of the burn where the slope was rather easier. There was much loose rock; with both hands and feet employed, the care necessary helped us forget the labour of ascent. Within an hour from the Lairig we reached the lochan. The ridge above was all boulders and stones, many of them loose, but a steady plug took us to the cairn within another hour.

Something of exultation crept in now. We knew victory would be ours. There was still a long way to go, but there was only one way – across the plateau where Braeriach beckoned. Indeed it was the quickest way home, for the mighty cliffs to the east prevented any descent till the goal was reached.

The spell of the high tops was on us. We bagged the next summit, Angel's Peak, in twenty minutes. Onwards from there is the finest high level walk in all Britain, never falling below 3,750 feet and much of it over 4,000 feet. It was easy going, a desert of sand and gravel, with green cushions here and there which would soon show the vivid pink of the moss campion. We strolled on, ever admiring the imposing precipices of Braeriach. Then the lady announced that we must pay tribute to the Goddess of the mountains by bathing our faces in the Wells of Dee. Mighty refreshing it was! Strange to think that this was the true source of the Dee. No other river in the country has such a source as that spring 4,000 feet up on the bleak plateau, where a powerful stream gushes forth.

On now, a gentle rise to Braeriach where the cairn emerged from steep snow. Our last top was won. We had been seven hours on the way from Cairngorm, and could trace our entire route, scarcely believing we had come all that distance. We could see the Shepherd's Hill and the pass of Ryvoan. Our haven lay there, nine long miles away.

"How long do you think we'll take to get back?" I asked. "Three hours," she replied. Just that plus half an hour for a halt. From Braeriach we could have gone due east where a good stalker's path leads down to about the highest point of the Lairig Ghru, but at all costs I wanted to avoid that, for the Lairig – the so called public footpath from Aviemore to Braemar – is just a stony horror at its summit. We were also reluctant to lose the height we had gained, hence we made along Sron na Lairig, the ridge which bounds the path to the west, exulting – all labour was ended, it was just a walk home.

"All labour ended," did I say? We had thought so, but found the final descent to the pass the worst part of the day, for deep heather with hidden boulders is just about the worst thing the hill walker can face. Reaching the pass at about 2,000 feet, where it changed from a wilderness of boulders to a mud bath, we followed it for about a mile and a half to the upper reach of the Rothiemurchus Forest, then had a mile of bog marching south-east to get to the Army Ski Club Hut. Surely we were entitled to our first smoke of the day? We sat down, well contented, and puffed away. Within two minutes we were jumping up and prancing around, for the ground was alive with ants!

What a change now was that stroll through the forest, with the cheepings and whistlings of the birds, after the bleakness and silence of the great plateaux! From the west end of Loch Morlich we were on a road for the first time of the day, sore on the feet for boots with nails of case-hardened steel. Human beings we saw once again, for we had encountered none on the hill all day long, and really seemed to have had the whole vast range of the Cairngorms to ourselves.

When I totted it up I found we had taken twelve hours and fifty minutes, which included one hour and fifty minutes of halts. She finished quite fresh. To my great surprise so did I. Was it the honey or the challenge of youth? I still cannot decide. Now she wants to do the six highest Cairngorms in a day. Heaven help me!

A final comment from his companion adds some poignancy to Ben's reference to the sounds of birds, and to the silence and bleakness of the plateaux:[70]

"After a day out I sometimes used to drop him a note to thank him and mention anything he would have missed on account of his deafness. Once or twice he added my comments in his articles and I remember being surprised when he wrote back to say that I had helped make the day come alive for him. As Ben rarely thanked anybody for anything, this was a very special occasion indeed."

8

THE CAIRNGORMS

For many years Ben contributed regularly to the Souvenir Programme of the annual Braemar Highland Gathering. In the 1975 edition, under the heading "It All Started In The Cairngorms", he began with this preface:

> Nowadays every Education Authority, many colleges and other organisations have their own out-of-door training centre, but the first of them all was started at Glenmore Lodge in the Cairngorms in 1947. The seeds, however, were planted long before that. At a time when such training was more or less unknown, pilot ventures were run in Glen Affric in 1938, and at Gordon Castle in Morayshire in 1939, at both of which Lord David Douglas Hamilton was Warden. Then, also, the late King George VI (when Duke of York) started annual camps for boys from public schools and lads from industry. The last of these was at Abergeldie on Deeside in 1939, and the King himself took a group of boys up Lochnagar.
>
> The Cairngorms also figured largely in war-time Commando training. In January 1943, the Fife Arms Hotel, Braemar, was requisitioned and training started under the charge of the late F. S. Smythe and other expert mountaineers. The object was to toughen the men to be able to go anywhere and do anything. At the same time the Highland Fieldcraft Training Centre came into being in Glen Feshie, and men trained in the Cairngorms led the onslaught in the invasion of Normandy in 1944.

Long before those words were written, it had been accepted that the mountain warfare training carried out during the Second World War formed an important link in the chain which led to the growth of outdoor training. But when he introduced the subject in this 1975 article, Ben was not writing simply with the benefit of hindsight. The National Outdoor Training Centre outgrew its infancy at Glenmore Lodge while he directed *The Open Air in Scotland*. One of that magazine's early issues contained an article from the man who had been in charge of the Commando training in the Cairngorms, the Everest climber Frank Smythe.[71] Never the strongest of men physically, Smythe had nevertheless

climbed in 1933 to a height of 28,000 feet on Everest, equalling the
highest point then reached, and later became famous through his books,
mountain photographs and lectures. He died in 1949, three years after
the publication of this particular Cairngorm story, at the early age of
forty-nine.

The larger extent of Commando training was based at Achnacarry in
the Spean Bridge area, and as the result of the location of the Commando Museum and Memorial there, this region has tended to attract
most attention in recent years. Smythe's short account of the allied, but
less publicised, episode at Braemar is beautifully written. It deserves a
place in Ben's story for several reasons. Ben suggested its inclusion in
The Open Air in Scotland, and the author clearly espouses the values which
were important to him, ideals which were similar to those he had put
forward when promoting the hostel movement. The article also forms
an essential prelude to the long Cairngorm period of Ben's life, for with
the worth of outdoor training in the promotion of self-reliance and
initiative thus clearly demonstrated, the development at Glenmore Lodge
became an inevitable sequel, as did his own involvement there. In articles
written over a period of thirty years he refers repeatedly to the Commandos and their training, particularly to this group. Even many years
later there were repercussions when he was involved in controversy
regarding cairns and shelters on the Cairngorms, including the possible
demolition of the high level shelters, "St Valery" and "El Alamein",
erected by the men under Frank Smythe's command.

Smythe's story begins with the war moving into its third year, as he
first sets the scene for the commission he had received:

MOUNTAIN TRAINING IN THE CAIRNGORMS

"In the autumn of 1942 Brigadier (now Major-General) Laycock, then
commanding the Special Service Brigade, invited me to form a school
at which Commandos would receive a training in mountain and winter
warfare. The spirit of the offensive had been born and raids were
already being carried out on enemy-held coast-lines, including the famous 'heavy water' raids which wrought such vital destruction to the
enemy's war potential. Many of these coast-lines, especially those of
Norway, are rocky or mountainous, and my instructions were that
Commandos must be trained to go anywhere, and do anything, whatever
the difficulties of the ground. I was given a free hand in the selection of
a training area and chose the Cairngorms. Better mountaineering is

possible in the Western Highlands, but the Cairngorms are more suited to winter warfare training.

"Our base was Braemar where we requisitioned the Fife Arms Hotel and there in December the instructional staff, which included expert mountaineers and ski-ers, assembled. Training was all too short. It began in January 1943 with a three week course designed to train under-instructors, then the main body of the Commandos received some six weeks.

"We had hoped for much ski-ing. The stores were packed with Greenland sledges and much else. There was even talk of a dog team to be raised from the local canines – which included anything from Alsatians to Scotties and Pomeranians! But the winter of 1942–3 was an unusually snow-less one. Instead, it blew. It blew as it does in Tibet. There were five full gales a week and one hurricane. What happened on the seventh day no one cared – it was our rest day. The men, drawn from every walk of life, had one thing in common, a tremendous keenness. They were ready to endure anything if it redounded to the discomfiture of the Hun. Yet, they approached such a training with some qualms and apprehension. It was our job to disillusion them. In this we succeeded, and more than succeeded. Out of increasing fitness was born a zest and out of a zest an enthusiasm, and in many cases a genuine love, for the hills.

"The secret of such a training is simple. You must place yourself in the position of someone from the streets of Glasgow or the Old Kent Road, who has never trodden or wanted to tread a hill in his life, to whom climbing is a 'sweat' and pavements preferable to mountain tops. Then you must set about inculcating a great pride and confidence. To achieve this he must be started easily. There must be no mention of 'toughening courses'; that is bad psychology. He must never be worked to the limit of his powers until the end of training when he himself will want to see how much he can do.

"It is easy to teach a man to climb. Later, in Wales, men were taught to lead 'very difficults' after only a week or ten days' instruction, while in the Canadian Rockies many of the Lovat Scouts became expert ski-ers in a matter of weeks. What is far more difficult is to teach an appreciation of country, and weather, route finding, use of ground, observation and map reading. Two years at least are necessary to turn out a mountain soldier in the Continental sense.

"But the men who were trained in the Cairngorms learned many of the essentials of mountain craft and the tricks and dodges of campaigning, camping and bivouacking. They learned to scramble on the rocks of Lochnagar, to use rope and ice axe in the gullies of the Beinn a' Bhuird, to steer their way across the central plateau of Ben Macdhui in blizzards which would have tested the hardiest and most skilful of mountaineers. Long and arduous cross country patrols, nights spent in rain storms and snow storms with no more for cover than a gas cape and fir branches, exercises in bitter winds and storms, nothing came amiss to them. If they had any fears, the greatest was to fail the course and be returned to their units.

"Their reaction to the most unpleasant circumstances was always flavoured with humour of the kind that has carried the British soldier through many wars. I well remember one instance. We were ascending from Derry Lodge to Loch Etchachan in one of the worst hurricanes I have ever experienced. Loaded as we were with some 70lbs of clothing, equipment, food and camping gear it was all we could do to face the driving squalls of sleet and hail. I was ahead, prospecting for a camping site, when, suddenly, a gust whirled me off my feet and dropped me on a rock yards away. As I lay there recovering my wind I saw the leading section plodding up the slope beneath me. It was led by a typical Cockney sergeant, one of those inspiring old grumblers whom our Continental friends and enemies have never fully appreciated. Suddenly, another terrific gust blew every man off his feet. Slowly they struggled upright and I saw the sergeant looking towards me. There was a momentary lull in the gale and through it I heard his voice: ' 'e can 'ave 'is Everest, every . . . inch of it!'

"For all their windiness I grew to love the Cairngorms. They provided us with but a few days ski-ing, mostly in the neighbourhood of the Devil's Elbow and on Glasmaol. Then the thaw came, and little snow work was possible other than in the gullies and corries where snow normally collects to an Alpine depth.

"Military cares and responsibilities interpose a spiritual gulf between man and mountain, but there were days of escape and many gleams through the murk of war when it was possible to appreciate the hills to the full. Two instances are outstanding in memory. In one, with a single companion I was engaged on that most disagreeable of mountain tasks, a search party, a wasted effort as it proved since the errant one returned to Braemar but an hour after the searchers had left. It was a bitter night of occasional snow showers and brilliant moonlight. We were searching the environs of Lochnagar and had crossed the shoulder of Carn Beag in order to descend to the loch. Suddenly and dramatically the great face of Lochnagar appeared. The moonlight slanting down and across it revealed the gullies as dark folds rifting a great curtain of radiant ice and snow, and high above a cornice gleamed like a thin twisted diadem against the deep velvet of the night sky. It was a view reminiscent of the high Himalayas, and as we stood looking across the level floor of the frozen loch I could imagine myself confronted with some cold and ethereal giant of Sikkim or Garhwal.

"Another incident occurred when I was searching for the Medical Officer on the fringe of Rothiemurchus Forest. A man had been injured near Loch Einich and I had gone to find the MO, who was supposed to be camped near the path to the Lairig Ghru. In the dark, and with my electric torch refusing duty, I managed to souse myself in the swollen stream of Glen Einich. It had been a day of blizzards, and it was snowing heavily as I made my way in pitch darkness along the edge of the forest. But presently the storm thinned, and one by one the stars appeared. And with them there broke forth through the darkness an inexplicable ghostly radiance. It was the aurora. As the snow storm slowly withdrew so did the aurora grow in splendour until the whole northern sky upwards to the zenith was glimmering and pulsing with waves and beams of pearly light. A few snow flakes were still falling, and to my imagination they resembled luminescent flower petals floating silently to earth.

"Despite the rigorous nature of the training many Commandos vowed to return to the hills after the war. As I write, the Commando Climbing Club has just been formed with Major-General Laycock as President and Lord Lovat, Brigadier John Hunt and myself as Vice-Presidents. This club is symptomatic. A feeling is growing, a revolt against materialism, and I venture the prophecy that there will be, as there must be, a renaissance in human affairs, a return to fundamentals, to the simpler things, to Nature and to beauty. Many who have toiled and moiled over the Scottish hills at the dictates of war will return to them of their own free will in times of peace. It is the duty of this and succeeding generations to see that those hills remain unspoiled, and that they are freed from selfish interests, so that they may be enjoyed in all their pristine beauty and simplicity. On them both young and old must continue to find not only the spirit of initiative and adventure, but refreshment and peace of mind."

RETURN TO THE SHELTER STONE

The vast amount of Ben's time and energy during his Cairngorm years went into voluntary endeavours. His work on behalf of Mountain Rescue steadily increased, with thoughts concerning safety on the hills leading him towards the campaign on accident prevention and the *Adventure in*

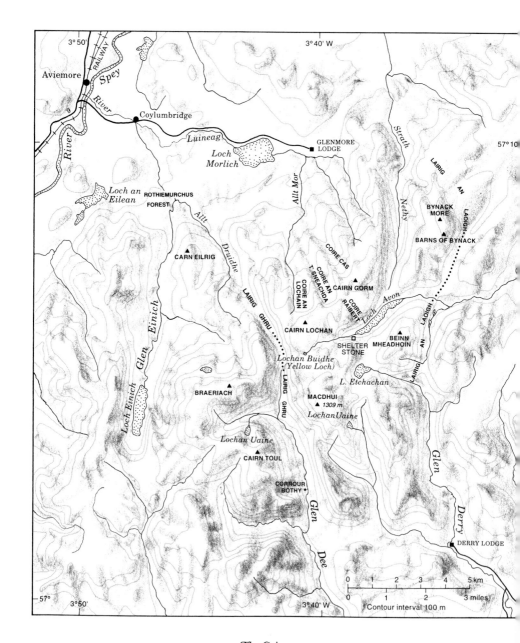

The Cairngorms.

Safety Exhibition. The National Outdoor Training Centre at Glenmore Lodge, his work there as a voluntary instructor, and the creation of a heather and alpine garden at the Lodge became the remaining focal points of the last three decades of his life. Countless publications on these topics, along with others on the surrounding area, helped him earn a living, but that really was of secondary importance.

"Will you take a bivouac party to the Shelter Stone?" the Warden asked me. I was delighted. Of all possible bivouac expeditions, that to the famous Shelter Stone by Loch Avon would have been my own personal choice. My thoughts flew back. It was exactly twenty years since I had been there, in that wonderful first year of mountain exploration when every hill was new to us. The memory of it all is still crystal clear.

Starting from Aviemore on a Sunday at the end of September, we walked to Glenmore (little thinking of what that name was to mean to me in later years), climbed over Cairngorm to reach Loch Avon in the early afternoon, and found the Stone unoccupied. Peak-bagging being our object in those days, we dumped our packs and went off to climb the nearby Beinn Mheadhoin. Eight men had arrived by the time we returned, so that we were ninth and tenth in a shelter with reasonable accommodation for six. Yet my diary does not record an uncomfortable night. I noted . . . "With four candles and two stoves going, the Shelter was a cheery haven, while the Visitors' Book provided countless stories of adventure."

Before dawn we were awake, made a hurried breakfast while the others slept, and crept outside. It was cold, dark, wet, and misty. Loch Avon, a sheet of black awfulness, lay below us, while the waters of Feith Buidhe and Garbh Uisge thundered down. We had a long journey before us and could not delay. In the growing light we climbed Ben Macdhui, spent a freezing ten minutes by the cairn, and scrambled down through the snow to the Lairig Ghru and a welcome blink of sunshine. Then we plodded for over thirty miles southward, through Glen Dee and Glen Tilt. We left Loch Avon at half past six on the Monday morning and reached Blair Atholl at 2 a.m. on the Tuesday morning, meeting no one by the way.

Douglas Scott has clear memories of the first visit to the Cairngorms in 1930, of the long trek from Loch Avon to Blair Atholl, and of how he and Ben tried to orientate themselves by torchlight in Glen Tilt. The map they used is now over sixty years old, but the scribbles on the margins are still legible, communications to his deaf companion in the dark – "I can hear the Falls of Tilt near," and other comments.

> In the years that followed I often climbed among the peaks of Glencoe and Lochaber, of the Central Highlands, of Skye, of Wester Ross and Sutherland, and visited the French and Swiss Alps, but never again was at Loch Avon or the Shelter Stone. Now I had to take a party of eight students there.
>
> The weather at least was the same as we toiled up the Cairngorm path, for the "windy ridge" still lived up to its name. Once again Loch Avon was hidden in thick mist, making compass bearings necessary, but I remembered the route of old. The Shelter Stone itself showed no difference; once more I revelled in the Visitors' Book. I had recorded my name in the second volume – now it was in its eighth!
>
> Towards dawn something wakened me. A strange unreal light was filtering in and lighting up the interior of the Shelter Stone. I crept outside while eight students slept on. Loch Avon lay below, glassy and calm. A glowing sky in the east heralded the dawn; never shall I forget the wonder of it. The waters of Loch Avon became a sheet of burnished gold. The gaunt black crags above took on a dull red tint, while the snow that still lingered at the head of the corrie became bathed in a warm rosy alpenglow. A perfect day followed, by Loch Etchachan to the summit of Ben Macdhui and that grand traverse over the plateau to Cairngorm. The Cairngorms had captured me. For the next twenty years I spent up to three months each year as voluntary instructor at the Lodge, usually for a month at a time, both in summer and in winter.

The above passages come from Ben's two part story of the Shelter Stone of Loch Avon, perhaps the most famous outdoor howff in the world. They also describe one of his earliest outings from Glenmore Lodge. Outdoor training is nowadays taken for granted, and is a thriving industry available in many forms. As he rightly stated, on the Scottish scene it began in earnest on the Cairngorms, with thousands of students and schoolchildren receiving their baptism on the surrounding hills. He was never happier than in those early days. Few he met at Glenmore forgot him, and many became lifelong friends. His account of the first twenty-five years of The National Outdoor Training Centre, which was published in 1975, is the story of the Lodge and its permanent staff [72] as seen through the eyes of one of the many voluntary instructors. I have interspersed recollections from students, friends and colleagues throughout the narrative in order to highlight his own very individual contribution:

THE GLENMORE STORY

I was editing a quarterly magazine when I received an article called "The Central Council of Physical Recreation Comes to Scotland". It told of the Council's first training course, held at Loch Lomond Youth Hostel at Easter 1946, during which parties rowed across Loch Lomond and climbed Ben Lomond. Later Charlie Cromar of the Council's Edinburgh staff came to see me and asked if I knew of a place in the Highlands which could be used as a training centre. All I could suggest was Forest Lodge by Loch Tulla, then (and still) in private hands. The problem was solved by Lord Malcolm Douglas Hamilton[73] who at the end of the war was Scottish Commandant, Air Training Corps. At Christmas time that year he obtained the use of Glenmore Lodge and ran two outdoor courses there, and it was he who suggested it be taken over by the CCPR (shortly afterwards changed to the Scottish Council of Physical Recreation). Lord Malcolm is acknowledged as the founder of the scheme. I think all of us agree that no finer place in Scotland could have been chosen – the whole vast range of the Cairngorms to explore, snow climbing, rock climbing and ski-ing, with Loch Morlich nearby for sailing and canoeing.

Two experimental seven-day courses were held in August 1947 and were such a success that the Lodge became a full-time centre in 1948. The first Warden was the Rev. A. V. Clark of Fort William, a member of both the Lochaber and Scottish Mountaineering Clubs who had done a lot of good work in Mountain Rescue on Ben Nevis and in Glencoe. The Lodge owes much to him for setting it on its way. For the first two years there were Holiday Training Courses for adults only, plus others for Service groups. The Lodge staff was very small and it could never have survived without the help of voluntary instructors from Mountaineering, Ski-ing and Sailing Clubs. Around Easter courses were mainly for skiers, and 1948 marks the beginning of what is now a great industry. It is difficult for those who know only the Aviemore of today to visualise the conditions at that time. Then Aviemore was just a small village which had come into being around the railway junction, with one hotel opposite the station and a row of shacks with corrugated iron roofs as shops.

The road to Glenmore was single width starting with a difficult and dangerous bend under the railway, and from Coylumbridge full of pot holes (many car springs were broken on that road). There was no ski road. The path up Cairngorm was a narrow twisting one through the forest by the Allt Mor, a very steep climb to the cairn at Clach Bharraig then by a way we called the Windy Ridge to the summit. For skiers there was almost more carrying than ski-ing as it took more than an hour to reach the site of the present sheiling. There were, however, splendid Nursery Slopes just beside the Lodge. The greatest mistake made was to build the present Reindeer House on that slope and thus destroy the only Nursery Slope below tree level.

At one of the early courses a young girl fell and struck her head on a boulder and was killed. There have been no ski-ing fatalities on the Cairngorms since that time. As a Memorial to her, her parents provided the funds to build a hut – Jean's Hut – for the use of students from Glenmore Lodge, a little way to the west of the present sheiling.

In 1950 it was decided to open the Lodge for school children during school terms and keep it open the year round. The guiding spirit was Dr Stewart Macintosh, Director of Education for Glasgow and for many years chairman of the Lodge committee. My own first visit was at this time. Mr Clark by then had returned to the Ministry and Charlie Cromar had taken over as Warden.

Robbie Murray, now a schoolmaster in Skye, attended one of the first adult courses and became so interested in the scheme that he joined the Lodge as Field Study Instructor instead of going on to Teacher's Training College. Jack Thomson also arrived at that time and the Lodge owes an immense debt to these two. Robbie set the lines of all Field Study Work, while Jack, a man who could turn his hand to anything, became chief Sailing and Climbing Instructor. Jack recently completed his 25th Year at the Lodge and is as tough as ever.

I arrived at the same time as the sections for Jean's Hut and was press-ganged into helping with transport. The Lodge had an ancient Nansen Sledge, relic of a Polar Expedition. The smaller sections were piled on this and a squad of boys hauled it through deep snow by that narrow track to the limit of the forest while Robbie and I manhandled the much bigger roof sections. I still remember that as about the hardest work I've ever done in my life!

For two years from 1950 the school children were all from Glasgow, the groups coming for periods of four weeks. Dr Macintosh chose children from the poorer schools, a great many of whom had never been out of Glasgow in their lives, so that it was a strange new world for them, a world without cinemas or fish and chips, without even a single shop. The only vehicles the Lodge then had were an ancient truck, seemingly bereft of springs, and an equally ancient Land Rover. What excitement on arrival at the station as all were packed into that old truck, which the children christened "The Sardine Tin". And what a jolting they got on that awful road!

That first night they were divided into four patrols, with ten in each – Gordon, Glenmore, Macdhui and Morlich. The first three days were the same for all the groups. First day – a short talk on maps and map reading, the meaning of all conventional signs, and how to judge distances etc. Then outside for wayfinding, setting maps and following a route described to them, this all on by-roads or paths. As this was the first such scheme in Scotland we had no precedent to go by. Most of the voluntary instructors, though themselves seasoned veterans, had little or no experience of introducing children to the hills. I suppose most of us developed our own methods. Mine began by giving each boy or girl a chance of finding the way over a short distance. When they came to any feature marked on the map, a bridge, a burn, a croft, etc., all had to stop, set maps and show just where they were. At a fork on the road they always tended to stop and wait for me to show them the way. I told them it was their job, not mine. There was often much argument. If they took the wrong path – and they often did to begin with – I just let them go ahead for quite a distance then pointed out their mistake so that they had to return to the junction and start again. They soon learned that a wrong choice meant more walking, and the leader who had selected it got a bawling out from the others. After that first day we chose a leader and second for each patrol but later left it to the boys or girls themselves – invariably they picked the best person.

On the second day they were introduced to the compass, which most of them had never previously seen. I would then give a talk on grid references and how to take them, bearings, adjustments to the compass to allow for magnetic variation, and choice of routes. Then outside each in turn had to lead over a short distance. The dense trackless forest was ideal for such a purpose, travelling from tree to tree till the set objective was reached, the instructor tagging along behind and helping out when mistakes were made. Compass work in such surroundings is the best method of training for future travel on a mountain in mist.

One Glenmore student, identified only by a number, wrote:

"We were going out for a wayfinding and map reading expedition with a very gloomy looking man, who actually turned out to be very nice and quite good fun. How dull wayfinding sounded after a day's ski-ing. How different it turned out to be, however, and we returned in a jubilant and rather learned state of mind."

Other friends who first met Ben at the Lodge remember him as an enthusiastic instructor, and in map reading and compass a hard task master – especially to students who were not too keen to get involved. Wayfinding was a bit of a task for some to begin with, but he would never allow any to shirk it. As they gained experience they started to appreciate the hills far more, finding his deafness little handicap. Ben compensated by missing absolutely nothing with his eyes, and his knowledge of nature constantly amazed the students. Alex Small tells of coming upon him with a party on the Cairngorm-Macdhui plateau in thick mist, and of thinking he was having a fight with his group – ". . . but no! They were arguing in sign language about the compass bearing! Shortly afterwards, in clearing conditions, he had them practically on their hands and knees looking for heathers of different varieties."

On the third day each patrol was divided into two for a wayfinding competition. By this time patrols had a very definite identity, with intense rivalry between them. Each section started at intervals having only a set of about six six-figure grid references – a lochan, a path junction, a stile etc. and always in an area they had not previously visited, the total distance being around ten miles. By now they were on their own, and had to choose routes either direct by compass or longer by path according to their own judgement, it being a rigid rule that each section must keep together, the pace being that of the slowest. Instructors were stationed at each point to be reached and I have many memories of hiding up a tree or lying in a hollow on the Nethy moors checking their arrival or calling them in by whistle if any went astray. A census showed that fewer than ten per cent had ever seen a one inch Ordnance Survey map at school, while the Silva Compass was entirely new to them – yet on that third day most parties managed that course on their own!

A typical month's course in those days included sailing (ski-ing if in winter), wayfinding, campcraft, field sketching, surveying and map making, hill walking and the principles of bivouacking, even bird watching, with time left for a day of independent exploration by the children. Always the final three days were given over to a bivouac expedition. At first girls were only allowed a two day bivouac but they went on strike and claimed equal rights! There was no rock climbing for the school groups at that time. At the end of the month they were all fully fit, and those three day trips are among the brightest of my memories. We ranged all over the Cairngorms – no peak was unknown to us.

Ben quickly spotted the best and most enthusiastic of the students, those who responded to the hills as he himself had done. Many became his protégés, among them Elizabeth Lindsay, Robin Smith and Margaret Somerville. Elizabeth, later dubbed the Cairngorm Amazon, recalls her first meeting:

"I first met Ben when I was on a course at Glenmore Lodge. I had been warned that he was completely deaf just before I met him in the lounge of the old Lodge during one of their famous ceilidhs. Just as well, because he would never tell anyone himself, and new acquaintances could be left floundering in his wake wondering what was going on – perhaps this wee man with the odd voice was drunk? I was introduced to his famous notebook that first night. I also had several dances with him, and he was darn good at picking up the beat, I suppose from the feel of the floor. Later he took me climbing on the Cobbler, and on the Trossach hills. He was a fund of information on the geology, flora and fauna, and I didn't realise at the time how privileged I was."

After two years Lanarkshire, Clackmannanshire and other authorities sent up groups, but only for a fortnight at a time. With these we fitted in camping with bivouacs. Groups were located at Coire an t' Sneachda, Coire an Lochain, the Shelter Stone and the Etchachan Hut, and on the second of two days all had to meet on the summit of Ben Macdhui by noon, where the tent and bivouac parties switched over. With teachers and instructors we then would have a party of about fifty at the cairn.

When Charlie Cromar returned to teaching in Glasgow, Murray Scott took over as Warden and most of the expeditions mentioned were during his reign. Canoeing was introduced about this period. I well remember a day between courses when Murray decided on an Instructors' Day and forced the old Land Rover to Nethy Bothy. There I witnessed the ease and grace of John Cunningham as he led most of the climbs on the Barns of Bynack, and remember how we ran the whole way back to the bothy.

One mid-summer day at this time I had a group of girls at Rothiemurchus hut, then crossing the Allt Druidhe on stepping stones and climbing Carn Eilrig, all in blazing sun. About noon ominous dark clouds appeared over Braeriach and it became quite eerie as the

Cloudburst near Glenmore Lodge, 1956. Photo: W. N. Connolly.

girls' hair stood up on end as if caught by a vacuum. It was obvious that something special in the way of storms was coming and soon the heaviest rain I have ever known came down vertically. I hustled them off the hill to get across the river before it rose in spate, and we were wading through water most of the way back to the Lodge. I went upstairs to change. What a sight when I came down! The dam behind the Lodge had burst, water was roaring down, with the kitchen staff trying to sweep it out the back door. The road up to the Lodge was a river which swept across the road at the site of the present shop. Cars trying to get out of the camp site were trapped, some of them on the road with water running in one door and out the other, while the whole camp site and the area down to Loch Morlich was under water. The Allt Mor was also in spate, and though we did not know it at the time the bridge had been washed away.

Next day there was no water supply in the Lodge and for days afterwards all the burns ran brown and frothy. We decided the course must continue normally, and children were sent down to a burn to wash in the morning. I had a party of boys on a compass route that day, the last lap being from Lochan na Beinne to Clach Bharraig and the Allt Mor. Only then did we find the burn still in spate and the bridge washed away, while the path through the forest used as the route up Cairngorm for well nigh a hundred years was under water. We had to make our way well above the forest before we could cross safely. A second cloudburst occurred many years later after the Ski road had been built, and the bridge was washed away again, so the present one is the third bridge on the site. It was on that day of the cloudburst that Bobbie Brown[74] and another teacher had gone to spend the night on the summit of Macdhui and had to get back in the height of the storm. Bobbie was a grand hillman and the best of the teachers who ever came up with the children. It was he who later brought up a party of his schoolboys on a Friday night, and covered the four highest tops on the Saturday – as far as is known the first time this had been done, Glenmore to Glenmore, by a school party.

Bobbie Brown remembers those days well:

"Ben was a truly remarkable and wonderful character whom I met in the early 1950s when we were both voluntary instructors at the old Glenmore Lodge. I went out with him on a number of occasions, and despite his deafness and the difficulty in communicating, we seemed to understand each other. I had the greatest confidence in tramping with him deep into the Cairngorms. I recall vividly one wonderful bivouac when Ben, John Cunningham and I and a party of 5th and 6th year pupils ascended Cairngorm, camped on the shores of Loch Avon at the Shelter Stone, proceeding then to Ben Macdhui, and descending into the Lairig Ghru and back to Glenmore. In those days it was a very rough road from Aviemore station up to the Lodge, and ski-ing was very much in its infancy. We seemed to get a lot more snow then also, and I recall skis outside the doors of the cottages as one made one's way up to the Lodge. (I don't think anyone would dare to leave their skis outside nowadays.) At the ceilidhs in the evenings Ben seemed to derive great pleasure from sitting at the back of the hall and watching others enjoying the music and dancing."

One January we were completely snowed up and I took a party of girls to Aviemore to buy provisions, walking the whole way. It must be remembered also there was then no ski road and every expedition to the plateau meant a climb of 3,000 feet first. Other incidents also stand out. A party of boys were with me at the Etchachan Hut on the second day of an expedition, while a group of girls were at the Shelter Stone with Alan Cathcart. I got my boys off by 8 a.m. up to Loch Etchachan and then down to the Shelter Stone. The girls were at breakfast, but obviously had no intention of sharing with us! A small figure rose up from a corner of the upper cave – none other than Professor Graham Brown, of Brenva fame, out on his own. He too helped much as a voluntary instructor and later I had the pleasure of climbing with him. Alas, within a year Alan Cathcart died of leukaemia and the Lodge lost one of its best instructors.

During one Christmas Course for adults a young lad came to me and told me that his father knew me. He was Robin Smith, then in his final year at school. His father and I had played in the same lawn tennis team before he married and went to India. Robin was with my group for three days, the first day to the Barns of Bynack and Bynack Mor. We crossed over the Lairig an Laoigh, but when a violent snow storm blew up from the north we had to give up, and had a very, very, tough fight against it, with one lad affected so badly we had to halt at Nethy Bothy. Murray Scott insisted we try again next day – via Eagle's Corrie in deep snow and across the Nethy on ice. A younger instructor with me fell through, thigh deep in icy water and had to return. This delayed us quite a bit so that we only reached Bynack Beag, but Robin made light of both trips. The third day called for a climb, but the gullies in Coire an t' Sneachda and Coire an Lochain had been inspected and condemned as avalanche risks so it had to be that steep inner corner of Coire Cas. As far as I know those were Robin's first snow climbs. The climbing world knows and still talks of his epic climbs in Scotland and the Alps – he became one of the foremost climbers in Britain until he met his end with Wilfred Noyce in the Pamirs in 1962.

There were many adult courses and I chiefly remember those from the Colleges of Physical Recreation. They were up for a shorter time, and did not take part in such long expeditions as the school-children. My chief memory of them is foot trouble – for most had never worn boots before in their lives. I think I must have used yards and yards of Elastoplast for skinned heels!

Margaret Somerville[75] was a student of Ben's at one of those adult courses:

"I met Ben at Glenmore Lodge when I was on a week's training course for teachers-to-be from Jordanhill Training College. He was one of the instructors, and was also to be my leader in a two-day expedition to the mountains, to the Shelter Stone of Loch Avon. First impressions of this little man, already as bald as a coot and with a loud toneless voice, were rather off-putting. His total deafness was of course known to us, but his huge interest and obvious enjoyment in our group soon won us over. This ability to involve himself with a group of young, hearing adults with no previous experience either of the hills or of communication with the deaf was testimony to his confidence, his skill and his determination. It was obvious from the beginning that he was a character; he would go to great lengths to avoid doing any food preparation, and was quick to join any group whose members were prepared to share their food with him. That weekend was my first introduction to the great outdoors, and I responded with total enthusiasm.

"Ben taught me a lot about the hills. For example, that a steady pace was better than an all-out attack on the mountain. One day he was delighted with me. We were out for a winter walk when a group of young lads passed us at speed. We just kept steadily on, and soon met up with the lads on the next ridge. This happened several times, until one of them asked: 'Is she an agricultural worker?' Since these were the Creagh Dhu boys, Ben was flattered that his protégé (me) was impressing the tough guys. Everything was an adventure with Ben. The Cobbler soon felt like a friend; the hills and ridges and mystery of Glencoe lost their strangeness. He wanted to show me the hills in their winter snow, and I remember a wonderful walk with him along the Aonach Eagach ridge.

"Wherever he lived – Dumbarton, then Rose Cottage at Arrochar, and finally Aviemore – he seemed to know everything about everybody, particularly in the world of Scottish climbing. I like to remember him –

vigorous, a man of the hills both for his own enjoyment and for others, always concerned that the hills should be accessible to all; a man of business, a splendid photographer, a fascinating companion, and of course a proud, independent Scot. I saw him for the last time at a party given by his brother John after Ben had received his MBE at Buckingham Palace. He was proud of the award, but was still just the same Ben I first met in 1951."

> There were also many days with rock climbing beginners at the Chalamain Gap and on Fiacaill Coire an t' Sneachda, and tough fights back over the plateau from Ben Macdhui in mist, rain and wind, and camps in the high corries in late spring at 3,000 feet, with still much snow around. The toughest camp we ever had was in Strath Nethy one January with schoolboys, when the Lodge recorded a temperature of 30 degrees below zero. The trek through deep snow took a long time and one just had to keep the boys busy all the time at camp, clearing snow, building big snow walls around. The old tents were very good with much stronger ground sheets than is common today. At night the boys had to take their boots in between their outer and inner sleeping bags. One lad left his overtrousers outside the tent, and in the morning they were like corrugated iron and stood up by themselves! The burn nearby was frozen over and water had to be brought from a lochan some distance away, breaking through six inches of ice to get it, with the buckets starting to freeze by the time they reached the tents. We would not have tried such a camp had they only been there for a week, but by the longer period they were well toughened.
>
> The Lodge owes much to its well chosen permanent staff and the great number of voluntary instructors who gave freely of their varied skills, setting it on its way to the world-wide reputation it has now gained. Yet looking back to those early days it is of the children from the cities and their reaction to an entirely new world which is my most vivid memory.

That reaction is evidenced by comments from unknown Glenmore students, identified again only by numbers. I found them among the detailed notes which Ben kept about every single group in his charge:

"It has been wonderful up here. I am afraid I cannot really express the feelings I have . . . As I think of going back to Glasgow with all its busy streets and factory chimneys, and then think about the hills and forests around Glenmore, it makes me want to hide away in the hills till the train is away from the station."

"Never will I forget all the experiences which Glenmore gave me. I think I shall be able to face the world's hardships with more confidence in myself, than I would have done had I not come to Glenmore."

"The saddest moment of my life is just the fact of leaving the Lodge, my new life, my home, everything the Lodge represented. The thought of going on the train makes me want to scream. I'm not going on the train. I want to stay here."

It says much for the staff that more than 3,000 children took part in those summer and winter expeditions with never any hint of trouble – and that long before the Mountain Leadership scheme was even thought of. During that time also about 6,000 adults took courses at the Lodge.

By 1956 Glenmore Lodge as an outdoor training centre had proved itself, and consideration had to be given for the future when the ten-year lease from the Forestry Commission would expire. Though the old building had many deficiencies, especially in the way of accommodation for instructors, some of us regretted it when the decision was made to erect a new building further up the glen. My memory of the old Lodge will always be of that cosy wee staff room with its wonderful outlook, and of Graham Brown in his favourite corner, puffing away at that old pipe. But the change had to be made if progress was to continue, particularly to ensure more privacy by getting away from the ever-growing public camp site.

The new Lodge was the first in Britain designed for its purpose and we soon realised its immense advantages and comfort. The official opening day in 1959 was a memorable occasion, with many VIPs from all over Scotland, including of course Lord Malcolm Douglas Hamilton and his sons. For a year or two the old routine continued, but there was a gradual change as more and more education authorities set up their own centres, so there were fewer and fewer school courses, with in the end only Glasgow still remaining faithful.

The finest winter was in 1960 when Glasgow schoolboys were up for the whole month of January. For weeks on end snow lay deep outside the Lodge, with the sun shining in a cloudless sky, and there was ski-ing all over the forest trails. I got a group of boys and we built the first igloo outside the Lodge. It remained for three weeks and became iron hard every night. Later the north wing of the Lodge was almost covered with snow and snow holes were built in the passage outside it. We had much more snow then than in the winters of recent years, and the winter expeditions became quite arduous – though we never went over the plateaux. I remember one in the lower reaches of the Lairig Ghru. The Rothiemurchus Hut was cut off because of deep snow and supplies for the army group there had to be left at the roadside at the east end of Loch Morlich, so it meant a trek for us through deep soft snow up to the hut then across to the Allt Druidhe, with hard work clearing snow before pitching tents. Boots supplied at that time were nothing like the splendid ones available today so many of the boys got their feet wet. With lots of dead wood nearby we solved the problem with a huge fire.

On the return journey one boy was going poorly and I stayed behind with him, allowing all the others to get well ahead. Just after our return to the Lodge an officer and a sergeant appeared complaining that much of their supplies left at the roadside had disappeared. The boys had helped themselves! I can still remember the woebegone look on their faces when we routed them out and sent them back at once to replace all unopened tins and uneaten chocolate (mighty little of the latter) for they were looking forward to a change and tea, and now had another three miles to trek – that's your Glasgow schoolboys!

The best school course then was the Senior Schoolboys' Exploration Course each August. One year they carried out a bathymetrical survey of Loch Avon from a camp at the lochside, using inflatable canoes; another time a geological survey of the plateau from Cairn Lochan to Ben Macdhui, with a camp in the upper reaches of Coire Domhain. On both these occasions the weather was bad but the jobs were completed.

Murray Scott, who had proved a splendid Warden, moved on to a bigger job as HM Inspector of Schools and Alex Dalrymple took over. In his time we had the toughest ever school course. This was for selected senior boys from all the chief grammar schools in England who had been told to expect a very hard time of it. Jimmie Hutchison, Field Study Instructor at that time, was in charge – the course objective being to keep a full weather station going near the summit of Ben Macdhui, and also to make a bathymetrical survey of Lochan Uaine. On the first day there was the usual map and compass training. Later that same night all groups were tested in a wayfinding course finishing at 2 a.m., so that most of it was in the dark. Next morning, half the course of thirty boys with three instructors went off to establish the high camp, carrying all the gear for the weather station and inflatable canoes. After three days the remainder of the boys took over and the job was completed within six days – then the camp was maintained for a further week for rock climbing.

For the whole time there was no sunshine at the camp, rain and mist every day, snow still around and temperature near freezing point

As many Glenmore students may remember him.

at night. A comparison showed that rainfall was nine times more than at the Lodge, proving the point that it may be winter any day of the year on our higher hills. The hill walking day for these boys was not just the usual one of round the corries of Cairngorm. "No need to get them back for afternoon tea," said Alex. "Give them a long day." So I took my group through the Eagle's Corrie to Strath Nethy then via the Saddle to Loch Avon and the Shelter Stone, up to Loch Etchachan and Ben Macdhui and back over the plateau to Cairngorm returning to the Lodge by 6 p.m. Boys on that course were the fittest and toughest of any I have ever been out with.

Alas, Alex's reign was short. Leukaemia claimed him. After hospital sessions, when he knew that death was near, he returned to the Lodge. It was typical of that fine man that he and his wife insisted that the course at the time be carried on normally and the boys not be informed – actually they were taking part in a run round Loch Morlich when he died and knew nothing about it.

Changes came with the arrival of Eric Langmuir, a former president of Cambridge University MC, as Warden. He it was who started the now-famous winter survival courses. The first one was in April, too late in the season, and in blazing sun the men were able to dig snow holes stripped to the waist with a battery of press photographers around. Now the course is held in February or early March and involves two nights out in snow holes on different parts of the Cairngorm range, attracting men from the three Services and Mountain Rescue teams throughout Britain. The new Lodge also became an official mountain rescue post. Every year now at special mountain rescue courses new gear is tested, and new techniques are tried out.

Eric Langmuir came to know Ben well during his time as Warden:

"By the time I came to Glenmore Lodge in 1963, Ben had begun to limit his involvement in the more strenuous expeditions from the Lodge. With his great knowledge of safety matters I think he realised his own limitations in taking full responsibility for looking after a group of young people on the hill, and increasingly he devoted his energies to rescue and safety aspects of the more specialised courses, to wayfinding as he called it (now orienteering), first aid, and of course to the development of his beloved Cairngorm garden at the front of the building. It must have been quite difficult for him at this time, travelling up from his home in Arrochar and working, sometimes for two to three months at a time, in return for travelling expenses and board and lodging. In time we were able to pay him for some of his work, but never anything approaching

An unexpected ski-ing accident, June 1960. Photo: Harvey Grainger.

a working wage and certainly never reflecting the huge amount of work and enthusiasm he contributed."

The first time a helicopter was used was a great event, the whole Lodge gathering in the Pass of Ryvoan to watch Jack Thomson being winched up. Now Army and RAF helicopters are common and we have two of them at every course, landing and taking off in front of the Lodge, with every student having the experience of being winched up. Up till this year 60-foot ropes were used and usually vertical lifts but last October there was a lift from the rock climbing wall by the Army Parachute Regiment using a 200-foot rope. There is now very close co-operation between the Lodge and the RAF Rescue Team at Kinloss. The fine piloting of the helicopters is a constant wonder to us. On twenty occasions in 1974 they lifted casualties from scenes of accidents in Scotland, thus saving the Rescue Teams the long hard work of the carry back to base.

Full credit has scarcely been given to the work of the Lodge staff in actual mountain rescue. Late one summer night when word came through that a lad was stuck halfway up the cliffs of Coire an Lochain, Jack Thomson on his own lowered him down to safety, the precarious position of the boy being such that it was doubtful if he could have lasted much longer. On one survival course in November a group returning down Strath Nethy in gale conditions came upon three hill walkers, one of them lying exhausted in deep snow and another in poor condition. They got all three back to the Lodge, one life certainly, possibly two, being saved. One Hogmanay the Lodge staff were called out at 8 p.m. Nearing Coire an Lochain, in thigh deep snow, they found a lad wandering around looking for his companion, and then, at 2 a.m., found the second lad exhausted and almost unconscious lying in the snow. Two lives were saved that night, and on more than one occasion during a mountain rescue course all students and staff have been out the whole day in searches. Now the control of all incidents on the north side of Cairngorms is in the hands of the Principal of the Lodge.

Following these descriptions of the rescue efforts of the Lodge staff, "The Glenmore Story" moved on to an account of further changes prior to 1975, by which time Fred Harper had taken over as Principal. Coincident with slowly enlarging accommodation, many new innovations, courses and training techniques had by then been introduced, notable among them the institution of avalanche studies under Eric Langmuir,[76] and the intensification of instruction in canoeing and winter mountaineering. Ben

also documented the steady increase in permanent staff, always acknow-
ledging their individual talents. His own latterly consultative role in
mountain rescue affairs was scarcely mentioned, preference being given
to recording visits from such as Dawa Tensing . . . "We took Dawa up
on the chair lift and he said he wished they had that on Everest!"

The Glenmore story continues today. Ben would be delighted, though
not surprised, with the range of courses offered. His very last comment
was that by 1975 the Lodge could almost be termed a University for
Outdoor Training. The word "almost" has become superfluous. Now
designated The Scottish National Sports Centre, and in its forty-seventh
year of operation, the Lodge has continued to expand its activities.
Excellent new indoor facilities complement the wonderful outdoor opportunities of the region, while instruction extends beyond the Cairngorms in numerous areas such as advanced rock climbing, kayaking and
ski-mountaineering, with courses conducted in the Alps.

The seeds planted in pre-war years, the initiatives of the Douglas
Hamiltons and the late King George VI, the success of Commando
training – all were important in their turn, necessary connections along
the way towards the development at Glenmore and the progress of
outdoor training in Scotland, yet another field in which Ben contributed
in his own individual way.

It is appropriate to end the Glenmore section with this final remembrance from Murray Scott:

"At this stage perhaps the best contribution I can make is by way of
a magnificent black and white photograph of an incident in June 1960,
when Ben was unexpectedly involved in the rescue of a skier who had
broken through the lower end of the Coire na Ciste ski run and fractured
his leg. There were no helicopters in those days, and when the alarm
was raised a small stretcher party set off from Glenmore Lodge, getting
assistance from a training group already in the field. The victim of the
accident was none other than Frith Findlayson, who was later to become
a major figure in the development of Scottish ski-ing.

"The photo I think captures wonderfully well the effort involved in
rescue in those early days, and is particularly significant as it shows Ben
at the working end of a stretcher, instead of being the man behind the
camera as he invariably was in later years . . . As far as his activities at
Glenmore are concerned, I could go on and on, for he loved the place
and the people, but the expression on his face says it all for me."

A Cairngorm Rock Garden – the early days.

Winter conditions at Glenmore Lodge.

A CAIRNGORM ROCK GARDEN

When the original Glenmore Lodge was replaced in 1959, Ben conceived the idea of constructing a heather garden to the east of the entrance to the new building, on a plot of land originally some 50 by 20 feet in size. In that garden today you will find a wooden bench carrying the following inscription:

> *In Memory of Ben Humble, MBE, who created this Alpine garden in the shadow of the hills he loved so well. A pioneer of mountain rescue in Scotland and for many years a voluntary instructor at Glenmore Lodge.*
> *16–4–77*

How did he develop professional expertise with heathers and Alpine plants? The answer to that question is simple. Just as he had done in every other area of interest from his days as a dental student, Ben taught himself, evidence yet again of the sense of purpose brought to him through his deafness, and of the manner in which it focused his energies. When others were talking, he was busy looking and learning. Minute flowers on the Cuillin corries, which many might pass without a glance; tiny Alpine willows high up on the Cairngorms; heaths and heathers on their native Highland soil – all were a part of his delight and pride in the Scottish countryside. The more he saw, the more he read and absorbed. Soon after the end of the war he began to experiment with the propagation of heathers, and rock gardens later graced every house in which he lived – at Comely Bank in Dumbarton, Rose Cottage in Arrochar, and Feithlinn in Aviemore. When he visited our home in Dumfries in 1966, he walked straight past the seventy rose bushes I had laboriously and lovingly planted. Not even a second glance! He only had eyes for the small rock garden we had also started down by the back wall. "Aaaaaah! Where did you get these? . . . Not bad, not bad, aaaaaah!" From Ben that was indeed a compliment!

In 1959 he was able to put all his accumulated love and learning into a garden at the newly constructed Lodge, tending its growth for eighteen years, with his last visits only days before his death. He also created a second Alpine garden higher up the mountain, at the lower Cairngorm ski-lift, a project possibly not previously attempted at such an elevation in Britain. It was taken out of his hands in the mid-1970s, leaving him dismayed by the loss of associated perks, the free use of the ski-lift and free meals at the mountain top restaurant! Although somewhat neglected in recent years, what is now more of a wild garden still shows splashes of colour from the plants he introduced. His passion for heather never waned, for at the end of his life he was again consumed with fresh ideas, this time for a new tourist attraction for Aviemore, a *Wonderful World of Heather Centre*, to be located on a vacant plot of ground in the village. Many people were canvassed in his usual fashion, and many convinced, but he ran out of time. The plans, the enthusiasm, and the experience are still evident in his detailed notes – all that is yet needed is someone to put them into effect!

It was the Glenmore garden, however, that remained his pride and joy, the last of the all-consuming loves of his life. As his days on the hills became less frequent he spent increasing time there. The story of its construction is told in his own especial style:

"You're walking through a forest," I told the boys. One of them said afterwards that they thought I was joking, for we were 4,000 feet up the Cairngorms. So I showed them, spreading extensively among the granite screes at their feet, the Alpine willow, a true willow, with catkins and all, though barely an inch in height. "Would it grow down at the Lodge?" asked one. "It might," I replied, "If you give it its home comforts."

They knew we were starting to build a rock garden, so I had to explain how, while on the mountains, we noted plants and flowers adapted themselves to their surroundings, in a rock garden the process was in reverse – we had to adapt the surroundings to the plants. That meant carrying down a supply of the granite chips with the fine soil among them. Would they care to do so in that empty pack? They did, and that was the start of the summit plateau of our own garden.

Looking back now, it is difficult to visualise its appearance four years ago when the new Glenmore Lodge was built. At one side top-soil removed to make the foundations for the Lodge had been piled up on top of thick old heather. Two huge boulders were left on the ground, and it seemed natural to try and construct a heather garden around them – my first idea was simply a circle surrounding the two boulders. There was no real plan for one does not look for formality in a heather garden; the layout was dependent on the size of the ground and the position of the original boulders, which could not be moved. Tiers were built round these, and ultimately linked up, giving us a great many beds at varied levels.

Digging started – oh, the labour of it! All sorts of rubbish was revealed – lumps of tar and cement, bits of wood and sacking. All this had to be taken out, together with as much of the rotting heather roots as possible. The peaty top-soil had been removed when making foundations for the buildings, leaving stony and sandy soil below. While heathers will grow in poor soil as long as it does not contain lime, peat is its real life blood, so barrow load after barrow load of peaty soil was brought in from wherever we could find it. But that labour was light compared to that of finding suitable stones, for the barrow could only take one or two at a time. Many more boulders were required. How to get them in?

Forestry workers were making a fire-break along the road. Many boulders were upturned. I noted all the most attractive ones of grey or red granite, and then many of the instructors at the Lodge gave much of their free time – it became a sort of competition to see how big a boulder they could manhandle and roll into position. One we tried to drag behind the Land-Rover. The rope broke. We got it in with chains. The Head Forester became interested. When out with him one day I pointed out a huge boulder with a curious V-shaped cleft in it, regretting that it was too big to move, as that cleft would give rooting for plants. I thought no more about it. A few days later the boulder was in the position I wanted. I still don't know how they moved it. Now plants grow from that cleft.

Coincident with building was the first planting. I myself had been growing heaths and heathers for many years, and the first scheme was entirely a garden of such. Would anything else grow, for surely the site was one of the most exposed in the country, at a height of 1,200 feet, mostly facing west and exposed to the prevailing wind from the south-west. And how the winds blow up there! Forty-knot gusts are often recorded, and it can blow for weeks on end. A few heathers were planted, but we soon learned that sheep delight in the young plants. They broke in one night, ate many young shoots and pulled other plants out by the roots! Soon, too, we learned which varieties would withstand the harsh conditions, for all were not equally hardy. Some took to the garden at once, while others took much longer to acclimatise, a few dying out altogether.

Gradually the garden grew till we had three tiers in the centre mound. The top was dubbed the summit plateau, and here we tried to imitate the conditions on the summit plateau of the Cairngorm; many helped by bringing more and more granite scree down the mountain on returning from their day's outing. The Alpine willow took root and flourished. The lovely moss campion was slower to acclimatise, but eventually its vivid green carpets spread and flourished. Thrift from the eastern ridge took to the garden at once, and soon there was lots of self-seeding. Alpine lady's mantle was another success, though dwarf azalea did not do so well. All these five plants grow in profusion on the surrounding hills. We made it a rule that no rare Alpines be removed from the mountains.

Another circle was constructed at the top of the area, and the two finally connected up by making beds at different levels. Each bed had its own heath or heather, usually in groups of six plants to give a mass effect, and chosen according to height, colour, foliage, and season of bloom.

My great delight is the bed of *Calluna vulgaris aurea*, and it is indeed surprising that this variety is not more often cultivated; I could not find it even in the famous Kew Gardens in London. True, it bears but little bloom, but one can forgive it for that with the glory of its foliage – brilliant red all winter and spring, and a mass of golden, fern-like foliage all summer. Within two years it will cover the entire bed, while its sprays will grace any floral arrangement in the house. Maybe it would not be so effective in the south. It almost seems as if the climate and the harsh conditions of the Cairngorm make for more vivid colouring – I have not seen such striking foliage in the same plant elsewhere.

Next to this is the latest to flower of the white heathers – *Calluna vulgaris Serlei alba*. It gave abundant sprays of white up to the end of November, but even in mid-December I was able to cut some bloom which graced a bride's bouquet later that day. It provides a mass of vivid emerald foliage all winter. Such massed colour is most effective when all wild heather around appears dead. To contrast the green is the eye-catching *Calluna vulgaris Serlei aurea*, with its dense canary-yellow foliage, and *cuprea*, of the rich copper colour. *Mrs Pat* has not done so well, but I still have hopes; with its light green foliage and delicate pink tips to the shoots it is certainly well worth cultivating.

Of course, there are lots of white, many from my own garden, propagated by layering – *Mair's Variety*, with its long upright stems; and *White Mite*, a tiny one, and one of the earliest to flower, which was discovered by Jack Drake 3,000 feet up, on Sgoran Dubh. It was a proud day last August when the Highland panel visited the Lodge, and we were able to present everyone with a sprig of lucky white heather.

Bell heathers and cross-leaved heath, mostly local, provide bloom at an earlier date, while a white variety – *Hookstone White* – keeps in

Himalayan Iris in full bloom, June 1993.

bloom for a very long period. Then there is a dwarf one with its white flowers slightly flushed with lavender, which always interests the schoolgirls. No wonder, for its name is *Honeymoon*! One day I was telling them of Fred Chapple's classic description of perhaps the most curious heather of all, *Sister Anne*, with its "pretty pink flowers which curl up at the tip as though admiring the plant as a whole, like a girl peeping through a mirror to admire her beauty." They immediately wanted to see that one also, but I had to admit that the sheep had eaten two *Sister Annes*, and the other had died on me!

The showiest of the purple heathers is undoubtedly *Calluna vulgaris Alportii*, a variety first cultivated about a hundred years ago, and just about the best of all, with its sage-green foliage and deep, wine-red flowers. Last year there was still some bloom in December.

With the winter-flowering heaths I had rather miscalculated, forgetting the amount of snow which falls at Glenmore. Of course, I knew they would grow, for these are among the most wonderful of all our plants – gales, frost and snow, mean nothing to them. The wilder the weather conditions, the more exposed the situation, the better they grow. They bud in the autumn, then for months are encompassed in ice and snow. In March 1962 I dug carefully through two feet of hard snow and found them in full bloom below. Only if the thaw comes early do we see the full beauty of them – the rich crimson flowers and dark foliage of *Erica carnea Vivellii* contrasting with the wide spreading light green mats and masses of flower of *Springwood White*.

There is not much bloom in a heather garden in mid-summer. That meant other plants to give colour then. I fear I became a nuisance to my rock-gardening friends, cadging plants and roots from this garden and that, but always keeping to the hardiest and easiest growing varieties – Alpine phloxes, dianthus, rock rose, and rock geranium. Of these, the rock rose and rock geranium have done best. I did not think the spectacular lewisia would survive, but tried four, and when building planted them to grow horizontally. Yet they have flowered twice a summer, though too often the stems are broken by high winds. Dwarf brooms with their masses of creamy yellow flowers now add a blaze of colour in early summer.

Why not fill up the curve of the rockery with a paved area? That proved quite a job – to get it as level as possible and collect flat stones about two inches thick. No cement was used, the spaces between being filled up with fine gravel and scree. Now to carpet the slabs. If you go from Dalwhinnie to Newtonmore in summer you will see masses and masses of wild thymes by the roadside. Those we brought soon rooted and spread, and gradually some of the smaller stones are being removed to give a better effect. Mounds of mossy saxifrages also now grow from the paving stones.

To separate the garden from the grass we decided to make a border of crazy paving. As this had to be combined with a french drain, it proved the hardest work of all. A trench was dug about two feet deep and two feet wide. Larger stones at the bottom and smaller ones at the top, with a final layer of gravel and scree. Again no cement was used, and it was easy to bed down the large flat stones, all of which were collected locally. Sedums, stonecrops and thymes now grow happily from that gravel, while self seeding thrift appears here and there.

Someone said, "Why not try gentians?" While I knew my heaths and heathers, I had never grown gentians, taking them to be plants for the specialist. Yet surely a plant from the Himalayas would grow in the frequently Himalayan conditions of the Cairngorms? They would, in a way, complete the scheme, since gentians were introduced into Britain in 1912; the gentians are the glory of the autumn – the rock-gardener's delight. Many species are available. For me it had to be the easiest to cultivate.

"Plenty of leaf-mould," I was told. We had collected some leaf mould, but it would be a year or so before it was ready for use. I solved the problem by buying a bale of peat from a grain-merchant. This was sieved and thoroughly soaked. The soil in the chosen bed was then removed to a depth of eighteen inches and the entire bed filled up with this fine peat.

Two dozen *Gentiana sino-ornata* were planted in June 1961. They gave a few blooms that autumn, and amazed us a year later. There were no fewer than three hundred trumpets of royal blue, and the massed effect as one looked down from the windows was quite spectacular. This autumn they will fill the bed entirely, and runners from them will be propagated elsewhere and give further displays. They proved much easier to cultivate than I had expected, though we were always careful to keep them well watered in periods of drought in summer. Now we are experimenting with earlier-flowering varieties.

Various brooms have been planted round the grass border in the hope that they will ultimately act as a windbreak, and in the area between them and the rockery, dwarf conifers. Here we have aimed at foliage cover to contrast with the darkness of the nearby natural pines. The group of golden cypresses catches the eye, but it will be a long time before *Thuja occidentalis Rheingold* and *Picea albertiana conica* show their full beauty.

Now, with a measure of success, we are growing more adventurous. A drift of Irish or Connemara heath, and one of Cornish have been planted, and if a proportion of the many cuttings taken last year survive there will be lots of heathers to come. And maybe – the ultimate dream – cross fertilisation may produce a new variety of our very own. That indeed would be the supreme success, and its name would have to be *Calluna vulgaris Glenmore*.

If you visit Ben's Glenmore garden today, do not expect to find exactly the garden he described. It has grown since his death in 1977, overgrown in some respects. Native pines, willows and birch have sown themselves and now smother many of the smaller plants, while the original levels are difficult to visualise. Although still providing fair autumn colour, most of the callunas (heathers) are tired and straggly looking, probably missing his individual care. *Calluna vulgaris Serlei alba*, his source of a December bridal bouquet, remains clearly recognisable. The ericas (heaths), on the other hand, have done surprisingly well, especially *Erica carnea Springwood White*. *Hebe pageana* from New Zealand, together with many thymes and sedums, has survived, but of the gentians there is no sign – nor, alas, of the dwarf Alpine willow. Making up for their absence, however, from the more rare originals we found a black Himalayan iris (*Chrysographes*) in full bloom in mid-June, along with the South African native *Euryops acraeus*,[77] both in remarkable condition despite the fairly dry condition of the ground.

Although Ben's dream of *Calluna vulgaris Glenmore* was not to be, time has justified most of his original concepts. The garden still provides a fine display at the entrance to the Lodge; the dwarf conifers now show the full beauty he visualised; his plan of intermingling native plants with those from other countries has proved successful in the long term; and the shelter belt he started on the north side of the plot has undoubtedly been the main reason why smaller plants have survived with limited attention for so long. He has shown clearly that at this altitude, despite sometimes wild weather conditions, it is possible to make a very attractive and lasting Alpine garden, one which requires only minimal maintenance.

"Ben was a man who got things done," Tom Weir wrote in 1977 . . . "If you go to Glenmore Lodge, look at the Alpine and heather garden he built, and think of him."

9

ADVENTURE IN SAFETY

MOUNTAIN RESCUE IN SCOTLAND

One September many years ago, a newly married couple set off on their honeymoon by train, travelling north towards Skye. Arriving at Sligachan in the early afternoon they set off to climb Sgurr nan Gillean, both unsuitably shod and clad. They got lost in thick mist, and shivered and shuddered all night on the mountain. At daylight, when they were half paralysed with cold, they tried to descend a steep gully. The girl slipped, knocked her husband off his balance, and they both fell. The husband got a crack on the head, and lay totally dazed for about an hour. When he came to he found his wife unconscious on a ledge a few feet above him. He lifted her down, took his shirt and coat and wrapped them around her. He then staggered towards the hotel, which was nine miles distant, getting there about noon in a complete state of exhaustion, only just able to tell what had happened. It took another four hours for the rescue party to find the girl, and she was dead when they got to her. The husband himself was at death's door for several days, but made a full recovery, and later went on to have a distinguished career in the House of Commons.[78]

That story of a needless death was only one of many which Ben related over the years as he promoted the cause of mountain safety. With prevention as his overriding theme, he constantly reiterated the necessity for inexperienced hill walkers and others to know and abide by simple common sense rules. At the beginning of their life together a highly intelligent couple broke almost all of those rules, and paid the price.

Ben is buried in Laggantygown Cemetery, just north of Aviemore. Looking south-east from the cemetery, there is what he would have called a grand view of the Cairngorms, the same view he enjoyed from the windows of his home in Aviemore. His gravestone carries words which can scarcely be more justified, for the mostly voluntary work which he put in on behalf of mountain rescue was enormous:

He loved the hills and worked unceasingly for the safety of those who climb.

The earliest rescue post in Scotland was set up in the same year that he first tramped round Skye. As in all the different fields in which he became involved, he wrote and said a great deal about mountain rescue. Like other areas, here too his stubbornness often led him into argument, for he seldom backed away from a firmly taken position. There was little disagreement, however, over his insistence that safety must be focused around prevention. This message formed the core of the *Adventure in Safety* Exhibition which he helped co-ordinate in 1968, and might have been the subject of a further book, the possibility of which he discussed with more than one publisher during the last few years of his life. Such plans did not materialise, but a fine summary of the development of Mountain Rescue in Scotland can be presented through his published articles:

> The first attempt at a Mountain Rescue Post in Scotland was in 1929 when the Scottish Mountaineering Club built their Alpine Hut high up on Ben Nevis. It was equipped with a first aid rucksack and a stretcher. This stretcher was just a heavy iron bunk with four big detachable handles which hooked on. The theory was that the weight of the stretcher would keep the handles in position – quite all right with the stretcher in horizontal position, but this is seldom the case in mountain rescues. The writer's party had the first and only use of it in 1934 when a man broke his leg in one of the Nevis gullies. The handles constantly fell off, and the stretcher was condemned.
>
> In 1933 a Joint Stretcher Committee had been formed by the Rucksack Club and the Fell and Rock Climbing Club, charged with bringing out a report on the type of equipment which should be available for use in accidents on the hills. This led to the introduction of the Thomas Sledge Stretcher in 1936, and with improvements from time to time this became standard equipment in mountain rescue posts throughout Britain, and gave very fine service. Mountaineering Clubs were asked to raise funds for the purpose of providing and maintaining equipment at several centres throughout the country, and a wider permanent Committee called the First Aid Committee of the British Mountaineering Clubs was formed. This Committee first met in 1936, with the Scottish Mountaineering Club playing a leading role. Rescue Posts were established in Wales and the Lakeland, and in Scotland initially at Glencoe, Fort William and Glen Brittle in Skye. This First Aid Committee later changed its name to the Mountain Rescue Committee, and was registered as a charity. All gear and equipment was supplied from funds raised by

the climbing clubs, although then, as now, almost 75% of accidents were to non-members of those clubs.

Prior to the Second World War the Cairngorm Club (at Glen Derry) and the Scottish Ski Club (on Ben Ghlas in Perthshire) provided rescue equipment, but other projected sites had to be delayed with the outbreak of war. The war brought great difficulties in dealing with the few accidents which occurred, owing to petrol rationing and the fact that most climbers were on service. Appeals for help were answered by those climbers available, who had to find their way to the scene of the accident as best they could.

In the twenty-year period from 1927–47, the average number of accidents in Scotland was six per year, with two fatalities, so the problem was not a really serious one. When an accident took place the police would contact the Scottish Mountaineering Club Secretary who would call out any climbers available. I remember one such call on a Christmas Sunday at midnight, when about twenty of us got to Glencoe at first light on the Monday morning, and spent a day retrieving a body from Buachaille Etive Mor. There was no rescue training, but all of us were experienced climbers.

During the war years RAF Mountain Rescue Units were formed to deal with crashed aircraft, and fortunately for the climbing fraternity they were kept in being after the war. Nowadays air crashes are but few, and over the years the highly trained teams from Kinloss and Leuchars have rendered magnificent service when mountain accidents occurred. Mountain warfare training in Scotland introduced many to the mountains, and after the end of the war there was a tremendous increase in the numbers of young folk seeking the hills. The Association of Scottish Climbing Clubs was formed at that time and they ultimately took over the problem of rescue work in Scotland, with many new Rescue Posts being established.

With the marked increase in the numbers of climbers, accident numbers began to increase, and as more and more Rescue Posts were kitted out, it became entirely beyond the finances of the mountaineering clubs, so the Ministry of Health and the Scottish Board of Health took over responsibility for equipment, and for supplying replacements for all the official posts. At the same time individual Scottish Mountaineering Clubs were given responsibility for one or more posts, and for supplying men for rescue as required. This was good in theory, but it never really worked as the clubs are mainly based in the cities, and it took a long time to call out rescuers and get them on their way. By the time they got to the site it had often

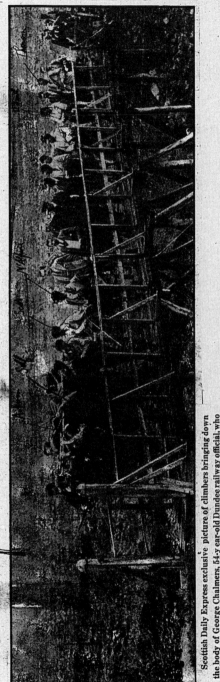

54-YEAR-OLD CLIMBER KILLED ON GLENCOE MOUNTAIN

Scottish Daily Express exclusive picture of climbers bringing down the body of George Chalmers, 54-y ear-old Dundee railway official, who fell to death over 600ft. precipice on Bidean Nan Bean, Glencoe.

Chalmers took part in rescue in January of two girls lost all night in the snow above Spittal of Glenshee. He is shown below (marked with cross) assisting as one of them was brought to safety.

FROM that excitement we returned to Fort William, heard that a climber had fallen over a cliff in Glencoe.

So followed a wild night drive round Loch Leven over a road I don't know, apparently a sanctuary for red deer, which are too big to hit with impunity.

The climber was on a spur of B.dean nan B an. With Constable JAMES McLEOD, of Ballachulish, we watched from the road the pin-point lanterns of search parties zig-zag across the huge black mass of the hill.

Five times in the two years he has been at Ballachulish he has taken part in searches for people lost in the hills around Glencoe.

WITH the dawn came tall, thin, grey-faced, dry-humoured Procurator - fiscal D A V I D STEWART, of Oban, to take charge. Came also mountaineers, men and women, from all over Scotland in cars. They pulled on their heavy boots, swung off up the hillside without talk or questioning, hurrying on the chance that their comrade might still be living.

* * *

WHILE we waited for more news a policeman borrowed a pail and washed one of the police cars. James McLeod told me ghost stories of Ballachulish—where the ghosts are so well-behaved they won't appear to policemen.

In return I told him what I could about the shinty cup final. He's a great fan, used to play regularly.

Helping in a stretcher recovery after a fatality in Glencoe in 1936. Photo from Ben's scrap book courtesy of National Library of Scotland.

RISKED LIVES FOR DEAD CLIMBER

Men Lowered Over 300 ft. Gully

Daily Herald

THE body of William Christie, the 25-years-old radio engineer who was on holiday at his home in Dunblane, was recovered late yesterday afternoon after it had been suspended for more than 24 hours over the Crowberry ridge of the 3,345-ft. Buachaille Etive Mhor, Glencoe.

Not

Climbers who had raced over treacherous roads by car throughout the night and shepherds and ghillies who had rallied to the call for help set out at dawn from Clachaig Inn and risked their lives on the treacherous icy slopes.

No!

No ice

No.!

When the body was recovered by the use of ropes from the summit, it was surmised that the victim's death must have been instantaneous, the result of his head striking a rock.

When the party returned to Kinghouse Hotel with the body graphic stories were told.

INCH BY INCH

No!

15 ft.

Ten crack mountaineers had led the way. Five went below and five others climbed to the summit.

Those above were lowered by ropes 300 ft. into the gully.

No.

Only the first to reach the dead man was Mr. J. Logan Aikman, secretary of the Mountaineering Club.

They found the body lying with the head resting on a ledge of snow and took it up by rope to the summit, from which it was lowered 300 feet below.

There it was roped to a stretcher and the difficult descent begun.

No,

"We had to thread our way inch by inch carefully along narrow rock ledges to the mouth of the gully," said Mr. Aikman to the "Daily Herald," describing how they reached the body.

"Occasionally the mist enveloped us and we had to stand in our tracks for

No mist!

10 or 15 minutes until it cleared. We made very slow progress.

"When we reached the top of the crevice one after another we went down slowly, almost a quarter of an inch at a time, as we were afraid the rope might catch on a sharp ledge.

"When we reached the foot we found Christie still in a dangling position. It seemed to us that he must have been dead at least 12 hours. We raised him carefully to the top."

Mr. Robin MacFarlane and Messrs. Ronald and Donald Reid, of Glasgow, who were with Christie on Sunday afternoon, and his brother, who had arrived that morning from Dunblane, were in the party of 30 volunteers who left the inn carrying ice axes, ropes and other equipment. They split into parties.

Mr. Christie's two brothers, who had been called to the district, met the rescuers as they brought the body down the hillside and were greatly affected.

fantastic

No!

No!

This article is absolutely full of inaccuracies. Aikman never gave such an interview as this

Typical comments by Ben on Press reporting of climbing accidents!
Photo courtesy of National Library of Scotland.

become a fatality that they had to deal with, and it was realised that only immediate or local rescue teams could save life.

I remember when Donald Duff took over as surgeon to the Belford Hospital in Fort William after the war, and climbers involved in accidents on Ben Nevis came under his care. Donald was a most experienced mountaineer, and when a call came for help he would at once lead a rescue party up the mountain. Part of police duty was the investigation of accidents, and police officers ventured high on Ben Nevis, but the then Chief Constable was reluctant to continue to send his men, poorly trained and ill-equipped, up the mountain. Better equipment was obtained, but this did not make them mountaineers, so Duff suggested he train them, and the Lochaber Mountaineering Club was formed, and subsequently the Lochaber Mountain Rescue Team, the first civilian one in Scotland. The weather in the Nevis region is very unpredictable, as witness the tragedy in Glen Nevis in November 1951 when four men died of exposure in one of the fiercest ever winter storms. Duff trained both civilians and police in mountain rescue techniques, and the result is the fine co-operation between civilian and police teams of today. He was the father figure of mountain rescue in Scotland, and also the inventor of the light weight Duff stretcher, which was widely used in Scotland and on Himalayan expeditions.

The Scottish Branch of the Mountain Rescue Committee was formed in 1962, with Donald Duff as their first chairman (the name was changed to The Mountain Rescue Committee of Scotland in June 1965). In addition to mountaineers, it included representatives from the Scottish Youth Hostels Association, the Red Cross, the Scottish Council for Physical Recreation, and Police and RAF Mountain Rescue, together with ex-officio members from the parent Committee in England. The main accident areas remained the Cuillin in Skye, Ben Nevis, Glencoe and the Cairngorms. When an accident occurred it was the duty of any climbers in the vicinity to give immediate help, further assistance then being called via the police or warden of the nearest Rescue Post.

The surge to the mountains had continued in the 1950s and 1960s and the accident rate had continued to rise. From the pre-war figures it rose to twenty per year during the fifteen-year period from 1937–1952, and more recently has been around fifty. More and more civilian rescue teams have been formed, and we now have trained teams in all the mountainous regions of Scotland, and these local teams have given outstanding service. The splendid RAF teams from Kinloss and Leuchars remain available for civilian rescue work, and in clear conditions the use of helicopters in recent years has greatly assisted the work of mountain rescue.

Glencoe was always a problem, as few folk lived in the glen, and calls often came through late on a Sunday when climbers up for the day had already headed home. But then at last Glencoe got a team of its own, formed by the almost legendary Hamish MacInnes after his climbing forays in New Zealand and the Himalayas. Hamish took over a croft in the glen, and a great burden of immediate rescue has fallen on the small team he trained. It is fitting that both he and Constable (later Sgt.) Whillans from the Glencoe team have been awarded the BEM for their services, for again and again they have saved lives under the most difficult and dangerous of conditions. Hamish has introduced search dogs for use on the mountains, where they are particularly useful in avalanche searches, and holds annual courses for the training of dogs. He has also been responsible for the invention of much new rescue gear, including a further advance in stretcher design. The MacInnes stretcher of lightweight alloy is particularly useful for work on steep crags, and can be carried up a rock face by one man.

Up till 1962 no local folk had been trained for mountain rescue in the Cairngorms. In that year, through the initiative of the Aviemore people, the Cairngorm Mountain Rescue Team came into being. Efficiently and quickly, by donations, dances, whist drives and so on, hundreds of pounds were raised and the men fully equipped with all the necessary clothing and gear. It was a very fine effort for such a small community. Since then they have had much training and have been called out on many occasions, and have to their credit a dangerous and hazardous rescue on the cliffs of Cairngorm.

As a result of a conference organised by the Mountain Rescue Committee in Edinburgh in October 1963 the first National Mountain Safety and Survival Training Course was held at Glenmore Lodge in the Cairngorms in April 1964. Now several courses of a week or more are held every year, volunteers coming from all over Britain as well as from the three Services and the police. The latter have played an increasing role in mountain rescue, and special mention must be made of Sgt. Duff in Aberdeenshire and Sgt. Smith in Ross-shire who are responsible for the police teams in their areas. However the police do not have, and never will have, the manpower to cope with all rescues. The brunt of the work remains with the voluntary civilian teams, and all of us owe them a great debt, for they have largely to raise their own funds and equip themselves. It is the searches for missing folk which cause the most trouble, as often they may be anywhere within a large area. Then hundreds of folk can be involved, police, civilian, and RAF and Army units. The vastness of the Cairngorms and the sudden violent changes of weather have made rescue work there arduous and dangerous for all involved.

Communication between rescue parties has always been a major problem. They may be spread out over a vast area. Most often searches are carried out in bad weather. Visible signs cannot be seen. Mist will hide flares, while the sound of whistles will not carry far. A major difficulty was always that the radios operating on the mountain rescue frequency were restricted to line-of-sight communication. The idea for the future is that there will be an automatic repeater station on Cairngorm relaying all messages to a low-level station, from which a whole search will be controlled.

This problem of recalling or keeping search parties in touch with each other would seem to be almost solved from the experimental work carried out by Pye Telecommunications in the Cairngorms in June 1964. "Walkie-Talkies" of course have been known for years, but until recently these radio units were bulky and heavy and not used to any great extent on the hills. Now we have bantam sets which weigh only four pounds, and they have an extensive range. The two day exercise used a control station on the summit of Cairngorm, with parties spread out over an area of fifty square miles giving their positions to control at hourly intervals. A mock accident was staged and brought to a successful conclusion with the much enhanced communication.

Although the Mountain Rescue Committee of Scotland now plays the coordinating role, it has ever been hampered by lack of funds. The Ministry of Health supplies the basic gear for Rescue Posts, but many other things fall on our Committee. We have to supply extra gear not on official lists, give grants to local teams, arrange for training and joint exercises, provide insurance for those taking part in rescues and searches (premiums for such coverage being very high), publish an official booklet annually and keep careful records of all accidents on Scottish hills. While recent grants from the Highlands and Islands Development Board and the Scottish Sports Council have been very welcome, the Mountain Rescue Committee of Great Britain remains a charitable organisation with only limited funds, subscribed and donated to mainly by Mountaineering Clubs and allied organisations. Should not this fine organisation which succours the exhausted and saves lives be regarded in the same way as the Royal National Lifeboat

Institution, and attract very much larger subscriptions from other than mountaineers? Saving lives on the hills is surely quite as important as saving lives at sea. The Government already helps by equipping the posts and making the services of the RAF teams available. Our voluntary system works well. It will continue to do so provided it continues to obtain public interest – and the public and official subscriptions it deserves and so urgently requires.

Our Committee have details of all accidents in Scotland since the 1920s. These have been carefully tabulated as to cause, and results show that 75% could have been prevented if normal precautions had been taken. Most accidents on the hills are avoidable. Since the days of Edward Whymper and the Matterhorn tragedy of 1865, the dramatic side of mountain accidents has brought them far more publicity than accidents elsewhere, and has overshadowed the prevention problem. Hence the writer suggested that concentration must be on prevention, and this led to our first Mountain Safety Exhibition held at the Palace of Art, Bellahouston Park in Glasgow in September 1968, under the theme, "Adventure in Safety".

Donald Duff, then in poor health, was an honoured guest at that Exhibition, and afterwards wrote to me urging that such good work be continued. So it was fitting that after his death the Exhibition in mobile form became a memorial to him, the Donald Duff Memorial Exhibition. We have staged major exhibitions in Edinburgh, Aberdeen and Fort William, and a goodly number of mini-exhibitions in other areas. Now we are venturing into England, and will have the full exhibit at the National Scout Camp at Gilwell in London for a reunion of 2,000 adult Scout Leaders, the very type we wish to contact. We feel that an intensive campaign over a five year period is essential with a rota of exhibitions held in all the main towns of Scotland and England, together with smaller exhibits in the climbing areas.

There are nowadays abundant opportunities for training our climbers, but not so many for hill walkers. Within a few years however, the problem of hill walkers ought not to loom so large as more and more take part in Mountain Leadership Training Schemes, such as those held at Glenmore Lodge. For these are the men and women – teachers and leaders from Youth Organisations – who will pass on their training to others, and we hope to see to it that all are aware of the essential rules of hillcraft. The present preventive work of the Mountain Rescue Committee must continue, however, and "The Powers That Be" must surely come to realise that prevention of avoidable accidents by education in the principles of mountain

Adventure in Safety

A guide to Mountain safety
with details of accident causes
and case histories of avoidable
accidents over many years
and a guide to the
Donald Duff Memorial Exhibition.

Published by
The Mountain Rescue Committee of Scotland

Donald Duff Memorial Exhibition, successor to the
Scottish Mountain Safety Exhibition, Glasgow 1968.

safety is the real solution to the problem; they must provide us with sufficient funds to carry on our work, thus saving young lives, cutting down the immense cost of rescue, and the thousands of man-hours involved by all rescuers. Let us hope that it may be so.

The *Adventure in Safety* Exhibition was planned by the Mountain Rescue Committee of Scotland, in co-operation with the Glasgow Education Authority. Ben and John Hinde were the joint organisers on behalf of the MRCS, with many other individuals and groups contributing, including members of the Scottish Mountaineering Club, the Junior Mountaineering Club of Scotland, the Glasgow Glenmore Club and Langside College, as well as Police and RAF Mountain Rescue personnel. The theme implicit in the title "Adventure in Safety" was clearly illustrated in three main halls devoted to prevention, training and demonstration, while a fourth housed a trade exhibition. A leaflet given to all who attended outlined ten brief rules of "Sense on the Scottish Hills", and also carried Edward Whymper's well-known words:

"Climb if you will, but remember that courage and strength are nought without prudence, and that a momentary negligence may destroy the happiness of a lifetime. Do nothing in haste; look well to each step; and from the beginning think what may be the end."

I attended the first day of the Exhibition at Ben's invitation, and have a very clear memory of part of the opening ceremony. Ben hovered in the background while Eric Langmuir gave a short introduction on behalf of the Mountain Rescue Committee. Giving Ben credit for being the moving force behind the Exhibition, Eric likened him to a wise old man who lived at the bottom of a high cliff, who for years had advocated a number of measures, including the erection of a fence, to prevent recurring injuries and accidents to unwary visitors – those who kept falling over the cliff despite the apparently obvious danger it posed. Ben had a quiet smile on his face as Eric was talking, and I recall suddenly realising, not only that Ben knew he was being talked about, but that he also knew what was being said – if not the exact words, then certainly their meaning. I also realised, perhaps for the first time, how little his deafness mattered in terms of what he was able to accomplish. Eric recently recalled Ben's contribution for me:

"We all did our bit, but Ben was really the conductor and composer as well, and worked mightily to get the show on the road. Those of us who were enthusiastically involved at first gradually drifted away, leaving Ben to shoulder the responsibility of managing the complex and time consuming business of a mobile exhibition (UK-wide) on his own. I think the exhibition marked the high point in a long campaign to improve awareness of mountain safety matters. There were a number of strands to that campaign: the work of Glenmore Lodge, the mountain leadership scheme and so on, but Ben's contribution was a unique solo eVort, much of it unsung and behind the scenes. The exhibition was one of the few public manifestations of his work."

Ben's contribution to safety on the hills came in many different forms. In addition to innumerable articles dealing directly or indirectly with the subject, he published many different series over the years giving succinct climbing tips. These often ran for many weeks in different Scottish newspapers, under several of his pen-names, and came under a variety of titles: "The Mountain Way", "Getting to the Top", "Peak of the Month", "The Climbing Game", "The Glory of the Bens", "Climber's Column" and "Technique of the Cragsman". They contained guidance for hill walkers and ordinary tourists, and short synopses of his rules for safety, as well as advice on technique for both novice and experienced climbers. It is impossible to guess how many were attracted by his simple style of writing, and led more safely into the climbing game as a result. In later years he also produced several invaluable maps for the hill-goer, of the Cuillin of Skye in association with Sandy Cousins, and of Glenmore and the Cairngorms from designs by Arthur Griffith.

One of his early references to safety contained two observations he repeated over and over again – on the inappropriate reporting of incidents on the hills, and the relative risks of climbing:

> If a man who had just learned to swim set off at once to swim the English Channel and was drowned he would be called a fool, with only himself to blame. Yet, when a novice, without experience, without proper equipment and showing total disregard for all normal precaution, sets off for the hills and kills himself, the affair is termed an accident to a climber. The analogy of the swimmer would be more accurate. Admittedly experienced climbers are sometimes killed, but so are experienced motorists, while experienced swimmers are sometimes drowned. Climbing is no more dangerous than any sport with an element of risk in it.

WINTER EXPERIENCE

Practice was almost as important to him as prevention, so when he was unexpectedly introduced in 1938 to a novel location which the avid rock climber could (perhaps) use for practice, he put his imagination to work in a less serious vein, and produced the following article for the *Glasgow Herald* under the title, "Alps in the Kitchen – A Cragsman Gains Winter Experience":

I had often wondered if it is possible for a cragsman to practise at home in winter-time when there is little opportunity for rock climbing. Then, not so long ago, I happened to be visiting a keen rock climber. After supper, I was sworn to silence and beckoned into the kitchen. Then I was initiated into the nightly ritual – a traverse round the kitchen walls without coming down on to the floor.

The whole scheme seemed quite impossible to me. The starting place was a small table by the window on the west wall ("a good platform belay," said the climber). Standing on the table he stretched out his left hand, opened a press door, and, with handhold on top of the door, stepped delicately onto the door handle with his left foot (avoiding a looking glass), and swung the other foot up on to the kitchen table on the north wall. In rock climber's jargon – which runs from easy through moderate, difficult, very difficult, and severe to very severe – this pitch would probably be described as of difficult standard.

The traverse along the kitchen table was easy; then he stepped up on to a narrow dresser and edged cautiously along. This had to be done very slowly, since he was almost doubled up because of the shelves above laden with heavy dishes (standard – moderate). Now came the crux of the climb, the traverse of the east wall by way of a press door and a kitchen door. While still crouching on the dresser he opened the press door wide, caught the top with his hands, and got an edge hold with the right foot on the handle. Next he swung across, caught the top of the kitchen door with one hand (being careful to avoid knocking down a clock on the wall), made a big step across and placed the left foot on the handle (standard – very difficult).

There the test reached its climax. The left foot was on the handle of the kitchen door and the right on the handle of the press door. He had almost to leap across and get the right foot on to the mantelpiece on the south wall, get a hold with his hand, and edge up cautiously, the mantelpiece being rather high (standard – very severe). The traverse along the narrow mantelpiece was not easy either, as there were no handholds above, and he had to avoid several tea caddies and china ornaments. (The standard of this pitch will vary according to the number of ornaments – perhaps, say, difficult to very difficult!) He next caught the top of the scullery door, swung his foot on to its handle, and stepped across to the starting place, the small table by the window (standard – difficult).

The whole thing had to be done without making any noise or knocking down any dishes. I managed the west wall and the kitchen table, and the dresser traverse along the north wall, but failed ingloriously on the stiff east wall. When I tried to do the swing movement with one foot on the press door and the other on the kitchen door, both doors moved simultaneously and I collapsed on the floor. Luckily, I remembered the rules and just saved myself from clutching convulsively at the clock and bringing it down on top of me. It did not seem expedient to make another attempt that night.

As time goes on the traverse becomes more difficult. One may find that a press door handle has fallen off and a key now serves as a foothold, the mantelpiece is beginning to sag, while one of the hinges on the scullery door is in a very suspicious condition . . .

Alas! My climber went to London. I received a letter telling me of the grand digs he had obtained. The next letter intimated a change of address. He had tried a traverse along the mantelpiece in his bedroom, and brought down part of the ceiling. Seemingly they do not build so substantially in the South.

Such a story appealed to Ben's sense of humour, but his message in mountain safety was a serious one, intended primarily for young people. There is still danger in the 1990s for the many hill-goers, despite the Leadership Courses in which he placed so much hope. Ever increasing numbers are on the hills each year, and the annual number of incidents has risen steadily, with 45 fatalities in 1993, the highest figures yet.[79] Some of the incidents in recent years have been associated with accidents in newer pursuits, such as para-gliding, mountain biking, and the use of all-terrain vehicles.

Whatever the cause of such tragedies, the foolish, the unwary and the uninformed still cause problems for others, and Ben's insistence that 75 per cent of accidents are preventable remains a largely valid assertion. It is appropriate, therefore, to set down in full the lecture he regularly gave to the student groups at Glenmore Lodge. Other instructors at the Lodge called it "the blood show", for it was interspersed with slides from his large collection of photographs taken at the site of hill fatalities. These were always accompanied by typical pithy comments, particularly when the unfortunate victims were other than Scots! The title was a favourite, chosen on more than one occasion to head articles describing the experiences which were gained in the early courses at the Lodge – by instructors and students alike:

EDUCATION IN ADVENTURE

For most of you this will be the first introduction to the hills, and I hope that in the future you will continue hill-going – both here and on greater peaks. It is up to you at all times to climb safely, and not to cause worry to others. In all the climbing areas in Britain the problem in the way of mountain rescue is increasing every year, and we must do everything possible to cut down the number of accidents.

In pre-war times the problem was not very great, as accidents were comparatively few. The number of climbers was limited in those days, indeed some thought it a foolhardy thing to do, and of little value. Many of us climbed a great deal, however, and the first mountain rescue I was involved in was in 1934.

When the war came, men were needed to form the spearhead of the attack for the liberation of Europe, and it was realised that the training of the mountaineer was essential. So came into being the Commandos and Mountain Warfare Training. Our own Cairngorms were one of the chosen places to begin with. The idea was essentially simple, to prepare men to go anywhere and do anything no matter what the difficulties of the ground and weather conditions, and at all times to encourage initiative and self assurance. Training was incredibly tough – the men often spent nights out on the bleak windswept plateaux, and of course without tents. You can still see the rough shelters they built on Ben Macdhui to this day.

So it came about that there was a surge to the hills after the war, and many new clubs were formed. The Scottish Council for Physical Recreation started to run training schemes here at Glenmore Lodge. Then came the successful Everest Expedition in 1953 and its world wide publicity – this caused greater interest than ever in mountaineering, and with the Duke of Edinburgh scheme schools started to play a big part. The surge to the hills continues, with new training schemes and clubs being formed every year.

Our accident statistics are clear. Look at the figures. In the twenty years to 1945, there was an average of six incidents per year, with two deaths. From 1945–1960, this had risen to average twenty incidents per year, and in the last three years thirty-five, with twelve deaths. Last year the figure had risen to forty-two, and this year (so far) to thirty, with eight deaths. This past Whitsun weekend there were six accidents.

All this has brought many problems to everyone involved in

Mountain Rescue. The trend is obvious. Mind you I don't think the accident rate now is any higher in proportion to the numbers climbing, but the press tends to dramatise mountain accidents and the general public gets the wrong idea of the climbing game.

Any worthwhile sport has an element of risk, and climbing is no more dangerous than small craft sailing, motor cycling or canoeing. A man breaks his leg in a city street – he is safe in hospital within half an hour. A man breaks his leg high up on a mountain – hundreds may be called out, and it may be twelve hours or more before he reaches hospital, and shock and exposure can supervene.

Mountain safety depends on following a few common sense and well established rules. These have been listed many times – you ought to know them all by this time, and you should all copy them into your log books from the notices here. Yet again and again fools disregard them and get into trouble. We have records of all accidents in Scotland over many years, and one fact stands out – 75% of all accidents are to non-members of Mountaineering Clubs. Hill walkers and casual scramblers are the most accident prone, hence it is wise insurance to join a club if you plan to continue. No matter where you live in Britain, there will be a climbing club in the area. Now – here are the chief causes of accidents:

1. UNSUITABLE CLOTHING AND EQUIPMENT. Warm and windproof clothing is always needed. Wet and cold are the enemies; it can be winter at any time of the year on the peaks up here and the tearing winds can be terrifying. Always carry extra clothing. It is also essential to have proper footwear and proper gloves. On tourist paths poor footwear is often responsible for many slips, producing injuries to ankles and legs, while on steeper ground more serious injury or even death can result. Remember that many of today's rubber soled shoes can slip easily on steep grass, and even more easily on wet grass. Here are some typical examples:

One day in winter my own party met three youths on Ben More in Perthshire. They were cyclists, and were in the usual riding gear, open neck shirts, shorts, sweater and jacket, with thin shoes. They had no gloves, no head gear, no ice-axes, and carried no extra clothing. Their story was that when they were well up on a snow slope one man slipped and fell some distance. His head and forearm were cut and bleeding. All were by then feeling the cold, so we saw them safely below the snow line. They had taken a chance and got off with it.

It was on the very same day that two men with somewhat similar equipment lost their lives on Cairngorm. Just a fortnight ago a party of young folk made for Ben Macdhui wearing jeans and wellington boots – just about the worst possible type of footwear for the hills. After what you have learned here, at least none of you will make that type of mistake.

I recently noticed the foot gear of a party coming from the top of the chair lift to the summit of Cairngorm – they were wearing quite a mixture: town shoes, golf shoes, gum boots, sandshoes, winkle pickers, and one lady had what seemed to be smooth soled house slippers. This in cold and snow. Like so many they gave no thought whatsoever to what conditions might be like on the summit.

2. NO KNOWLEDGE OF MAP AND COMPASS. A very frequent cause. Sometimes advice is given that when you encounter mist on the hills you should sit down and wait for it to clear. If you did that you might either starve to death or die of cold, for mist can stay on the hills for a week at a time. Mist is a normal part of our mountain scene, and everyone who goes on the hills ought to be able to travel safely through it.

And if you have a compass, you must know how to use it properly. It's no use blundering into mist and then starting to use a compass, for that means you don't know where you came from, just the point you are now starting from. Always anticipate mist and prepare a point to point route card with compass bearings. Mist on the mountains is rarely so thick that you cannot see some distance ahead, but it often destroys all sense of direction. The seasoned climber would not think of going on the hills without a map and compass.

Hills with little rock on them are the best place for training in this route finding game. Mist may lie above five hundred feet and the greater part of the mountain be unseen, yet climbers, by using their compass and interpreting the map correctly, can steer themselves to a cairn. Mistakes are more often made when the mist comes down when one is on the mountain top. The slightest change of direction at the start will make an immense difference lower down. Hence it is wise to consult the compass very carefully before leaving the known point – the cairn.

Over the last four years there have been twenty-eight parties lost, none with compasses, and all causing an immense amount of worry and trouble to others. That group on Macdhui a fortnight ago had no compass either, and search parties involving over a hundred were called out. None of you should leave Glenmore Lodge without knowing how to use map and compass.

3. SOLO HILL WALKING AND SEPARATING FROM ONE'S PARTY. Never go on your own until you have experience, and don't split up. If you are going to be lost, it is better to be lost in company. There was a classic case here years ago where two men got into an argument on the summit of a mountain as to the best way down. They separated. Both got down safely, but on opposite sides of the mountain. Both organised search parties for the other, and large parties spent all day on the hills unnecessarily. Then just a month ago a party of three separated on the summit of Cairntoul as they couldn't agree on the best route back. Two got back safely, the other was found dead next day.

4. LEAVING NO WORD OF AN INTENDED ROUTE. In such cases especially here with the vastness of the Cairngorms immense problems are caused. At Easter 1960, a couple left their car at Loch Morlich Youth Hostel. The alarm was raised the next day when they had not returned home. Kinloss and Leuchars RAF teams, police and civilians manned many search parties that afternoon and on the two following days from both the south and the north sides of the mountains. Many hundreds were involved, and searches continued every week-end until June, the bodies eventually being found in the Lairig an Laoigh area. In this case, of course, the search was almost doomed from the beginning, as the pair had omitted to take the primary precaution of leaving behind a note of their outward and homeward route. All that was known was that they had been seen at noon on the first day on the summit of Cairngorm. No one had any idea of what direction they had taken after that. It seemed that they were on a fairly regular trek – over Cairngorm to Loch Avon, and down the valley of the Avon, to return via the path over the Lairig an Laoigh, and had met with very bad conditions. Had a note been left, the search would have been directed to that area at once. After that we had letter boxes erected at the camp site and Cairngorm car park, with notices asking folk who were going on the hills to leave note of their route, approximate time of return, and bad weather alternative.

Yet even still foolish folk ignore them. On Hogmanay Saturday a hill walking party of four passed two of these boxes and ignored them. They climbed over Cairngorm to the Shelter Stone of Loch Avon, then tried to return in the dark, and lost themselves entirely. All night they wandered lost, and on the Sunday two of them came by chance on a skiers' tent high up on Cairngorm. They were helped down by the skiers, and a search party organised for the other two.

The searchers were mainly our instructors here, who were out from 10 a.m., and the two missing men were not found until 2 a.m. on Monday morning by Jim Hutchison and his group. One had collapsed and was almost buried in snow. It was the Lodge Staff that saved their lives.

5. BENIGHTMENT. A frequent cause, due to poor judgement of the time required for expeditions. It is often advisable to stay put until dawn rather than attempt to get off the hill in the dark if the ground is difficult below. Always carry a torch. Two years ago a party were benighted on the plateau, but managed to reach Sinclair Hut in the Lairig Ghru. They knew a search party would be organised by their friends, hence they left at first light and were back in time to stop search parties setting out. This group had consideration for others, but lack of this often causes us much worry, with searchers out needlessly all day. The problem of recalling search parties is not fully solved – "Walkie-Talkie" sets have been used with success at times, but communication is defeated by intervening hills. The future will surely bring improvements in this type of equipment. Flares, too, are used, but mist can defeat them. Better not to be lost at all!

One lady claimed great "experience" on Ben Nevis. She had been benighted there many times! The first problem caused to others resulted in her being escorted off a steep snow slope when seen to be equipped with an umbrella, which she claimed would be as useful as an ice-axe in stopping a slide. Several months later she was admitted to hospital in Fort William with a head injury, and the last time we heard of her she was found after spending two bitterly cold November nights in a rude shelter near the summit, which she had reached after trudging through calf-deep snow in shoes covered with plastic bags. The RAF team who found her reported the case to the Home Department. She was visited by police officials at her home in Glasgow, and warned against her activities. She promised not to climb Nevis again until the following April, but refused to buy an ice-axe.

6. SUDDEN ONSET OF BAD WEATHER. A party has to decide according to its own ability whether to press on and brave the changed conditions, or to find some temporary shelter. If your equipment is good you can ride out a storm. A rude shelter can be made on the lee side of a boulder with a wind break of stones and turf, and in winter snow holes are possible. But these are often last resources, and such a night out can never be pleasant.

7. A SIMPLE SLIP. Simple slips are the cause of a good many accidents, and can result either in slight injury, serious injury or death. It is very noticeable that almost all slips by hill walkers occur when descending. A person can often be eager to get off the mountain in failing light and apt to be careless. Rushing down scree slopes has also caused many falls. The expert can take a scree slope quickly, but the novice can so easily get into trouble. Remember what I said about correct footgear.

8. CASUAL SCRAMBLERS. Such folk can be a menace, and have often caused us much trouble. A hill walker, or even just a tourist seeking a view, sees a little crag, thinks it quite easy, and tries to scramble up. A girl did so on the Arran peaks last year, and as so often happens got stuck on a ledge – could move neither up or down – eight hours went by before a local rescue team extricated her. Two years ago a girl from a picnic party at the Green Loch of Ryvoan went up the steep area on the far side of the loch and got stuck. Her father went to bring her down, but got stuck as well, and instructors from the Lodge had to bring them both down.

Last July three well equipped walkers reported that a poorly equipped companion had gone ahead from Glen Einich towards the great cliffs of Sgoran Dubh despite their protests. The three had taken an easier route, and later reported the fourth missing. Sixty of us were out the next day from 9 a.m. to 6 p.m. in bad weather. The man was found dead. He was wearing a T-shirt, flannel slacks and sandshoes, and had fallen a great way down the cliffs. Almost every single rule of the game had been broken, but why should it take the loss of a life to drive these lessons home?

9. ROCK CLIMBING. Almost 20% of accidents occur during rock climbing, and most of these are to folks under twenty. Rock climbing is a highly specialised sport, as you will have realised after your day of it here. But that was only a beginning. The most frequent cause of an accident is of a person trying to climb beyond their standard, for which they have neither knowledge or training. A boy boasted of his rock climbing at Glencoe Youth Hostel one night and was allowed to lead on the Crowberry Ridge the next day, one of the classic British rock climbs. It was far beyond his standard. He came off and was seriously injured. I could quote you dozens of such cases. If you think of continuing in this game you should join a club, for clubs are jealous of their own reputation, and you will find leadership

there. Climb behind an experienced leader for a season. You will learn much. Then start your own leading on easier routes, before working up to the more difficult ones.

There are, of course, unavoidable accidents in rock climbing such as a hold coming away, or a boulder moving, but these are comparatively few. By far the most important thing is to be able to judge just what you yourself can do with safety. Always climb within your own powers. New rock and snow climbs of great severity are done in Scotland every year. There is no record of the experienced men who venture these coming to grief. They have served their apprenticeship, they know their job and climb safely. I have had the pleasure and privilege of climbing behind some of the finest climbers of our time, some members of the Himalayan expeditions. I cannot remember any occasion where any of them took more than a justifiable risk, but I can remember quite a few occasions where a leader has turned back.

10. WINTER AND THE USE OF AN ICE-AXE. Winter brings other problems, but also greater joys. There is nothing finer on this earth than the perfect day on the high tops in snow. But train yourself for those days first! Always have an ice-axe in winter they say, but with its three sharp points it is a lethal weapon unless you know how to use it properly.

Many fools still go on the hills in winter without ice-axes. Well, if you start to slide, there is no means at all of stopping yourself. You will slide down either until the slope eases off, or till you crash into a boulder or go over a cliff. Even if the slope does ease off, you'll be lucky to escape injury for one always tends to swing round and go down head first – to have skin stripped off one's brow or nose and chin is not at all pleasant. Some winters ago four tried to descend at the head of Coire Cas, none with ice-axes. All fell; all were injured – arm, shoulder, face and skull injuries, while one man had the skin stripped off his brow and nose, with his nose just a bloody mess. I understand his wife was very annoyed when she saw him!

Slips often occur on steep snow when one has an ice-axe. Everything depends on one's instant reaction and knowledge of how to stop oneself. It is dangerous to buy an ice-axe and go off to the high tops without first well practising its use. Here are two reports from our files.

a) A novice, first day on snow, and first day with an ice-axe, slipped high up on Ben Nevis and threw the ice-axe away. He was killed.

b) A lone climber joined a club party and descended behind them in steps they had cut. Suddenly he hurtled past them with his ice-axe swinging uselessly. He did not seem to know how to use it, and was seen to clutch at the snow with his hands. He fell a long way, and was seriously injured.

We have dozens of reports like that.

Glissading is one of the greater joys of winter climbing, but has been the cause of many deaths. Some people think that glissading is just a matter of sitting down, sliding, and chancing it. A party of five did so on the summit of Ben Nevis. All went over the cliffs and all were killed. They broke the rules, having no knowledge of how to control pace by breaking with the ice-axe, and having no knowledge of the slope in front of them. Experts can glissade down a slope where a novice could be killed. Here again it is a matter of practice. Practise on lower slopes, preferably a short slope. There was a splendid nursery slope beside the old Lodge in the old days. The greatest mistake was to build the present Reindeer House on that slope, and hence destroy the only nursery slope below tree level.

So here again are the rules: Practise on a safe lower slope until you are proficient. Even when you are proficient, never glissade down a slope you have not climbed that day. Never glissade down a slope when you cannot see the whole way to the bottom, and never glissade when there is any hint of ice. Often when the snow is very hard it is even impossible for an expert to stop, so you must gain knowledge by experience.

11. DROWNING. It may seem strange to mention this, but six men have lost their lives, including three engaged in searches for lost climbers. In each case the cause was lack of knowledge of Scottish hill streams. Two were drowned crossing the Dee near Corrour Bothy. A burn that was easily crossed in the forenoon may become transformed after a few hours of heavy rain, and suddenly be very, very dangerous. Normally one can step across the burn at Loch Avon on the way to the Shelter Stone. Last week the bivouac party had to wade across waist deep.

One midsummer day a tremendous storm blew up when I had a party on the summit of Carn Eilrig, at the junction of the Lairig Ghru and Glen Einich streams. I hustled my group down at the start of the cloudburst, and we were across the Allt Druidhe before it had time to rise. Later that day it was a raging torrent 30 yards broad. One year later a party of schoolboys with a teacher from the

Rothiemurchus Hut crossed at the same place in the forenoon, and went up Glen Einich. Very heavy rain came on and the stream was in great spate by the time they returned. The teacher tried to cross, but was swept away at once and drowned. The boys moved down stream and were trapped at the confluence of the River Einich and the Allt Druidhe. This took place at 3 p.m., but it was not until six that someone saw them and raised the alarm. The police contacted the Lodge, and Jack Thompson and Alan Cathcart went off with ropes, crossed the river and then roped them all safely across. We always carry a coil of rope on expeditions up here.

Well, there you are. You have started the climbing game. I hope many of you will keep it up, and I hope many of you will return to see these great hills in all their winter glory. The climbing game is the finest game in all the world, and provided you keep to the rules it will last as long as life itself. Climbing begets longevity, and longevity begets climbing. At the Easter Meet of my own club, the Scottish Mountaineering Club, there were fifteen over sixty, and two over seventy, yet they had a long day on the hills.

Advances in mountain rescue in recent years have largely come by way of improvements to equipment or services which Ben had seen introduced in his day; there is now vastly improved communication over long distances, as he envisaged; survival gear and clothing have been transformed; helicopter rescue services are used in responding to the majority of incidents, with Rescue Teams no longer required to justify their call out as in the past; and rescue dogs are now more widely available for help in avalanche and other searches. Seventeen years after Ben's death, however, the simple rules of safe hill walking and climbing remain the same, and in spite of all the lessons he taught – lest any think that they no longer need repeating – no better example could be given than that of the timeless story of the Belgian tourists in the Cairngorms, splendidly told by John Hinde.

In a way this incident is a reflection of Ben's career. He first read of a death on the hills on his earliest visit to the Shelter Stone of Loch Avon, in his first climbing year. He later published an account of the history of the famous shelter, mentioning it repeatedly at other times in his writing, and frequently led groups of students there on bivouac expeditions from Glenmore Lodge. Now just a few short months before his death here was a group taking refuge at the Stone, and in the process breaking all the rules he had spent the better part of his life proclaiming:

ESCAPE FROM A STONE TRAP

"It is surely time we had learned from Cairngorm accidents that these mountains are killers and that no expeditions should be lightly undertaken. It now seems that even Speysiders are lulled into unawareness by the recent months of good weather and that foreign tourists can be given misleading information.

"After weeks of blazing sunshine two wreaths of eternal snow still resisted the power of the sun, lying at the foot of rugged granite crags in a high remote corrie facing east above the headwaters of the river Dee. Now, in the first weeks of September, gale-driven snowstorms have augmented these snowfields and they will certainly last till the next hot summer. Few indeed are the years when they vanish entirely, and if the average temperature was only two degrees lower there would be great glaciers filling the higher Scottish corries.

"Similar corries surround the head of Loch Avon, a spectacular place where vertical crags impend about the water or ice of the two mile long loch, whose surface is well above the sea. Great boulders of clean hard granite, much bigger than houses, have fallen from the 800 feet cliffs and now lie in a chaotic jumble, like a giant's rockery, near the loch side.

"One of these boulders, hard to distinguish among scores of others just like it, is marked on maps as Mountain Shelter Stone. It is a natural shelter, the most famous howff in the world, a part of British folklore, and used by climbers for a hundred years. Small gaps have been filled in with stones and peat; good weather users have lined the uneven floor with heather and sheets of polythene, and many editions of the Shelter Stone visitors' book have been completed – yet at best it is a dark hole, high enough to avoid smashing your head on the single huge roof block, if you kneel down. During torrential rain a rush of water gurgles from a deep recess and keeps you awake all night as well as wetting the floor. The only advantage over a tent is that the solid block does not move in the gales – you hope!

"The Stone is just over three miles from the Cairngorm car park, which is visited by thousands of tourists throughout the year, and yet it forms a disguised trap; it shelters on the one hand, and may save your life; but to escape in bad weather means to cross the Cairngorm plateau in a bitter hurricane, or to cover more hard miles than you are capable of, to other remote places.

"Last week, Chris and Peggy – experienced capable mountaineers – were settling down for a night in the shelter, a planned visit, and they had all the paraphernalia that makes for comfort in the mountains; plenty of spare dry clothing, dehydrated foodstuffs, primus stoves, dry matches, sleeping bags, groundsheets, insulating ground mats, and all the travel gear: maps, torches, whistles, compasses, gaiters, balaclava helmets, woollen mitts, windproof suits and climbing boots.

"Their coffee was bubbling in the mess tin, their sleeping bags occupied dry places in the cave, a candle lit all but the deepest corners, all set for a cosy stay, when they were accosted by seven distressed Belgians asking directions to the Shelter Stone. They were soaked to the skin and were all wearing cotton jeans, which are absolutely taboo among mountaineers, and had committed an even unholier crime by wearing plimsolls or light street shoes. The very best equipped wore wellington boots, which have themselves caused many an accident on slippery mountainsides.

"The seven Belgians had been given a weather forecast at the Glenmore camp site, 'bright and dry', the notice read – perhaps everyone was too casual after such phenomenally dry weather. The holiday-makers had wanted a nice walk out, somewhere to spend the night, and then a nice walk back the following day. They had been directed to the Shelter Stone, 'which would take seven comfortably' – and there they were, cold and wet in the dour Scots boulder heap, with no sign of the comfortable Alpine style hut they had been used to, and which they had been expecting, perhaps with a drying fire and a friendly warden.

"They were all in their mid-twenties, three girls and four men, close friends who had shared several holidays together. One couple, a doctor and his wife, just about to celebrate their first wedding anniversary, should have known all about accidental hypothermia, or the dangers of cold, wet exposure which every year causes deaths in European slums as well as on bleak Scottish mountains – mountains that appear insignificant on the maps, only 1,200 metres high, but which can be as Arctic as the Alaska Range.

"The tourists all crawled into the dark howff and draped their wet shrouds of pathetically light clothing around the rock walls, sharing their largely unsuitable sleeping bags. The cave, cold as a tomb, was now jammed full of people, and there was no way to avoid the wet places. All the spare clothes they had were things like Bermuda shorts. For their evening meal, which should have been hot soups and stews with plenty of sweet biscuits, cheese and hot tea, they ate hard boiled eggs, bread and jam and dry biscuits. Each one had canned beer – a useless waste of weight because there is mostly too much water for the asking.

"So they spent a comfortless and restive night, discussing their plight, with the leak spouting like a tap and the snow piling up at the entrance, one of the worst nights of the year covering all the boulders in three feet drifts with wet snow blown down off the high plateaux. In the morning the Belgians had half a boiled egg each for breakfast, left over from the previous night, with corn flakes, apples and jam. Chris and Peggy gave them hot drinks, because they had no stoves of their own.

"They left the Shelter Stone at ten in the morning to cross to the Cairngorm car park by Coire Raibeirt, a steep funnel in its lower stretches, prone to avalanches after new snow. Four hours later they had covered just over a mile and climbed just over 1,000 feet, and they were in real distress. They were at 3,500 feet on the Cairngorm plateau with the gale force wind blowing into their faces, snow falling, and visibility down to zero intermittently, real 'white out' conditions. The weakest man had collapsed. He had been dragged along for a few yards with his head flopped and feet trailing in the snow, but could obviously go no further.

"Chris and Peggy would have been all right without the Belgians. They could have done the whole journey in two or three hours, and they had not wanted the responsibility of escorting seven strangers through the boulder drifts, but they had been appealed to for help and were now regarded as guides. Their dependants had followed as best they could, but one of the girls shed a tennis shoe, which only was found after a search in the snow deep in a crevice. Another had a light plastic jacket torn apart by the gale. It had the makings of a tragedy which was only averted by the prompt actions of local rescuers.

"The collapsed man was left behind with the doctor and one other, these two being the strongest men. A scoopshelter was gouged in the snow for them, and they were protected from the wind with rucksacks, sleeping bags and a groundsheet wrapped around them. The girls and the other man carried on – only 500 yards to go to the plateau edge and the descent down to the broad ridge known as the Fiacaill of Coire Cas, tacking into the wind first one way and then the other. The lucky ones had hoods pulled across their faces to protect them from the driving snow, but they had no gloves and had lost all feeling in their hands and feet. They were wet and very cold, with blisters like those of 'immersion foot' beginning on their limbs.

"Chris was ahead, guiding them north-west on a compass bearing, but the other man had almost given up. He could see nothing at all and kept throwing back his head and staggering. The girls were magnificent. Two were in the middle of the group helping themselves, but Peggy and the doctor's wife supported the half blinded man, half carrying him, half dragging him, and constantly encouraging him. It was in truth a feminist triumph. Often we have heard that women survive better than men, and this seemed further proof, but of course the women were lighter and smaller, and proportionally they had probably had more to eat than the males.

"Throughout the Belgians had tried to help each other. It was true that none had wanted to be left behind, and there was the constant urge to keep pressing on, especially the women, but never did they deteriorate so badly that it was a question of every man, or woman, for himself. They finally got there. At 3,300 feet they were at last below the cloud base, with Coire Cas clear below them. It was still very hard work, but they made it to the car park, with a uniformed policeman helping them for the last few hundred yards.

"Chris had gone right down once they were in the clear to alert the rescue services. For the women the last bit was something of an anticlimax; they had been fighting for seven hours, and now escape for them was certain, but they still had the anxiety, particularly the doctor's wife, for their three men left on the plateau.

"Rescue was efficient and speedy, and has been reported elsewhere. A helicopter could not get right to the bivouac because of the bad conditions, but it helped in transporting rescuers, as did a snow vehicle. All three men were carried down that same night, not a lot worse for their cold exposure. The whole party were dried out and fed at Glenmore Lodge, with hot baths and a night's lodging. Afterwards, comfortable and warm, they gave Peggy and Chris a warm ovation, regarding them as saviours. They must have learned a lesson from their 'pleasant walk'.

"It is easy now to look back and say what should have been done, but the Belgians were indeed fortunate that a capable couple had planned to spend that particular night at the bleak Shelter Stone, beside the gloomy Loch Avon, with towering crags beetling in the snow storms."

Ben's published articles make no mention of his own role in the evolution of the Mountain Rescue Committee of Scotland, and only by inference of much other work on behalf of Mountain Rescue.[80] I am grateful to Bill Murray for the following brief summary of these contributions:

"The lasting value of his contribution in this area, publicly recognised by the award of the MBE in 1971, stemmed firstly from his long and persistent fight during the 1960s to maintain the independence of the Mountain Rescue Committee of Scotland as a voluntary body. This campaign, of paramount importance in itself, was complemented by the written record of mountain accidents which he culled annually from the rescue teams for some twenty years, adding to the details he had uncovered from as far back as 1925. His dedicated work has been the foundation of

Outside Buckingham Palace, 1971.

so much which has followed in accident prevention and mountain safety."[81]

Not the least remarkable aspect of Ben's life is the fact that in every one of the totally different fields in which he became involved his opinions have always been reinforced by time; this is evident particularly since he never hesitated to commit his views to paper. The pattern remained the same even down to his very last communications, which concerned the use of the ice-axe. His final words on the subject were published in the letters to the editor section of the *Glasgow Herald* on the day of his death, and in the *Scotsman* on the day of his funeral. They differed only slightly, hammered out along with many others on his ancient typewriter at Feithlinn during the penultimate active day of his life:

> Sir, – Possession of an ice-axe when climbing the hills in winter does not necessarily mean safety. Indeed it becomes a liability if one does not know how to use it.
>
> The Mountain Rescue Committee of Scotland keeps very careful records of all accidents in Scotland, and records over many years show clearly that the main cause of winter accidents is slips on snow slopes, snow ice, or ice, and inability to control such.
>
> There were three successive accidents in the same area. One wore vibrams, one wore nailed boots, and one wore crampons. All had ice-axes. When the slip took place the end result was the same. All three were killed.
>
> Slips can be controlled according to one's instant reaction and proper use of an ice-axe. The Mountaineering Council for Scotland arranges from time to time weekend training courses for members of clubs and others in the use of ice-axe and crampons, but far too many carry ice-axes with no idea of how to use them. Complete records for 1976 show that almost all winter accidents to hill walkers in snow involved ice-axes. This was also the case, though to a much lesser extent, among climbers.
>
> Our Committee again and again repeat the rule laid down many years ago by the American Alpine Club that all who seek the mountains in winter, and particularly beginners, should have had at the beginning of each winter season one or more days' training under skilled instruction on the proper use of the ice-axe on safe lower slopes before going high. Were this followed out in Scotland there would be a much lower accident and fatality rate on our hills.

One does not have to look far for confirmation from today's statistics on that oft-repeated advice. In a report on trends in Mountain Rescue in Scotland presented in 1991, John Hinde noted that by the end of the first six weeks of that year there had already been 25 per cent of the highest previous annual total of Scottish Mountain fatalities, adding also that "at first glance it seems that the major cause has been poor ice-axe braking on hard snow."

10

THE FINAL YEARS

FEITHLINN

The River Spey is recognised as one of the fastest running rivers in Scotland. Ben chose a plot running down towards the Spey for his Aviemore home, with a clear outlook towards the Cairngorms, and named the house Feithlinn, from the Gaelic *Feith* or *Feithe* (a bog, or slowly moving stream) and *Linn* or *Linne* (a pool). Investigating the appropriateness of that choice recently, I found shoulder high nettles barring the way towards the river from the bottom of his old garden, but later came across the direct path along the bank from the south end of Dalfaber Road, through masses of wild lupins and brooms. Not too far from the lower fence of Feithlinn is a backward pool in the river, largely bypassed by the main flow, where you can look directly up towards the Lairig Ghru. Here Ben must have found the name for his house.

During the course of its construction in 1970 he managed to drive the builders quite round the bend, along with anyone else whom he could get involved. Sandy Lindsay, the brother of the Cairngorm Amazon, was ruthlessly roped in as an unofficial Clerk of Works, and held accountable for all manner of things. The house turned out more or less as planned, but the door of the garage, with its concrete weight and pulley mechanism, proved a disaster from the start. Possibly it remains so today.

Being resident in Aviemore allowed him the opportunity to spend even more time at Glenmore Lodge, and he used every excuse to go there to work on his garden and catch up on all the gossip, either from the Lodge staff or from Sandy and Morag Lindsay at their nearby store. A chat at Geordie Paterson's shop at the Dalfaber Road end of the village also became a daily ritual. Just as suddenly as he would drop in, he would be gone again, the constant need for communication temporarily satisfied.

Before long Feithlinn boasted a fine rock garden, many of the heathers and alpine plants propagated in his own nursery bed, others brought by friends. The large living room window gave a panoramic view of the mountains, and a striking enlargement of his favourite photograph, *Sunset from A'Cioch*, dominated one wall. There were an astonishing number of visitors to the house. In the seven years he lived there more than seven hundred names were entered in the Visitors' Book, representing twenty different nationalities – climbers, hill walkers, runners, foreign visitors, former students from Glenmore Lodge (now with their spouses and children), family members and friends. "I do like to have a crowd around the house," he wrote in one letter, delighted at last in being able to repay the hospitality he had received from others in previous years.

I stayed there on visits home from Canada on a number of occasions, often without a car, and had the chance to re-acquaint myself with Ben's habits as a driver. All found this something of an experience. Many of his friends referred to the topic in their letters to me, for it was not easily forgotten. Some of the memories are worthy of a temporary digression, even at this late stage in his story, since his response in this area was no different from any other aspect of life – always distinct unto himself.

Because he could not hear the engine, he was never quite certain a car was actually running. His simple solution was to rev it furiously until the vibrations were obvious, and in practice this resulted in the noisiest imaginable start, the vehicle shaking as if in protest. Gear changes were something which had to be felt, and the rules of the road were at times adapted for his own purposes. One climbing acquaintance told me of catching up with Ben in the early morning on the way north. His car was weaving from side to side across the road as he drank in the view of each successive and familiar peak, quite oblivious to the possibility that others might need to share his road. Sandy Lindsay remembered Ben's solution to an unexpected impasse caused by raised pavements and road divisions – the car was simply re-directed over any offending obstruction and the journey happily resumed. He also recalled the amusing story of an occasion in Glasgow when Ben had his car stolen. Shortly after its disappearance, while he was a passenger on the top deck of a tram, he spotted the vehicle being driven alongside. He gave one of his great roars, and frantically charged down the stairs in an effort to get *both* drivers to stop, temporarily reducing the occupants of the tram to a state of complete turmoil! Another incident found him involved in a damaging car accident. As could happen under these circumstances, his speech became very loud, and his behaviour so bizarre that the police took him away for further questioning under suspicion of impaired driving. Only later when he had quietened down was the real situation understood. His driving licence was brought into question at that time; it was only retained, I seem to remember, with the help of some string pulling on my father's part.

We spent part of two family holidays at Feithlinn during his final years, although never for long enough to satisfy him. He was constantly planning travels abroad, with Canada, the USA, Australia, the Cayman Islands, Rhodesia, South Africa and Kenya all being considered at one time or another. Latterly his plans tended to alter from one month to the next, and only two trips finally materialised, first to Canada in 1973, and then to Kenya the following year.

In a way the Canadian holiday was an extension of his life at home, for it simply meant reunions in different locations with old friends and younger members of the family – something he always greatly enjoyed. I have two lasting memories from that visit. One of him at Sicamous, in central British Columbia, his head covered by a knotted handkerchief in the tremendous heat – "My . . . this is the hottest ever!" he said. And then of his excitement about the opportunity to meet and talk at our house in Edmonton with Dr Bill Taylor, Norman Collie's biographer. "A grand party!" he told me. The familiar expression which accompanied both of these short comments gave them their intended full meaning.

Diane Standring accompanied Ben on both overseas holidays. Not long after his death she set down these recollections:

SAFARI TO KENYA

"Travelling with Ben wasn't always easy. He was almost seventy in those days, his stamina and constant curiosity the things I remember most. Perhaps because of his hearing difficulties he was continually fussed and worried about departure times, passports, luggage and the like; nothing had to be left to chance. On both trips we carried rucksacks, Ben humping an old Army bergan and a lightweight case, with one of his famous battered tweed hats perched on his head. In airport lounges, once it was clear that we had plenty of time before leaving, he would relax and start passing comments to other travellers, usually witty, but as per normal loud enough for everyone around to hear, and followed by his loud cackle. The totally alien African environment in Kenya didn't bother him a bit. We had to use buses to save money. They were always jam packed with locals, and boiling hot inside. Ben didn't bat an eyelid, just grinned and took it all with excellent humour. We stayed on the outskirts of Nairobi at the Club House of the Mountain Club of Kenya. He had to sleep on the floor, and there were minimal washing facilities, but he never moaned.

"There were several highlights on that holiday. A day trip to Lake Naivasha to see the massed flamingos. He was thrilled by that. Then we were fortunate to be invited to join a group on a weekend camp on the

Aberdares. High up on the plateau, cool in the mornings, exploring the bush by day, and sitting round a campfire at night – it was super and he did enjoy it. We went to visit his nephew Graham, who was managing a tea plantation up country, and stayed there for a few days. I was interested in bird watching and Ben entertained himself wandering around the estate watching what was going on, always asking the African workers questions. Then we packed into a Volkswagen Beetle and had a long drive to Lake Rudolf. Graham kept Ben on edge by telling him about some locals who had been arrested by Ugandan police, as we had to cross the border at one point. He coped well with the heat and the dust on the journey and was very impressed by Graham's driving on the frightful roads.

"After that journey, the coast at Mombasa was the other memorable time. For the few days we were there he thrived on the ease of living: having tea brought in the morning, and superb meals; being able to lie out under a palm tree and look at the endless beach; and floating about in the swimming pool – he wasn't keen on the sea because of his ears; best of all, long walks on the beach before the coming of the sudden darkness, with the sky all colours. My main memory of Ben in Kenya is of his great interest in everything, and his lively sense of humour. One day near the end he took the bus into Nairobi as he wanted to do some last minute shopping before returning home. He came back with some excellent batiks and carvings at much better prices than most of us would have paid, and he knew it – his deafness was no bar to his ability to bargain with the Indian traders."

". . . This has been the grandest holiday ever," Ben scribbled in his diary at that time . . . "Diane has many old friends here who have helped, and as a result I have seen much more of Kenya than any normal visitor. We stayed for almost a week with Graham at Kericho, and then had a wonderful few days at the Fishing Camp at Elyre Spring at Lake Rudolf in the Northern Frontier Region. Graham did wonderfully well getting the little VW there and back on the horrendous roads. His was the only private car, all others flew in. We slept out under palm trees."

I asked my brother about his own memories of Ben's visit to Kenya in 1974:

"The highlight for Ben was undoubtedly the safari to Lake Rudolf. He enjoyed every minute, and was very impressed by the fact that we were the only people there who had come by car. It took about eight hours hard driving to get from Kitale to the Lake. Because of the

A day on the Scottish hills. Photo: Diane Standring.

On safari in Kenya, 1974. Photo: Diane Standring.

possibility of having to spend a night on the way we had to carry some basic camping equipment and enough petrol for the round trip, so it was quite a squeeze – an unexpected rain storm up in the hills could turn an almost dry river bed into a raging torrent, with then nothing to do but wait for the water to go down. In those days the road went through Uganda for about thirty miles, so one had to be prepared for Idi Amin's none too sober soldiers pushing the wrong end of a rifle through a front window. Ben was very taken with the little Volkswagen's performance over the bad roads. 'What a road, what a road . . . aaaaaah!' he said as we went down two horrific escarpments, and he was amazed by the way the VW was able to 'sledge' over the loose sand where a normal vehicle would dig in its differential and get stuck. Apart from one puncture we had no serious problems. As my friend Alistair Burn was a part owner of the Lodge at that time we had free accommodation in the best cottages, just paying for food and drink, but Ben would have none of that, and insisted on camping out – a howff at Lake Rudolph, I suppose! We stayed one night at Kitale in both directions, Ben and Diane thought it a super place ('no wonder I enjoyed my five years there,' they said). Afterwards I put them on the Peugeot taxi for Nairobi, and they went down to the coast from there."

LETTERS FROM FEITHLINN

During the years he lived in Feithlinn, Ben wrote me more than thirty letters, the frequency increasing markedly towards the end. The letters reflect his extraordinarily busy life of constant travel, involvement and organisation. If he wasn't occupied with exhibitions, committees, and courses, or writing to all and sundry, he was busy with his heathers and alpine plants. Failing that, he would usually be trying to organise other people into schemes which he devised. Only latterly did he begin to run out of steam.

Shortly after the Kenya holiday a note of concern about the future started to appear in the letters. Camouflaged at first by talk of other things, by 1976 it was obvious that he was suffering from a severe depression, the main problem of loneliness compounded by his inability to look after himself when on his own. Yet through all of this he remained involved in many affairs, as extracts from some of the letters show:

June 1974:
  . . . Had a grand party here last weekend of Presidents and ex-Presidents of SMC. I am very busy with helping edit a new edition

of the Guide to Glenmore Forest Park – about 6,000 words of typing which gets me down a bit, but quite well paid and they are taking eight of my photos – hope to get this job finished this month but it keeps me indoors in this fine weather.

Inflation still continuing and today's news worse than ever. Heaven knows when it will all stop – my capital almost halved. I have lost my job at the garden up the mountain. They have given it to someone else, and I miss that as it meant free lunches and free use of the chair lift etc.

. . . I don't look forward to the winter here now . . . Had the Cairngorm Hill Race on my hands last Saturday. As the founder I had to start the race, and later present the prizes. Winner went up and down in 1 hour 13 minutes (ten miles and 3,000 feet of ascent and descent).

Ben had retained his interest in running from his early days as a Dumbarton Harrier, when he was noted primarily for his stubborn stamina. Hill races gave him great pleasure, and he frequently became involved as an organiser. Ian MacPhail recalled that their friendship had begun at a cross-country race on Hamilton Racecourse in the late 1920s. After finishing around 120th, Ian stood watching the remainder of the field of 200 runners complete the course, and recognised the very last of all to finish as the already balding Ben Humble. More than forty years later they were present together at the 1970 Commonwealth Games in Edinburgh, where Ben was tremendously excited by the victory of Vale of Leven runner Lachie Stewart in the 10,000 metres.

October 1974:

Just completing a week at the Lodge. Very hard work with an enormous amount of weeding at garden . . . Last Sunday we lifted five Army youths from 3,000 feet by helicopter – one ill and others all suffering from exhaustion and exposure. Far too much of this sort of thing with Army exercises up the mountains – lads often unfit, try to do too much, and with no proper gear. I can now say I have climbed with the first Britisher to get to the summit of Everest, Dougal Haston, and also with other members of the expedition – Peter Boardman, Allen Fyffe and Hamish MacInnes. A pity tragedy marred their very fine effort. This will be the only year in twenty-five I have not even been to summit of Cairngorm – can't manage uphill now unless very slowly.

October 1974 (2):

. . . I was lecturing at Heriot-Watt University in Edinburgh last week, and go again to Edinburgh University this Thursday, overnight

there, then to Melrose next day where we are having the first of our
District Training Mountain Rescue Meets which will take in all teams
in South of Scotland, plus Leuchars RAF, dogs and helicopters –
this will last till Sunday night, then the big ten-day Rescue course
at Lodge. We'll have police and men from all three services with
teams from all over Britain, so I hope to get up in a helicopter again
– far better than a plane! Every student has to be winched up. We
did not get proper insurance for them last year but negotiating for
it now.

Have just received invitation to give main toast to guests at the
annual dinner of the SMC in Edinburgh 30th November, where we
will have men from all the main clubs in Britain. I may be in Edinburgh quite a lot in December keeping an eye on the designer of
the new Mountain Safety Exhibition. He is taking far too long to
do the job, and I want to fix dates for next year as we have requests
for it from all over Britain.

February 1975:
Had a bad fall at home a few weeks ago, two ribs broken – all
my own fault, crashed down unexpectedly five feet. Bruising down
all left side, cuts etc. Managed to rest and write most of the time
while recovering. Then had to go to Glasgow. Civic Authorities in
Glasgow, police and Scottish Film Council wanted to see the Civil
Defence films I made in Glasgow from 1941–1944 as had transpired
these are the only filmed records of Glasgow at that time. I last saw
them in 1944. I got something like VIP treatment, all expenses paid,
Assistant Chief with big police car met me at the station and took
me to the studio. Quite a crowd, police and other officials, director
of Film Council, City Archivist and so on. Two hour show . . . What
a different Glasgow with big water tanks and shelters in George
Square – exciting scenes of rescuing from a three storey tottering
blitzed building. They think they may use them in the forthcoming
800th centenary of the granting of Burgh Charter to Glasgow – all
voluntary work on my part and I provided all my own gear!

December 1975:
Next year may be my last summer here. I simply can't stay on
alone and don't know what I can do. The garden will go to rack
and ruin. Feeding and cooking the main problem when alone, yet
I don't want to give up. A pity I sold the wee cottage at Arrochar
then I could have sold here and moved back, and a shame if I had
to give up as I have found an outlet for my heather blooms. Small

sprays of white heather with tartan ribbon in small cellophane envelopes. Made twenty at end of the season, and they sold at once at Visitor Centre. Planning pressed heather on cards, could make much cash out of this next summer.

Would put up cash for you all to come over again next year, and Bob and Aileen from Toronto. My chief joy is of having others stay here with me – it means a lot to me.

February 1976:

It has not been a happy winter for me as I am so very doubtful about the future. Health a worry, may have to go down to London for full medical investigation, but perhaps not till May.

March 1976:

Had fine time at London Dunbartonshire dinner. Ian MacPhail was main speaker, got a great reception. I was asked to speak also at last minute, and did so briefly. London is far too expensive. Charged me 75p for a haircut and I said they must have included a search fee!

Have examination arranged for London hospital in early May, then have to be back here to speak at Royal Medical Commission for Prevention of Accidents. Twenty-four speakers on all aspects of the outdoors. I will be giving presentation on hill walking and general joys of being on the hills in safety.

April 1976:

How I can manage here now I just don't know. Can't cook. Find the future very bleak and can't settle to anything. I am not feeling at all well. Have lost all appetite, really don't know what to do. Have five articles commissioned, but no concentration and have not been able to settle to any of them. Also now a chance of book on history of Mountain Rescue, and a smaller monograph of 15,000 words on heathers, but must have peace of mind before I get down to them.

May 1976:

Can't see any prospect of staying on here alone in the future and can't afford the wages of a full time house keeper. Now no sleep without drugs. Am eating very little. Never feel well when no one else in the house, as so many things may happen which I don't hear of. When engagements pending have to wait up most of night if possible so I won't sleep through the time. I will advertise and see if I can get a part time person . . . so not looking forward to next winter particularly. Only pleasure when visitors here. The garden is beginning to go to ruin as I can't cope with it.

August 1976:

This has been a most difficult summer for me. Quite impossible for me to run the house and big garden on my own. If you can make it over next summer may try and hang on. Not so bad in June and July when I had quite a few visitors. But now again loneliness and cooking problem. Very lethargic during the day and nights always the worst. Thought of Old Folks Home but that would finish me off . . . Finest summer weather ever here, all village packed, but mine the only empty house. Doubt if I will be still alive for the Commonwealth Games in Edmonton.

September 1976:

Travel south Friday for full examination and small operation at St Mark's . . . Will be OK when I get back as I go to the Lodge for a fortnight and will be well fed. Doctor says trouble is mainly dietary and that I can't stay on alone, but still no word of any possible help. I dread the winter. A pity, too, as I have at last found a market for the heather as I told you last year. Sold over 300 in two and a half weeks. More or less an order for 1,000 if I can get them early for next year.

I am counting on you to come over at once if anything should happen to me and help clear things up. Some friends again advising an Old Folks Home, but that would be a living death for me . . .

Many friends rallied around during the last winter of 1976. Some stayed at Feithlinn for short periods, others gave him meals. When the house was full, all was well, but he felt totally isolated on his own, and was constantly worried about his inability to arrange any kind of domestic help, despite advertising and following up on many possibilities.

January 1977:

Had my usual party on January 3rd. At one point I asked a lad to count how many in the dinette and kitchen, and he counted twenty-seven, while there would have been more than that in the lounge. Two Everesters here as last time, and though I laid on a lot of beer and whisky I finished with more when they left!

March 1977:

Still very depressed about the future. Most certainly I will not be able to stand another winter here alone, even this summer looks as though I'll have few visitors compared to last year.

A few weeks at Glenmore Lodge towards the end of March provided a tremendous tonic; there he was nearer the mountains, and fully occupied by his garden. Somehow aware that he was running out of time, he returned to Feithlinn and launched himself into a last frenetic burst of activity.

April 1977:

Just back from six weeks at Glenmore Lodge. Finest Easter weekend ever with perfect snow cover, and they say 10,000 folk were in the Cairngorms. A very curious thing happened when I got back home. I got the writing bug again, although I have not written at that pace for ten years. Typed 17,000 words in one go from 2 p.m. till 3 a.m., then 9 a.m. till 2 p.m. next day, all at great speed with hopeless typing. It's strange how when one gets started memories come back from the subconscious mind, memories from my childhood – the whole story of Bellfield and my father's way with the Forge. Actually the story is in a way about the family name of Humble. Many folk have written me with details. You'll be glad to know you are descended from a Baron Humble created by Charles II! Synopsis now gone to publishers in London. I have a copy here which you will get some time.

Have meeting of Mountain Rescue Committee at Loch Eil on Sunday, then I go to London Monday to follow up on all leads *re* new book. Have to be at Ministry of Defence, *The Times, Daily Mirror*, Middle Temple, publishers and many others. All this grew up within the last few days. Today letters to *Scotsman, Glasgow Herald, Mirror, Times*, and long, long stuff for Ministry of Defence. I've been typing continuously since noon so time to stop as now about 10 p.m.

Best wishes,
Bennie.

Ben suffered a sudden stroke the following morning, while working at his typewriter on a letter of resignation from his position of Accident Recorder of the Mountain Rescue Committee. He did not regain consciousness, and died in hospital in Grantown-on-Spey two days later. His last letter reached me in Edmonton just as I had completed my final arrangements to fly to Scotland for his funeral. I still recall the strange sensation of seeing, and then opening, that totally unexpected envelope with its familiar handwriting. This time there was no trace of depression, only enthusiasm for his final project.

MEMORIES

When we began the task of clearing up the contents of Feithlinn in the days following the funeral, my Uncle John [82] and I were quite unprepared for what we were to find. Nothing of any apparent consequence in Ben's life had ever been discarded. We discovered first the letters to his parents from Skye, so pivotal to the understanding of his life, and then the American letters from his father which held further important keys to his character. Unmarked envelopes yielded mementoes of the two sorrows from his childhood, the deaths of his brothers: a lock of George's hair and his birth certificate, and all of Bobbie's letters from World War I. From his youth, too, came report cards from Glasgow High School, and three speeches given to the Academical Debating Club of Dumbarton in the early 1920s, the motions debated illustrating once again how little things change with the passage of time.

Every cupboard was packed to the roof with files and boxes containing accepted and rejected manuscripts from as far back as 1930, together with many professional papers and voluminous correspondence on all manner of topics. Three large scrap-books held every single published article,[83] every review of each of his books, every letter to a newspaper and periodical, everything he had written outwith his books, in fact, in more than half a century. Only in later years were the newspaper cuttings loose and unentered into the scrap-books, with articles published in the 1960s and 1970s still in the magazines or journals where they had appeared, the habits of a lifetime finally slowing down.

It was natural that much concerned his climbing world. Aside from a large collection of books, and his own countless publications, we came across box upon box of transparencies and photographs, with negatives even from the earliest hill walking days. Alongside lay stacks of papers and records on mountain rescue, his handwritten summary of fatalities on Scottish hills from 1925–1945 being of particular archival importance. The entries in faithfully kept climbing diaries [84] gave clear reflections of his personality, while another enormous scrap-book provided further evidence – if any were required – of a capacity for constant enquiry and record keeping. Containing clippings of press reports of mountain accidents on the Scottish hills,[85] this personal archive had been started in the early 1930s. Handwritten comments and exclamations covered almost every page, a scathing commentary on four decades of unreliable and unduly dramatised reporting which Ben considered almost always counter-productive to the work of those involved in rescue.

I did not realise the significance of one special treasure of Feithlinn until many years later. This was a small black notebook, entitled "Scraps of Verse – Frivolous and Serious", into which a young Ben had entered nearly ninety verses or maxims. Despite the title, the quotations were almost exclusively serious, taken from a wide range of literary sources including St Augustine, the Sanskrit, Plato, Shakespeare, Wordsworth, Shelley, Galsworthy, Robert and Elizabeth Barrett Browning, Lincoln, Disraeli, Stevenson, Burns and the Rubaiyat of Omar Khayyam. Other lines came from less well-known and anonymous authors, one brief verse holding special meaning from his schooldays.[86] Most related to life and work, or to character and friendship; significantly, the first entry was the poem *Work*, by Henry Van Dyke, a one word personal maxim.

As we worked our way gradually through the house, Ben's life began to come alive, taking us back in turn to each of his six great loves: to Tayvallich first, then Bellfield and the Dumbarton of his childhood, Skye and the Cuillin, Arrochar and the Cobbler, the Cairngorms, and finally the Alpine garden at Glenmore Lodge. The picture was completed by the remarkable output of the final few days, the biographical notes in which he preserved in outline his own story and that of his father and seven brothers, a narrative made all the more fascinating by the inclusion of recollections about many prominent people with whom the family had been associated. Three possible titles headed the final manuscript: "*I, Benjamin, A Victorian Autocrat, or A Victorian Socialist or similar.*" The typing could only be described as appalling, as he warned both John and me in separate letters, but it proved possible to put the twelve closely typed sheets together into the sequence which forms the heart of this book. A single page, sadly, was missing, leaving a tantalising reference to an important old memory of his father incomplete.[87]

One arresting sentence bore no relation to the family history, but provided further evidence that he *knew* he had not long to live. He talked to me briefly about this feeling on one occasion, and mentioned it repeatedly in the letters of the last year. While such thoughts can be related to depression, remarks made at a time when his outlook was entirely positive are less readily explained. "I have not much time left," he told Hamish MacInnes in one of his last letters, and then – a matter of hours away from a catastrophic stroke – he hurriedly interrupted the typing flow of his notes to insert these words. *"It is now 3 a.m. In case I am unable to finish this, I had better say now who else comes into my story."* One can only speculate, on the seventh son again, perhaps, since his doctor confirmed that apart from depression, to which his death was unrelated, he had not been under treatment for any kind of life-threatening illness . . .

The story of *I, Benjamin* leaves still other lingering questions. In sending me their recollections, many friends echoed Bill Murray's sense of wonder at Ben's constant industry:

". . . a vast amount of his time and energy went to voluntary interests, mostly profitless in money-terms, and far beyond what ordinary and other mortals could possibly sustain."

While this characteristic undoubtedly derived from his father's Victorian work ethic, and the drive for communication and involvement from his deafness, there may have been another dimension, brought out best through the words of someone who understood the hills equally well. Frank Smythe ended the preface to his book *The Spirit of the Hills* [88] as follows:

". . . the hills have a power for drawing out the best that is within us; on them we are given a full measure of happiness."

If those words ever applied to anyone, they surely applied to Ben. Smythe then went on in a later chapter to describe how he had discovered the true meaning of silence while climbing alone as a youth – the silence of high mountains in winter:

"The ear strains itself, but there is nothing to be heard. There is silence, not an awful silence or a silence of foreboding, but a silence that is the perfect negation of noise, something absolute, something detached from all human emotion. Those who dwell in the cities and never experience silence, although they imagine that they do, will be amazed by it. So profound is it that at first it seems to weigh too heavily on the senses, but very soon it will be accepted, not as something extraordinary, but as something natural, compared to which all man made sound is artificial."

Reading the closing lines of "The Deaf Can Hear" again in this different context, remembering that the enormity of Ben's silence excluded even the sounds of progress, one begins to realise how close he may have come to the feeling of ecstasy noted in a long-forgotten review of *Tramping in Skye*. Were the hills the ultimate source of both his physical and mental energy? If so, then looking back now at all of his life, rather than a handicap, did he not have the advantage?

> The hill-goer's memories are many and varied, and can never fade: of winter climbing when in the morning the tops are bathed in the rose flush of dawn; of the climb and maybe the hearty labour of step cutting; of gaining the summit and gazing around on a sea of

snow capped peaks sparkling in brilliant sunshine; of the descent and the exhilaration of the long glissade. Memories too of wild stormy days and the fierce joy of battle through the wind, rain, and the mist, and of perfect summer days and bivouacs high up on the mountains.

And the sunsets! After a long day on the hills there comes a pleasing sense of well-being and fitness, and the hill-goer appreciates the more those glorious West Highland sunsets. The lovely peaceful sunsets over Jura from the hills of Knapdale, the stormy sunsets over the mountains of Rum from Mallaig, and above all, the sunsets in Eilean a' Cheò. To see the mighty steel blue range of the Cuillin, splintered peaks against a crimson sky, is unutterably splendid.

These are just a few of the rewards of those who hear and answer the call of the hills.

Two weeks after his death, an appreciation by Tom Weir appeared in the *Glasgow Herald*. It contained these words:

"I write about Ben today because I attended his funeral last Saturday in Aviemore, when the sun shone on the snowy Cairngorms and the red-branched birches gleamed silver on the slopes of Craigellachie. Ben was seventy-three when he died of a stroke in the Spey Valley where he had lived out the last years of an exceptionally active life. When the perceptive Church of Scotland minister made the penetrating statement, 'His handicap was your handicap,' we recognised something that all of us felt deeply . . .

"I wish he could have seen the big crowd of climbers of all ages at his grave, and he would have loved to hear their talk afterwards. It was a cheery occasion. We were saying goodbye to a man who had enjoyed life, had enriched it with his presence, and gone out of it without pain."

Some months later the pages of the *Scottish Mountaineering Club Journal* [89] included a further acknowledgement of his contribution. These were its final paragraphs:[90]

"Ben's canvas of mountain interests was wide, and his energy and involvement did not diminish with advancing years. He was the only Club member for whom the President and *Journal* Editor were well advised to maintain an individual correspondence file. His letters came on all subjects – dinners, AGMs, huts, publications, politics, etiquette, and of course, accidents and rescue. Ben was into everything, right up to the end of his life. It was uncannily fitting that a letter from him appeared in the *Scotsman* on the day of his funeral. As somebody said, 'Ben always had the last word!'

"Perhaps the most remarkable thing about all this was that his opinion was always worth listening to and frequently later proved to be accurate. Eric Langmuir makes this tribute: 'I often took his advice on matters of Mountain Rescue. On those few occasions when I acted against his advice, I was always proved wrong. When you get down to it, Ben's life was one of unstinting service. The material rewards he obtained for his work were trifling compared to what he contributed.'

"He was probably best known for his contribution to Mountain Rescue and for his concern about accidents. This extended over some forty years or more and merited the award of an MBE. He used the first mountain rescue stretcher in Scotland and was influential in the founding of an independent Mountain Rescue Committee for Scotland, his views ensuring that this work became the responsibility of the rescue teams rather than the climbing clubs, as in England. He was a member of the Committee from its inception, and his consistent effort was to ensure the independence of the Committee and the Teams from control by those, such as the police, with a statutory responsibility for rescue. In this his work is of lasting importance, as he has helped to ensure that the control of mountain rescue work remains in the hands of those who actually do the job.

"Owing to Ben's work as Recorder for the MRCS, there exists today a complete record of incidents over more than twenty years. This is invaluable for any kind of investigation into accidents and rescue trends. Anyone involved in this type of work will appreciate the difficulties he had to extract reports and information from the Teams, most of which have a healthy unconcern with reporting and filing. It was a daunting task which he tackled with characteristic vigour and determination.

"As a close friend of Donald Duff, the pioneer of the Duff stretcher and another stalwart of the Scottish Rescue scene, he was the moving force behind the highly successful 'Adventure in Safety' Exhibition which opened in Glasgow in 1968 and was subsequently held in London (1969), Edinburgh (1970), Aberdeen and Fort William (1972).

"This exhibition gave large numbers of young people the opportunity to see at first hand the need for skill and care in their hill walking. This was especially important to Ben who had a profound concern and enthusiasm for ensuring that young people were introduced to the hills in the best possible way. He was associated with Glenmore Lodge from the early days when it was housed in what is now the Loch Morlich Youth Hostel. He acted as a voluntary instructor for over fifteen years and when he became less well able to lead the way on the hills he turned his boundless energy towards the creation of an Alpine garden in front of the Lodge. He cared for it steadfastly over the years and it remains a memorial to him and the things he cared for.

Laggantygown Cemetery, Aviemore 1977.

"Ben had a happy gift of establishing a rapport with those of a later generation than his own. Des Rubens says: 'I regretted the death of Ben Humble very much. Several of the Edinburgh University Mountaineering Club came to know him quite well in the last few years. I think it is worth noting that we were very impressed by his enthusiasm for his own latest excursions, both abroad and at home, and by his interest in the activities of young climbers[91] like ourselves. We in turn were fascinated by that remarkable scrap book, his other personal records, and not least by the eccentric manner of the man himself. It is our regret that these visits of ours to Feithlinn were to end so soon.'

"Ben valued his continuing links with Glenmore Lodge in the later part of his life. He was there a good deal, his arrival heralded by those great sighing 'Aaaaaahs' which one heard first as he came through the front door, his departure later announced by the fierce, clutch destroying revving of his car, by which he projected himself up the front drive and away home to Aviemore. He was a guest at a number of Hogmanay dinners where his recitation of the 'Ryvoan Rat Farm'[92] astounded and amused successive students.

"He was a grand man, and we miss him. One cannot but speculate what Ben might say if he could reach across the gulf and comment on what we have said. It might well be:

" 'Not bad, not bad, but if you had asked me to do it in the first place I could have done it better myself . . . Aaaaaah!' "

NOTES ON THE TEXT

1. David, the third eldest of the eight brothers.
2. A 1914 Dumbarton Voters Roll shows Robert Humble as a tenant of Bellfield, not as the owner. Even among the fairly well-to-do, it was common practice at that time to rent rather than own one's house.
3. During its history the firm was successively known as William Denny & Son, Denny Brothers, William Denny & Brothers, and from 1918 as William Denny & Brothers Ltd.
4. Humble, B. H. (1931). Preventive Radiology. *British Dental Journal*, 52, 1, 1.
5. Humble, B. H. (1931). Preventive Radiology. *The American Dental Surgeon*, 51, 4, 101.
6. Humble, B. H. (1931). Identification by Means of Teeth. *Proceedings of the 8th International Dental Congress*, Paris.
7. Glaister, J. and Brash, J. C. (1937). *Medico-Legal Aspects of the Ruxton Case*. William Wood, Baltimore.
8. Simpson, K. (1951). Dental Evidence in the Reconstruction of Crime. *British Dental Journal*, 91, 9, 229.
9. Humble, B. H. (1933). Identification by Means of Teeth. *British Dental Journal*, 54, 10, 528.
10. Polson, C. J. (1973). *The Essentials of Forensic Medicine*. Pergamon Press, Oxford.
11. Harvey, W. (1976). *Dental Identification and Forensic Odontology*. Kimpton, London.
12. Harvey, W. (1976) ibid.
13. My first cousin, Bob Humble, and his eldest son have both had excellent results from stapedectomies.
14. Highland tradition attributes "the sight" to the seventh son of a seventh son. Ben satisfies only the first of these two criteria. However since he often referred to his position in the family as the seventh son, I have used the title here deliberately, puzzling along with many of his friends over the sources of his remarkable perception.
15. A separate Scottish mountain 3,000 feet or higher.
16. Ashley, J. (1973). *Journey Into Silence*. The Bodley Head, London.
17. The Isle of Mist.
18. Humble, B. H. (1933). *Tramping in Skye*. Grant & Murray, Edinburgh.
19. Ben had several later meetings with Mackenzie before his death in 1934.
20. Sgurr Mhic Coinnich.
21. Humble, B. H. (1934). *The Songs of Skye – An Anthology*. Eneas Mackay, Stirling.

22. First two verses.
23. Iona.
24. Hillary, R. (1968). *The Last Enemy*. Macmillan, London.
25. Taylor, W. C. (1973). *The Snows of Yesteryear – J. Norman Collie, Mountaineer*. Holt, Rinehart and Winston of Canada, Toronto and Montreal.
26. The tea-room did not survive the war.
27. Although Ben does not specify the fact here, this voyage included a short stop on the island of Rum.
28. Humble, B. H. (1952). *The Cuillin of Skye*. Robert Hale, London.
29. Humble, B.H. (1936). *Wayfaring Around Scotland*. Herbert Jenkins, London.
30. At the early hostels the familiar triangular sign of the SYHA was mounted on a cleft birch pole.
31. See Chapter Eight.
32. Published in the *Weekly Scotsman* in September 1935.
33. This was certainly at the instigation of Sir Charles Rogers, one of the prime movers in the campaign to have the Wallace Monument erected. See MacPhail, I.M.M (1979). *Dumbarton Castle*. Donald, Edinburgh.
34. At the laying of the foundation stone of the Wallace Monument at Stirling in 1861, the sword was borne in the procession by the Master Gunner of Dumbarton Castle, walking in front of Dumbarton magistrates and councillors. (MacPhail, I.M.M (1979), ibid.)
35. Macdonald, H. (1854). *Rambles Around Glasgow*. Hedderwick, Glasgow.
36. The 1924–25 Empire Exhibition at Wembley, London.
37. Later named the *Queen Elizabeth*.
38. The deep water anchorage of the River Clyde.
39. A Dumbartonian.
40. From the poem, *A Hill*, this verse introduced the text of *On Scottish Hills*.
41. Buchan, J. B. (1913). *The Marquis of Montrose*. Nelson, London.
42. A round trip of almost fifty miles for Ben, and almost eighty for his companions from Glasgow.
43. Humble, B. H. (1948). *On Scottish Hills*. Chapman Hall, London.
44. See chapter 7.
45. Commonly referred to as ARP.
46. Humble, B. H. and Mearns, A. G. (1942). Colour Films in First-aid Training. *The Lancet*, 242, 1, 569.
47. William Joyce, popularly referred to in Britain as Lord Haw-Haw, who broadcast in English for German propaganda radio during the war.
48. Also stored at the Scottish Film Archive is a short film of the paddle steamer *Queen Mary II* on the River Clyde, taken in 1936 by Ben's brother, Dr John Humble.
49. This film was also a prize winner at the 1949 London Festival.
50. Even on semi-formal occasions, Ben sometimes could not resist temptation. One press report of a lecture and film show at the Burgh Hall in Dumbarton includes this comment: "Mr Humble enlivened the proceedings by showing the parade again in reverse."

51. Humble, B. H. (1945). Plan for a Park – What Might Be. *The Open Air In Scotland*, 1,1,15 (Winter issue).
52. Humble, B. H. (1948). National Parks for Scotland. *Today and Tomorrow*, 31–35.
53. Humble, B. H. (1963). Public Wilderness. A weekly five part series published in the *Scotsman* during March and April 1963.
54. Humble, B. H. (1964). National Parks – The Vision and the Reality. *The Climber*, December 1964 issue, 11–14.
55. Humble, B. H. (1965). Queen Elizabeth National Forest Park. *The Climber*, June 1965 issue, 27–28.
56. The route to Handa naturally remains the same today. For fine descriptions of the island, see Weir, Tom (1973). *The Western Highlands*. Batsford, London, and Murray, W. H. (1968). *The Companion Guide to The West Highlands of Scotland*, Collins, London.
57. But completely silent for Ben.
58. Unless the comments were relayed to Ben by his companions, he may have embellished these stories somewhat from his own imagination.
59. Nimlin, J. B., Humble, B. H., and Williams, G. C. (1940). Rock Climbs on the Cobbler – A Symposium. *Scottish Mountaineering Club Journal*, XXII, 130.
60. Humble, B. H. and Nimlin, J. B. – in collaboration with the Creagh Dhu Mountaineering Club (1954). *Rock Climbs at Arrochar*. The Scottish Mountaineering Club, Edinburgh.
61. Houston, J. R. (1971). *Climbers' Guide to Arrochar*. Scottish Mountaineering Trust, Edinburgh.
62. Howff is an old Scots word (often used by Burns) for an inn associated with good company and good whisky. Ben described the art of howffing as the ability to make oneself comfortable overnight, out of doors, at any time of the year (snow-holing and tenting excepted). He also wrote that it was Jock Nimlin who first applied the word howff to any sort of rude shelter used by climbers.
63. Although Ben made this comment, Ian MacPhail remembers that he was actually thrilled to have his name on a climb.
64. As with Lennox and Dunbartonshire, the boundaries of the Counties of Moray and Angus do not coincide with the limits of their ancient counterparts.
65. Dr George Beeching, Minister of Transport in 1963.
66. Loch Lomond is more correctly described as a seaboard loch. See Murray, W.H. (1968). *The Companion Guide to The West Highlands of Scotland*. Collins, London.
67. Now Mrs Elizabeth Freck.
68. Some younger readers may not realise that the term "par" is a creation of modern (North American) golf. It has replaced and demoted the older and historic word "bogey".
69. There are no fewer than five Lochan Uaines in the Cairngorm region. The two separately referred to in the text, one here and one in the following chapter, are those marked on the map.

70. Ben referred on another occasion to the sound of hobnail boots as being "music to the climber's ear", which only serves to emphasise how one can become involved in his story to the point of totally forgetting that he had no hearing.
71. Smythe, F. S. (1946). Mountain Training in the Cairngorms. *The Open Air in Scotland*, 1, 2, 6 (Spring issue).
72. The names of the permanent staff are at the heart of the success story of Glenmore Lodge. Ben detailed their many comings and goings in his account. In order to preserve the fluency of his personal narrative it has been necessary to omit some of these types of references, together with unduly extended details about a few of the early Glenmore courses. The instructors whose names are not included here, but whose role he specifically acknowledged, are listed in the Appendix.
73. Later Duke of Hamilton, who lost his life in an air crash in Africa.
74. Bobbie was then a teacher of Physical Education and a former International soccer goalkeeper, later to become Manager of St Johnstone Football Club and then Manager of the Scottish International Team.
75. Now Mrs Margaret Greenstreet.
76. Eric also played a large part in the inauguration of the Mountain Leadership Training Board.
77. This plant also continues to thrive at the Cairngorm ski-lift garden.
78. Rt. Hon. Walter Elliot, Member of Parliament for close to forty years, and holder of many Cabinet positions.
79. 1994 has begun in similar fashion with a massive search in the Cairngorms, a mirror image of events during the same period in 1993.
80. See also chapter 10.
81. Murray, W. H. (1993). Personal communication.
82. Ben was outlived by two of his elder brothers. Archie died at Perth, Ontario in 1979 at the age of 86, John at East Molesey, Surrey in 1985 at the age of 84.
83. The National Library of Scotland now stores the collection of all Ben's published articles. By way of a very individual and personal journey, these articles constitute an account of the opening up of the Scottish outdoors in the period from 1930 to the mid 1970s.
84. Now housed in the Library of the Scottish Mountaineering Club.
85. Stored in several volumes and available for viewing at the National Library of Scotland, George IV Bridge, Edinburgh.
86. By Nelson Downie. Ben added the note: "One of the most brilliant students ever turned out by the High School. Killed in a skirmish in the North-West Frontier in India at the beginning of the Great War."
87. Finally solved in 1993, with the help of Mr Graham Hopner, Local Studies Librarian, Dumbarton Distict Libraries.
88. Smythe, F. S. (1935). *The Spirit of the Hills*. Hodder and Stoughton, London.
89. *The Scottish Mountaineering Club Journal* (1978), XXXI, 169, 303.
90. Although this tribute repeats some details of Ben's career which have been

discussed in earlier pages, I have left unchanged the final paragraphs of this last appreciation by his colleagues.

91. Ben took great pleasure in friendships with many outstanding young climbers. He wrote on one occasion of how the late Dougal Haston had nursed him up a rock face when he (Ben) returned to climbing following an operation on his arm.

92. An idea originating from the presence of rats in the Ryvoan Bothy; the recitation outlined in rhyme how he might become a millionaire by breeding rats and cats!

APPENDIX

The following are the additional names of members of the permanent staff of The National Outdoor Training Centre at Glenmore Lodge whose contribution Ben acknowledged in his article "The Glenmore Story", originally published in 1975 in the August and September issues of *Climber and Rambler* (now known as *Climber and Hill Walker*):

Charlie Allan, Rusty Baillie, Bob Barton, Peter Boardman, Ian Brown, Martin Burrows-Smith, Liam Carver, Ingrid Christopherson, Sam Crymble, Clive Freshwater, Allen Fyffe, Adrian Liddell, George McLeod, Bill March, Steve Mitchell, Roger O'Donovan, Reg Popham, Tommy Paul, Duncan Ross and Dougie Stewart.